The Cognitive Neuroscience of Bilingualisı

The Cognitive Neuroscience of Bilingualism presents an introduction to the neural bases and cognitive processes of the bilingual brain. It covers foundational knowledge required for study in the area of bilingualism, including prominent theories and research methodologies, and the state of research in relevant fields of psycholinguistics, cognitive psychology, and neuroscience. Major topics include bilingual development and brain plasticity; aphasia and the bilingual brain; cross-linguistic effects of bilingualism; bilingual lexical and conceptual memory; and cognitive and neurocognitive effects of bilingualism. This book represents the first of its kind to bring together the various psychological and theoretical issues of bilingualism with respect to language processing and representation, while providing insight into the "reality" of the bilingual brain.

John W. Schwieter is Full Professor of Spanish, Linguistics, and Psychology, and Director of Bilingualism Matters @ Laurier and the Language Acquisition, Multilingualism, and Cognition Laboratory at Wilfrid Laurier University, Canada. He is also Adjunct Professor of Linguistics at McMaster University, Canada. Some of his recent books include *The Cambridge Handbook of Working Memory and Language* (2022) and *The Routledge Handbook of Translation, Interpreting, and Bilingualism* (2023).

Julia Festman is Full Professor of Multilingualism at the University College of Teacher Education Tyrol, Austria. Her main research focus is on multilingualism on the individual, cognitive, and educational levels. She combines psycholinguistic and neuroscientific methods for investigating learning and processing of multiple languages. Her latest book, *Second Language Acquisition and Lifelong Learning* (2023), is coauthored with S. Pfenninger and D. Singleton.

Cambridge Fundamentals of Neuroscience in Psychology

Developed in response to a growing need to make neuroscience accessible to students and other non-specialist readers, the *Cambridge Fundamentals of Neuroscience in Psychology* series provides brief introductions to key areas of neuroscience research across major domains of psychology. Written by experts in cognitive, social, affective, developmental, clinical, and applied neuroscience, these books will serve as ideal primers for students and other readers seeking an entry point to the challenging world of neuroscience.

Books in the Series

The Neuroscience of Expertise by Merim Bilalić
The Neuroscience of Intelligence by Richard J. Haier
Cognitive Neuroscience of Memory by Scott D. Slotnick
The Neuroscience of Adolescence by Adriana Galván
The Neuroscience of Suicidal Behavior by Kees van Heeringen
The Neuroscience of Creativity by Anna Abraham
Cognitive and Social Neuroscience of Aging by Angela Gutchess
The Neuroscience of Sleep and Dreams by Patrick McNamara
The Neuroscience of Addiction by Francesca Mapua Filbey
The Neuroscience of Sleep and Dreams, 2e, by Patrick McNamara
The Neuroscience of Intelligence, 2e, by Richard J. Haier
The Cognitive Neuroscience of Bilingualism by John W. Schwieter and Julia Festman

The Cognitive Neuroscience of Bilingualism

John W. Schwieter
Wilfrid Laurier University
McMaster University

Julia Festman
University College of Teacher Education Tyrol

CAMBRIDGE
UNIVERSITY PRESS

CAMBRIDGE
UNIVERSITY PRESS

Shaftesbury Road, Cambridge CB2 8EA, United Kingdom

One Liberty Plaza, 20th Floor, New York, NY 10006, USA

477 Williamstown Road, Port Melbourne, VIC 3207, Australia

314–321, 3rd Floor, Plot 3, Splendor Forum, Jasola District Centre,
New Delhi – 110025, India

103 Penang Road, #05–06/07, Visioncrest Commercial, Singapore 238467

Cambridge University Press is part of Cambridge University Press & Assessment,
a department of the University of Cambridge.

We share the University's mission to contribute to society through the pursuit of
education, learning and research at the highest international levels of excellence.

www.cambridge.org
Information on this title: www.cambridge.org/9781107197503

DOI: 10.1017/9781108178501

First published 2023

Printed in the United Kingdom by CPI Group Ltd, Croydon CR0 4YY

A catalogue record for this publication is available from the British Library

Library of Congress Cataloging-in-Publication Data
Names: Schwieter, John W., 1979– author. | Festman, Julia, author.
Title: The cognitive neuroscience of bilingualism / John W. Schwieter,
Julia Festman.
Description: Cambridge ; New York, NY : Cambridge University Press, 2023. |
Series: Cambridge fundamentals of neuroscience in psychology |
Includes bibliographical references and index.
Identifiers: LCCN 2023016432 (print) | LCCN 2023016433 (ebook) |
ISBN 9781107197503 (hardback) | ISBN 9781108178501 (ebook)
Subjects: LCSH: Bilingualism – Psychological aspects. | Neurolinguistics. |
Cognitive neuroscience.
Classification: LCC P115.4 .S39 2023 (print) | LCC P115.4 (ebook) |
DDC 404/.2019–dc23/eng/20230612
LC record available at https://lccn.loc.gov/2023016432
LC ebook record available at https://lccn.loc.gov/2023016433

ISBN 978-1-107-19750-3 Hardback
ISBN 978-1-316-64779-0 Paperback

Contents

The color plate section can be found between pages 150 and 151

Figures

Tables

Acknowledgments

We would like to thank our editorial assistants, Malcolm Brockett and Ali Jasemi, for their excellent work during the preparation of the manuscript. We gratefully acknowledge that financial support to hire them was provided by the Office of Research Services at Wilfrid Laurier University in Ontario, Canada. We would also like to thank the commissioning editor, Stephen Acerra, the peer reviewers, and the entire team at Cambridge University Press for their support and expertise in the development of this book. Schwieter is very grateful to CNN Chief Medical Correspondent Dr. Sanjay Gupta for his enthusiasm about our research and this book. Several topics in this book were discussed in our April 2022 interview "How language lights up the brain" (available at https://cnn.it/3781qVG). Finally, we are extremely appreciative to Jubin Abutalebi, Roberto R. Heredia, Alina Leminen, and Ping Li for offering their kind words of endorsements that appear on the back cover.

CHAPTER ONE

Theories and Methods in the Cognitive Neuroscience of Bilingualism

An Introduction

Learning Objectives

- Identify the differences between the definitions of who is a bilingual and understand the impact of this discrepancy and the consequent need for uniformity of research on bilingualism.
- Learn about various neuroimaging methods and the research questions for which they are suitable.
- Become familiar with the advantages and disadvantages of research methods in the cognitive neuroscience of bilingualism.
- Develop an understanding of the notion of ecological validity in research on bilingualism.

1.1 Introduction

Cognitive neuroscience is a discipline that aims to understand the relationship between the brain and the mind. It is fundamentally based on human neuropsychology, which focuses on revealing the neural bases of cognition and describing mental processes in the human brain; however, cognitive neuroscience goes beyond these foci. Moreover, it is nourished by a strong interdisciplinary combination and integration of approaches and knowledge from neuroscience, medical science, cognitive psychology, and computer science.

In this book, we set out to explore the brain's mental capacities, and in particular, one aspect of cognition – language. Our primary aim is to examine how the neurological organization and functioning of the brain supports bilingual language acquisition and language processing.

1.2 Theoretical and Empirical Issues of Bilingualism Research

1.2.1 Bilingualism Research: Who Is a Bilingual?

Sixty percent of the world's population knows two or more languages. It is estimated that 43 percent of people are bilingual, and an additional

17 percent know at least three languages (iLanguages.org, 2023). The word *bilingual* is composed of the prefix "bi-" and the adjective "lingual." Both parts of the word are derived from Latin, with "bi" meaning "two," and "lingual" from the noun "lingua," meaning "language." The adjective *bilingual* refers to two languages. While the direct translation into one's dominant language, for instance, seems easy and its meaning clear-cut, up until now, definitional issues regarding bilingualism have not been solved. In this section, we dive into the world of definitional difficulties concerning the term *bilingualism*. Unfortunately, this definition is rather confusing. At first glance, *bilingualism* appears to be dichotomous, but a closer look shows that it is much more complex. However, examining and characterizing bilingualism is of great importance, and, as will become clear throughout this book, many dimensions shed light on the complicated term *bilingualism*. For research (in particular, grouping of participants and clear-cut research findings), an accurate characterization of bilingualism is vital. Many of these dimensions are intermingled or even intertwined, and therefore looking at only one dimension and using its extrema for selection purposes in studies on bilingualism is often too short-sighted.

Differences in the interpretation of bilingualism are based on various aspects:

1. The level of fluency (proficiency):
   - According to an early, extremely restrictive definition of bilingualism by Bloomfield (1933), a bilingual has "native-like control of two languages" (p. 56). A perfect, ideal native speaker speaks the language fluently and has a rich vocabulary, perfect command over complicated sentence structures and norms of the language including spelling, perfect grammar skills, and mastery of communicative conventions and stylistic variation. Clearly, only proficiency level was used here as a criterion, ignoring all other dimensions of bilingualism (Dewaele, 2015).
   - But, of course, not all "native" speakers show this high level of language command in their "native" language. Consequently, would individuals who do not have perfect command over two languages be excluded from being labeled as a bilingual?

This leads to several more questions:

- What is the minimal level of language competence acquired by a speaker to be categorized as bilingual (i.e., are language learners in their initial stage already bilingual or should the term *bilingual* refer only to advanced language learners)? For Haugen (1953), a bilingual is an individual who produces "complete and meaningful utterances in other languages" (p. 6), whereas for Diebold (1961), a bilingual is someone who begins to understand utterances in another language, though not yet able to produce utterances in this language. Is it enough to just know a few words such as "good morning" or "thank you" in another language to be bilingual, as suggested by Edwards (2004)? These criteria are – although very vague – flexible and could thus be considered a first step toward viewing **bilingualism as a continuum** rather than a category (Dewaele, 2015).

- Is high proficiency required in all four linguistic skills (speaking, listening, reading and writing) or only in some of them?
- What about languages that do not have a written form, for example, some Arabic and Chinese language varieties? Would someone not be called a bilingual because he/she is unable to write in these languages?
- There is also the issue of speed and accuracy (or, in psychological terms, speed–accuracy tradeoff): In the definition of bilingualism, does fluency include accuracy, or can a speaker be accurate, but not very fluent when speaking a language and still be called a bilingual?

2. Relative competence in both languages:
   - Balanced bilinguals are speakers with an equal mastery of two languages. But does this necessarily apply to all linguistic skills and domains, topics, settings?
   - Unbalanced bilinguals have an unequal mastery of two languages; that is, they have a higher proficiency in one language, which is their dominant language, than in the other, nondominant, language. Are these individuals not classified as bilinguals when they speak a dialect or language without script as their first, dominant language?
   - Balanced bilingualism does not necessarily imply a high level of proficiency; for example, two non-native languages can be mastered at an intermediate level of proficiency. If an individual learns two languages but has not yet reached full competence in these languages, is he/she not considered a bilingual according to the definition in point 1?

3. Frequency of language use:
   - According to a more recent, less narrow definition by Grosjean (2010), a bilingual is someone who uses two (or more) languages in everyday life.
   - Does a bilingual use the two languages on a regular (maybe even daily) basis and to the same extent?

- Are the languages used in private context and/or in occupational situations and are all four linguistic skills regularly used?
- Are heritage language speakers considered to be bilingual if they do not use one of their languages often, given their life circumstances?
- Do individuals count as a bilingual when they do not speak the language regularly but "only" read in it frequently?
- What is more intertwined with language use frequency – length of residence in a country where the second language (L2) is spoken (suggesting little language exposure and L2 use) or length of exposure to an L2 (suggesting more active language use in L2)?

4. Number of languages:
    - Does bilingualism refer to the knowledge and use of **exactly two languages** or can it mean "two or more" languages (often referred to as multilingualism/plurilingualism)?
    - What is a language? Do dialects, sociolects, and so on count as languages?

1.2.1.1 Dimensions for Classifying Bilinguals

In studies across all disciplines involved in research on bilingualism, important factors for categorizing individuals as bilinguals (such as the language proficiency attained in the languages, language use frequency, and the number of languages) are still quite problematic, because they are not precise, as illustrated by the many questions raised in Section 1.2.1.

A factor that is apparently already accepted in research communities of linguists, psychologists, and cognitive neuroscientists and is widely used is **age of acquisition**. There is some agreement in the field that the cut-off line for early bilingualism lies in early childhood, but it is not exactly clear at what age – around the age of three (according to McLaughlin, 1984) or somewhat later, say, at the age of six? What is more, De Houwer (1995) distinguished between *bilingual first language acquisition* (BFLA) and *bilingual second language acquisition*, with the former referring to regular exposure to two languages within the first month of birth and the latter to exposure starting later than one month after birth but before the age of two. Hence, even the chronological division in bilingualism terms is difficult to define (see Section 3.3.3 for an overview and further discussion).

This being said, a more recent **life-span-oriented perspective on language acquisition and learning** offers a close, detailed description of subgroups, of early as well as late language learners, including adolescent, adult, and third-age learners. For instance, Pfenninger, Festman, and Singleton (2023) suggest that general language use, frequency of use per linguistic skill, and language switching habits may vary across a lifespan depending on social settings and change along with mobility and new living conditions in speech communities and workplaces. Language attrition (i.e., the decline or loss of a language once mastered to a certain degree) can happen to languages acquired after birth within the family or from a family member who is no longer around; it can happen to languages learned at school, languages learned in the course of migration through different countries, or languages learned for work-related needs or during a temporary stay abroad. Bilinguals use their languages in different ways, their frequency of use dynamically changes, and it seems that this frequency plays a critical role in language skill development.

Some additional factors (listed in Table 1.1) as well as an understanding of their effect on bilingual language processing are equally important. Hence, more and more studies include (at least some of) these factors when describing their bilingual participants. Failure to do so leads to research findings being hardly comparable to other studies and blurring of the overall picture of the cognitive neuroscience of bilingualism.

1.2.1.2 What the Classification of Bilinguals Means for Research on Bilingualism

Given the number of important factors influencing bilingual acquisition, learning, and use (mentioned earlier, but not necessarily complete), it goes without saying that **each individual bilingual has a unique combination of different bilingual characteristics**. Bilinguals differ not only in their personal language acquisition history (i.e., the setting, amount, and quality of exposure to two languages), but also in their personal use patterns and preferences, and the dynamic changes of language use, proficiency, and so on. Surprisingly, even speech motor areas vary individually; that is, there is a "high degree of variation across subjects in the mapping of motor and sensory aspects of human language" (Andrews, 2019, p. 28). For example, before bilingual patients undergo brain surgery (e.g., related to epilepsy or tumor), the areas related to language production (motor) and comprehension (sensory) are located by a highly invasive method, cortical stimulation mapping (CSM), during object picture naming. An overview of the data from CSM, accumulated since the 1970s and extensively examined by Ojemann and Whitaker (1978), revealed variability from brain to brain in how the language centers are organized

Table 1.1 Relevant dimensions for classifying bilinguals

Dimension	Categories and characteristics
Acquisition context – chronological details	
• Age of acquisition	• **Early (simultaneous) bilingual** = parallel acquisition of two languages in early childhood (**simultaneous bilingualism** of two first languages before the age of three, McLaughlin, 1984) • **BFLA** (regular exposure to two languages within the first month of birth) vs. **bilingual second language acquisition** (exposure starting later than one month after birth but before the age of two) (De Houwer, 1990) • **Early sequential bilingual** = acquisition of two languages with the L2 usually before the age of six (Beatens Beardsmore, 1986) • **Late bilingual/late language learner** = **sequential acquisition** of two languages with the L2 usually after the age of three (or six) (e.g., Lambert, 1985; McLaughlin, 1984)
Acquisition/learning context – environmental details	
• Circumstances of acquisition/ manner of acquisition	• **Informal** (natural setting) = at home, in the family • **Formal** (educational, institutional setting) = at school, with textbooks
• Sociocultural environment	• Migration status and experience • Length of residence/exposure • Socioeconomic status (SES) • Communicative habits of the speech environment (two separate cultures with one using only one language vs. one culture that uses both languages)
• Linguistic environment	• Amount of time spent with monolinguals and with bilinguals (using one language only) or using both languages (De Houwer, 1990) • (Continuity of) exposure to each language (e.g., Byers-Heinlein, 2015) • Quality and quantity of input (e.g., Unsworth, 2016)

Table 1.1 (cont.)

Dimension	Categories and characteristics
Language use context – social psychological details	
• Language status/prestige	• Both languages valued = **additive bilingualism**; both languages and cultures bring complementary positive elements to a person's overall development
	• One language (usually the minority language) being socially devalued, social pressure to avoid its use, replacement through prestigious language of the majority = **subtractive bilingualism** (e.g., Lambert, 1975)
Language outcome/competence – language skill details	
• Language dominance	• **Balanced bilingual** = same level of proficiency in both languages: "native-like" competence in both (Haugen, 1973) or same ability in both but not "native-like"
	• **Unbalanced bilingual** = language dominance in one language (better skills in that language compared to the skills in the other language)
• Level of language fluency	• **Beginner, intermediate, advanced learner**
	• **"Native speaker," "native-like command"**
• Literacy	• Ability to read and write = **literate**
	• Lack of ability to read and write = **illiterate**
	• **Monoliterate** vs. **biliterate bilingual**
Language use/contact – language use details	
• Individual speaking habits	• Daily language use, frequency of language use per language
	• Ease with translation and interpreting and frequency of acting as translator/interpreter
• Switching habits	• Weinreich (1953) considers bilingualism "the practice of alternately using two languages" (p. 1); see Rodriguez-Fornells et al. (2012) for language switch habits
	• More recently, different language contexts have been suggested (Green & Abutalebi, 2013):
	• In **single-language contexts**, each of the languages is used separately (e.g., home vs. school),

Table 1.1 (cont.)

Dimension	Categories and characteristics
	• In **dual-language contexts**, the languages are both used but separately with different interlocutors, and • In **dense code-switching contexts**, speakers switch freely between their languages with their multilingual interlocutors.
• Domains of language use and context of exposure	• Family, leisure, work (e.g., Grosjean, 1998); superior knowledge in certain domains of language use (and topics), e.g., work, school

(for review, see the excellent chapter by Andrews, 2019). More recent research adds to this "dynamic nature of language mapping" by shedding light on the language organization of a single patient having undergone multiple surgeries (see Serafini, Grant, & Haglund, 2013).

We go along with De Groot (2011) who states that "the bilingual community is a colorful lot" (p. 5), and we also keep in mind that individuals categorized as monolingual speakers of a language are a colorful lot, too. De Groot's book is about both individuals who have reached the "end point" of language proficiency (i.e., following the definition focusing on level of proficiency) in both languages *and* language learners/users at different stages of proficiency and with different lengths of exposure (focusing on the acquisition and timing aspects). Her book also includes studies published on bilinguals, that is, those who speak two languages, and on studies reporting on two (among possibly more) languages that individuals have been asked to use for a certain task.

The difficulty in experimental research – which applies to studies on bilinguals based on neuroimaging techniques (as shown in Section 1.3) – is that it usually involves comparisons of conditions. More specifically, researchers contrast an experimental condition with a control condition, and these conditions should differ in only one property. The change of a dependent variable can then be attributed to this property. Problems arise when these two conditions differ in more than one property. Consequently, explanations of experimental effects can stem from a number of properties and leave much room for interpretation and speculation. Confounding factors are those that covary with the independent variable and bring more "noise" into the original study design and argumentation.

Previously, research on bilingualism seems to have been easier: Speakers were categorized into one of the two dichotomous categories of bilingualism, for example, early bilinguals versus monolinguals, with the former being the experimental group and the latter serving as the control group. Both groups performed a certain task in the monolingual's language known to both groups. In such a **between-group design**, the performance of the participants was compared on a **dependent variable** (the variable that is measured). This study design was used to identify differences between mono- and bilinguals; bilingualism was used as the variable that influenced performance and as the genuine cause of the difference. It goes without saying that it was assumed that both groups were identical on all other variables.

More recently, it appears that we have come to grips with the impact of single factors and the "noise" caused by confounding factors. **Confounding factors** are those variables that are neither manipulated in terms of an independent variable nor measured in terms of a dependent variable. They influence the performance and results of the dependent variable in addition to the independent variable. In bilingualism research, a recent focus on individual differences and participant characteristics has elaborated on this issue (e.g., Lauro, Core, & Hoff, 2020; Pfenninger, Festman, & Singleton, 2023). Additionally, some variables have been found to confound others, in particular socio-economic status (SES), migration background, and lexicon size (for a review, see Festman, Czapka, & Winsler, 2023). However, one must be very careful to not hastily draw conclusions from this belief. Not everyone who migrates to another country is automatically poor, not everyone who is poor automatically has a small vocabulary, not all poor people automatically are educational underachievers, and so on. These conclusions would be simply inaccurate as they do not apply to all members of these groups, but rather stigmatize the individuals.

1.2.2 Language and Language Domains Relevant for Bilingualism Research

When we talk about language, we may refer to the *representation* aspects of language, that is, how different language subcomponents are structured and organized. With regard to bilingualism, this means how two languages are represented in the brain, where they are located, and how they are organized.

Table 1.2 Domains of language

Domain	Referring to
• Phonological	• Sound structure
• Orthographic	• Spelling
• Semantic	• Meaning of words, sentence, etc.
• Morphological	• Word-forming elements of language, often grammatical aspects such as gender, number (singular/plural), inflection, and prefixes and suffixes, etc.
• Syntactic	• Phrase and sentence structure
• Pragmatic	• Language use in various contexts
• Discourse	• Series of speech events or sentences

We may also consider the processing aspects of language, that is, how language and, more specifically, its different subcomponents are activated, how they interact with each other, and, concerning bilingualism, how languages interact with each other.

For research to be conducted in the realms of bilingualism and the brain, both must be examined in greater detail: Language is broken down into different subcomponents, which are usually mapped onto specific brain regions and linked to neural functions (Banich & Compton, 2018). This means that only very specific aspects of a bilingual's languages can be tested in a single study in the domain of cognitive neuroscience.

Language knowledge is commonly divided into different subcomponents: (a) **sound** (speech perception and production, sound patterns and contrasts), (b) **words**, **morphology** (word structure, grammatical knowledge related to word formation), and **semantics** (meaning), and (c) **syntax** (phrase, sentence and discourse structure). In particular, psycholinguistic approaches to studying language rely on an even more fine-grained distinction and division into different types of linguistic information. Table 1.2 briefly explains these different domains of language.

1.3 Methodological Considerations

From early on, researchers in the fields of linguistics, psychology, and sociolinguistics have largely been involved in the study of bilingualism (e.g., Weinreich, Fishman, Oskaar, Haugen, Mägiste, Obler, Paradis, Grosjean, Peal, and Lambert). Although these approaches to the study of bilingualism have set the stage for theories, models, and a scientific basis for the investigation of bilingualism, they can only shed light on the outcome, that is, the verbal output, but cannot reveal the processes behind it. The study of bilingualism from a cognitive neuroscience perspective necessitates the use of specific methods and techniques, as they offer a window into the brain. Technical advances have made it possible to develop various methods (mainly for clinical use) that can explain the structure and functioning of the brain. These modern techniques are already being used for research in the cognitive neuroscience of bilingualism and are employed to investigate, in particular, bilingual processing in the brain in real time. These methods can thus help to uncover how the brain processes two languages at a time or processes one language while knowing a second one.

Although we cannot describe the methods here in full detail, we try to clarify how each of them works and for what purpose they are used (see Section 1.4.1). Importantly, each method is unique and is usually employed because of its specific advantage over other methods for certain research questions.

Imaging techniques are one of the methods and techniques that are most relevant for the study of languages in the brain (and for the search for neural differences in the brains of mono- and bilinguals). They are commonly divided into the following types:

1. Techniques to **assess brain anatomy**: For example, structural magnetic resonance imaging (SMRI) and diffusion-tensor imaging (DTI).
2. Techniques to **detect current brain activity**: For example, functional magnetic resonance imaging (fMRI), positron emission topography (PET), and near-infrared spectroscopy (NIRS).
3. Techniques that **record electromagnetic changes in the brain related to language processing**: For example, electroencephalography (EEG) and magnetoencephalography (MEG) (see Banich & Compton, 2018, ch. 3, for an excellent overview).

Since all these techniques have specific requirements when used for recording language-related processes, their early days were somewhat shadowed by technical limitations that have now been largely overcome. For example, EEG experiments seldom involved overt language production due to artifacts that distort the signal; the quality of fMRI scans had the same problem with artifacts during speech, and additionally the limitation of capturing only a part of the brain until whole-brain scans were made possible. Today, technical advances and new types of analyses have greatly improved the quality of data.

To begin, we will take a quick look at many of the most relevant methods of research used in the cognitive neuroscience of bilingualism.

1.3.1 Focus on Neuroimaging Methods

Neuroimaging methods measure cortical activity when language processing is ongoing. The interpretation of data is based on the assumption that the neural areas which consume more blood are more highly active and are involved in specific processes necessary for current task execution and performance.

1.3.1.1 Techniques to Assess Brain Anatomy: SMRI and DTI

SMRI (structural magnetic resonance imaging): Brain anatomy, more specifically **grey matter**, can be examined with MRI, a technique in which researchers focus on the size, shape, and/or volume of different brain structures. Some studies investigate the difference in surface area of grey matter or the thickness of the cortical ribbon. In examinations of subcortical structures, both volume and shape are assessed. Mechelli et al. (2004) have provided a seminal structural-anatomical MRI study comparing bilinguals and monolinguals which demonstrates the changes of grey matter density related to L2 learning as modulated by proficiency.

DTI (diffusion tensor imaging): DTI is a newly developed MRI technique (introduced by Basser in the 1990s, see Basser, 1995) and a specialized form of magnetic resonance imaging. DTI informs us about white matter, more specifically about: (a) anatomical connectivity between different brain regions, and (b) integrity of white matter. Since water diffuses in nerve fibers (which can be measured with DTI), the main axis or directions along which water diffuses can be determined, yielding white-matter tracts. Consequently, the main directional orientation of white-matter tracks can be detected, as it is the axis along which most water diffusion is measured. The visualization of water activity in the brain's white matter is superior to that of a traditional MRI. It allows for the analysis of complex neuronal networks of the brain. The structural integrity of these tracts is indicated by the degree of diffusion of water. DTI has been used in bilingualism research, for example, to investigate white-matter development in bilingual children (Mohades et al., 2015).

1.3.1.2 Techniques to Detect Current Brain Activity: fMRI, PET, and NIRS

fMRI (function magnetic resonance imaging): For the study of language and cognition in cognitive neuroscience, fMRI has probably become the most important technique, despite being extremely expensive and sensitive to participants' movements, making it difficult to use for studying language production. What is more, fMRI measurements involve the production of loud noises, and due to the large size of the scanner and its testing restrictions, fMRI can be challenging to use when studying infants and children as well as certain adults.

For fMRI, a variation of the structural MRI technique is used. It is a noninvasive, oxygen-related technique (allowing for multiple scanning of the same participants) and is a widely available technique in clinics and research institutions.

When a brain region becomes active, it requires more oxygen and glucose which are delivered via blood flow. Thus, the oxygen-rich blood flow in this area increases to feed the metabolic processes of the neural structures. Blood oxygenation levels also change rapidly to facilitate the activity of neurons in a brain region, but there is still a delay of a few seconds, depending on the blood vessels in the respective area.

Therefore, fMRI measures changes in blood oxygenation over time, that is, how much oxygen in the blood is used in a certain brain area. The deoxygenated hemoglobin is measured and used as a correlate for the neuronal activity (Huettel, Song, & McCarthy, 2004). In short, **fMRI cannot provide any direct measure of neural activity, but of physiological activity, and thus is an indirect measure of neural activity.** Volume differences between increased oxygenated and decreased deoxygenated blood are detected, yielding a BOLD (blood oxygen level dependent) signal which indicates which brain regions have drawn more blood flow, demonstrating that activity patterns have increased.

The **spatial resolution** generated by fMRI is increasingly high, allowing for specific localization of brain region activity within millimeters. However, the **temporal resolution** is – compared to EEG and MEG – rather poor, only providing blood oxygenation level changes on a second-by-second basis, that is, every time data is averaged over a full second or more: "For this reason, precise temporal resolution for knowing what part of a sentence elicited an increase in neural activation in the particular brain area is not typically possible with fMRI. However, averaged activation patterns over the course of overall language use can provide a very detailed map of what brain regions were generally active" (Spivey & Cardon, 2015, p. 117; see Wattendorf et al., 2014, for an example of silent sentence production).

For fMRI scans, the participant must be situated in a scanner, a large machine which creates a constant magnetic field (classified according to the strength of the constant field, e.g., 3 Tesla). The response of atoms to perturbations in the magnetic field is used to create maps of brain structure (SMRI) and function (fMRI), since oxygenated and deoxygenated blood have different magnetic properties.

fMRI is usually employed while participants perform a task. This requires the set-up and performance of at least two conditions, with the first used as a baseline task against which brain activation in the second, the experimental task, can be measured and compared. Both for baseline and experimental conditions, multiple pictures are obtained, providing a massive amount of data.

To analyze fMRI data, **resting-state measurements** are included. The rest condition is often used as the control condition in which a participant is required to "rest" in the scanner, lying still with his/her eyes closed or while looking at a fixation cross. The problem with this is that the brain is always active – participants' minds may wander or might consciously be trying not to do anything. Therefore, the rest-state condition has been heavily criticized as an appropriate comparative condition to experimental conditions (e.g., Raichle, 2001). What is more, a closer look into resting-state data has revealed **resting-state networks**, named according to their usual function in a specific region; for example, visual, dorsal attention, limbic, and frontoparietal (see Yeo et al., 2011). The grouping of areas into these networks has been found to be consistent across participants, "suggesting that such groupings represent something fundamental about the organization of the human brain" (Banich & Compton, 2018, p. 84).

While fMRI can reveal the level of neural activation, a newer technique, called **multivoxel pattern analysis** (MVPA), allows for a fine-grained depiction of the pattern of activity. MVPA shows that the visual perceptions of different object categories each initiate a unique pattern of activity per object category (e.g., furniture vs. tools) (see Haxby et al., 2001). Xu et al. (2017) used MVPA to investigate unique patterns of activity in Chinese–English bilinguals related to reading in each language.

PET (positron emission topography): PET is a neurochemical method. It "works by altering molecules to have a radioactive atom and then introducing them into the blood supply so they can be carried to the brain. Those molecules are then taken up by the brain. As the molecule comes from a nonstable radioactive state to a stable nonradioactive state, two photons of light are emitted that are picked up by detectors around the head" (Banich & Compton, 2018, p. 78). This is an invasive method involving high-energy radiation, so it is not suitable for women of reproductive age nor for children. Its temporal resolution is very poor, as brain activity can be measured only over minutes. But PET does monitor the use of glucose from blood and regional cerebral blood flow (rCBF). Thus, it allows for a detailed analysis of how the brain uses specific molecules and can measure the absolute rCBF. PET has already been used to some degree in bilingualism research, see for example, seminal studies by Perani et al. (1996) and Price, Green, and von Studnitz (1999). Recently, a number of studies in the field of cognitive neuroscience of bilingualism have employed **FDG-PET** (fluorodeoxyglucose-PET) to measure brain metabolism and connectivity in order to reveal possible neuroprotective effects of bilingualism (Perani et al., 2017) or neural effects of lifelong bilingualism (Sala et al., 2022).

fNIRS (functional near-infrared spectroscopy): NIRS measures changes in the brain's oxygen level density (BOLD) yielding both deoxygenated and oxygenated hemoglobin activity, with a temporal resolution of 10 Hz. NIRS has a number of advantages over fMRI: It allows for infants and children as well as special populations of adults to be studied. NIRS is quiet and consists of a small, portable device that is relatively tolerable to participants' movement (Watanabe et al., 1998). Kovelman et al. (2008) further explain: "An advantage over fMRI is that, in addition to BOLD, fNIRS also computes the deoxygenated and oxygenated hemoglobin from the absorption measured at different wavelengths using the modified Beer–Lambert equation. While fNIRS cannot record deep into the human brain (~4 cm depth), it has good spatial resolution that is excellent for studies of human higher cognition and language, and it has better temporal resolution than fMRI (~<5s HR, sampling rate = 10 × per second)" (p. 5). Kovelman et al. used fNIRS during a semantic judgment task with Spanish–English bilinguals processing semantic information in mono- versus bilingual contexts.

1.3.1.3 Techniques Which Record Electromagnetic Changes in Relation to Language: EEG and MEG

EEG (electroencephalography): Since its early days, EEG has been an important method that has greatly increased our understanding of language processing in bilinguals (see Wicha, Moreno, & Carrasco-Ortíz, 2019, for an overview). It is a comparatively inexpensive, mobile, noninvasive method, with surface electrodes being placed on the participant's head. These electrodes measure the brain's electrical activity as a continuous wave, one wave per electrode. The EEG activity comes from the synchronous postsynaptic activity of a large number of neurons with similar spatial orientation (Luck, 2014).

While EEG recordings should be informative about language processing, they must be time-locked to the occurrence of a stimulus, for example, a real word, an erroneous word in a sentence, or other critical stimuli. Exposure to a critical stimulus is called an event, and continuous EEG recordings can be analyzed in relation to these events, resulting in so-called **event-relation potentials (ERPs)**. Spivey and Cardon (2015) stress one of the advantages of ERPs: "researchers are able to look at ongoing moments of real-time processing rather than just the end reaction or result" (p. 115) (with the "end reaction/result," these authors referred to behavioral measures, e.g., a reaction time task). There are a number of **ERP components** which have been identified in language processing (e.g., the N400, i.e., a negative deflection of the waveform starting at around 400 ms after presentation of the critical stimulus, which is the reaction to a semantic anomaly in a sentence, i.e., a word that deviates in meaning from what is expected; see Kutas and Federmeier (2011) for a review). These show a peculiar waveform and differ in degree of activity (amplitude), time-wise occurrence, length (latency), and location (topography). To obtain reliable information, EEG recordings of many participants and trials must be averaged and analyzed.

When applying this technique in language studies, it is necessary to rigorously design the experiment, and great care has to be taken when selecting task stimuli. Comparisons between different task conditions are vital, and, for studies on bilinguals, often a monolingual control group is included. More recently, other bilingual subgroups have also served as control groups (see e.g., Festman & Münte, 2012). EEG has **excellent temporal resolution**, that is, it allows for the study of ongoing cognitive processes on a millisecond scale and the time course by which linguistic information is processed in the brain. However, because of the barrier of the skull, spatial localization of neural activity is distorted (Cohen & Cuffin, 1983) and therefore challenging. High-density recording systems are used to partially reduce this problem, while dipole modeling procedures help to identify the source location of the neural activity.

There are two, currently still less frequently used but promising EEG approaches in bilingualism research. **Time-frequency analysis** of EEG recordings examines activity, which is locked to an event, over time. The strength of activity in different EEG frequencies is calculated and reflected in different frequency bands ranging from low to high frequencies. A time-frequency plot shows which frequency band was predominant at which time, following an event. For recent studies on bilingual infants based on time-frequency analysis, see Nacar Garcia et al. (2018). Moreover, there is an active new line of research on **resting-state EEG** in bilinguals compared to monolinguals (e.g., Bice, Yamasaki, & Prat, 2020; Soares et al., 2021).

MEG (magnetoencephalography): Like EEG, MEG is noninvasive. MEG records the **magnetic potentials** produced by brain activity and its fluctuations of magnetic fields. These fluctuations are generated by synchronous firing of large neural populations in the brain. For this purpose, a helmet is placed over the participant's head. In the helmet, highly sensitive SQUID sensor arrays are located (SQUID = radio-frequency superconducting quantum interference devices, Silver & Zimmerman, 1965), and consist of triplets of one magnetometer and two planar gradiometers.

Time-locked responses can be recorded and analyzed, resulting in **event-related fields (ERFs)**. What is more, MEG has a very high spatial resolution that is able to localize neural activity, because magnetic fields are less distorted by the skull (Hämäläinen et al., 1993). This means that it can go beyond the **localization of activation** possible in EEG (only limited to entire lobes, e.g., frontal, temporal): MEG can differentiate between particular cortical regions, for example, the primary auditory cortex. See Baillet (2017) for a description of MEG work in cognitive neuroscience. Recently, Zhu et al. (2020) published a study investigating executive control during bilingual language switching using MEG.

1.3.2 Real-Life Bilinguals and the Laboratory Setting: Questioning Ecological Validity

In their chapter on methods for studying adult bilingualism, Spivey and Cardon (2015) strongly criticized the lack of ecological validity when employing neuroimaging techniques for the investigation of bilingualism. They raised two major points of criticism: (1) the technics "generally require the participant to be immobile to prevent artifacts in the signal of neural activity, which takes away from their ecological validity" (p. 115); and (2) many studies are based on single-word stimulus material while bilinguals' communicative actions usually involve the production and comprehension of whole sentences. Spivey and Cardon therefore question whether this style of research investigates "processing language in a natural way" (p. 118). Some of the concerns expressed by Spivey and Cardon could – as follows from our detailed outline of technical options on brain measurements in Section 1.3.1 – be reduced. However, the ecological validity has attracted more attention recently (see Blanco-Elorrieta & Pylkkänen, 2018 for review; also see Holleman et al., 2020 and DeLuca et al., 2019a). What is more, there are attempts to study the neurobiology of language under more naturalistic conditions (e.g., Andric & Small, 2015) or endeavors involving multibrain perspectives on communication in dialogue (e.g., Kuhlen et al., 2015). Although these studies are related to monolingual settings, it is only a matter of time before the fundamental issues and technical challenges have been solved and such tricky methods can be applied to the study of bilingualism.

1.4 Summary

In this chapter, we have considered different definitions of bilingualism. This has underscored the fact that there are many differing aspects which should be taken into account when investigating bilingualism, designing studies, and choosing participants. Bilingualism is a complex construct, a continuum. Crucially, many key details about bilinguals' backgrounds need to be reported in studies to make the results comparable and clearly linkable to the specific study sample (see the seminal paper by Grosjean, 1998). Relative proficiency seems to be the most influential factor, but it is by no means the only relevant variable in studying bilingualism. Rather, individual differences and their variability, dynamically related dimensions and their interaction over time, speech environments and their changes, language use habits, socioeconomic background, and so on have been found to influence language processing and even brain function to some extent.

With increasing revelation of brain anatomy, neural functions of single regions, and of networks, our view of the brain and our knowledge improves continuously. From the description of the different neuroimaging techniques, it is apparent that each of them has advantages and shortcomings. There are various ways to overcome these. First, it has become clear that some less frequently used techniques could be highly informative when employed for research studies on bilingual participants. Second, the techniques should always be chosen wisely, for generating data with maximum validity (for an example of overt language production in EEG, see Festman & Clahsen, 2016) and ecological validity. Third, such techniques could be used in combination (although this would be technically challenging) (see Spivey & Cardon, 2015). Fourth, if this is technically not possible, it is definitely worth studying specific phenomena in the realms of bilingualism by drawing on results from different methods (for an example, see Festman, 2012; Festman & Münte, 2012; Festman, Rodriguez-Fornells, & Münte, 2010).

Review Questions

1. Explain the difference between mind and brain and describe how they are related.
2. Try to develop a working definition for bilingualism. Which of the characteristics mentioned in this chapter are most important? Which ones could be discounted? How can you justify your choices?
3. Think about one research question and argue which neuroimaging method you would choose and why you would pick this specific one.
4. Select one neuroimaging method and describe its advantages and disadvantages.
5. Why do some researchers call for more ecological validity in bilingualism research? Do you agree with this?

Further Reading

De Groot, A., & Hagoort, P. (Eds.). (2018). *Research methods in psycholinguistics and the neurobiology of language: A practical guide*. Wiley-Blackwell.

Field, A., & Hole, G. (2003). *How to design and report experiments*. SAGE.

Li, W., & Moyer, M. (2008). *The Blackwell guide to research methods in bilingualism and multilingualism*. Blackwell.

Pavlenko, A. (2014). *The bilingual mind: And what it tells us about language and thought*. Cambridge University Press.

Schwieter, J. W. (Ed.). (2019). *The handbook of the neuroscience of multilingualism*. Wiley-Blackwell.

CHAPTER TWO

Neural Representations and Language Processing in the Bilingual Brain

Learning Objectives

- Develop an understanding of key brain areas associated with language among bilinguals.
- Learn about the processes involved in bilingual language. Comprehension and, specifically, about word recognition.
- Explore bilingual language production, including picture naming, word production, and translation.
- Gain an understanding of the cognitive and neuroscientific methods used to study language comprehension and production.

2.1 Introduction

Researchers have been intrigued by the complicated nature of the representation of two languages in one brain for many years. To date, studies have uncovered a wealth of information by examining the bilingual brain using sophisticated imaging technologies (see Chapter 1). In this chapter we will look at **neural and neurocognitive representations** of multiple languages on one brain. In doing so, we will tackle difficult questions such as where languages are processed in the brain and which **neurological mechanisms** facilitate speech production and comprehension. Throughout the chapter, we will discuss studies that have made significant strides toward a comprehensive view of where languages are **localized and processed**, and also explore central themes, concepts, and assumptions, including those from neuroscience, psycholinguistics, language acquisition, and bilingualism, in order to formulate an understanding of **two languages in one brain**.

In Section 2.2, we discuss language lateralization in bilinguals and provide a general sketch of some of the important **brain areas** associated with language representation and processing. Following this, in Section 2.3 we address some key research on **language comprehension** among bilinguals. The research we review has employed widely-used behavioral experiments such as word recognition and sentence processing tasks. We will also highlight some advanced and fruitful technologies that measure perception skills and, as a result, have elucidated our knowledge of how language is comprehended. Section 2.4 transitions to processes of **bilingual speech production** through an exploration of whether spoken or written words provide unrestricted, restricted, or partially restricted access to both language subsystems. Finally, Section 2.5 concludes the chapter, by emphasizing that the neural representation of languages in bilinguals is affected by several **factors**, among which relative proficiency seems to be the most influential.

2.2 Key Language Areas and Lateralization in Bilinguals

Since at least the early 1800s, researchers have been interested in whether certain abilities, sensations, and behaviors are related to specific locations in the brain. This theory of **localization** was adapted to human language(s) in the brain and, by the mid-1800s, *language* was thought to have several neurological "hot spots." An enduring question in bilingualism research relates to whether languages are represented in such a way that one language is located in one hemisphere and the other language in another hemisphere. More and more, research is suggesting that this is not the case. Although there are several functional differences between the left and right hemispheres, to say that the **left hemisphere** is responsible for Language A and the **right hemisphere** for Language B is inaccurate.

In popular psychology, efforts have been made to assign certain abilities to either the left or right hemisphere. For example, you may have heard that the left side of the brain is the logical side and the right side is the creative one. While claims like this may have some validity, others are often incorrect given the variable nature of the human brain. In fact, many brain functions – including bilingual language processing – are distributed across both hemispheres. In Table 2.1, we list **some anecdotal functions** that have been suggested to be predominately executed by either the left or right hemisphere.

As Table 2.1 suggests, language abilities are executed in both hemispheres. However, many neurologists believe that for most right-handed people, for example, language is **lateralized** in the left hemisphere. The term *lateralize* refers to the area where primary function occurs. In other words, right-handed people may use their left hemisphere slightly more than the right hemisphere for language tasks. The opposite is the case for left-handed people, who more than likely have language lateralized in the right hemisphere. Stretching across both hemispheres are

Table 2.1 Primary functions of the left and right cerebral hemispheres

Left hemisphere	Right hemisphere
• Language: Linear reasoning such as grammar and word production • Logical reasoning • Temporal-order judgments • Analysis • Sequencing • Mathematics • Filling in forms: Letters and numbers	• Language: Holistic reasoning such as understanding metaphors and intonation • Spatial perception • Pattern matching • Creativity and imagination • Facial recognition • Holistic thinking • Feelings and intuitions

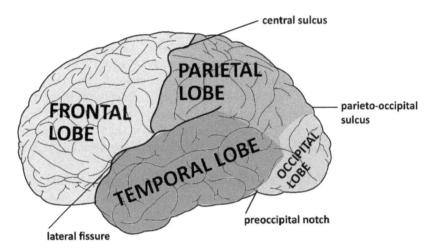

Figure 2.1 Lobes and fissures in the cortex
Note: A black and white version of this figure will appear in some formats. For the color version, please refer to the plate section.

several **lobes** of the brain: **Frontal, parietal, occipital**, and **temporal**. The lobes are anatomically divided by **fissures**: The parieto-occipital sulcus, the central sulcus, the lateral fissure, and the preoccipital notch (see Figure 2.1). In Table 2.2, we provide an overview of key functions of the brain's lobes.

While each of the lobes is involved in some aspect of language, there are a few particular areas in the left frontal and temporal lobes, if language is lateralized in the left hemisphere, that are especially important for both monolingualism and bilingualism. One area in the brain that appears to

Table 2.2 Primary functions of the lobes of the brain

Lobe of the cortex	Primary functions
Frontal	• Speaking • Voluntary movement and motor performance • Planning and predicting future consequences of current actions • Making the choice between good and bad actions • Controlling socially unacceptable responses • Differentiating and finding similarities between things or events
Parietal	• Reading • Integrating sensory information from various parts of the body • Knowing about numbers and their relations • Manipulating objects
Occipital	• Visual processing
Temporal	• Retaining short- and long-term memories • Processing auditory information including words and speech • Integrating sensory functions

be essential for language *production* is known as **Broca's area**. French surgeon Paul Broca (1861) reported on a patient who was completely unable to produce speech but could comprehend it relatively well. A postmortem examination of the patient's brain revealed that there was a lesion in the **inferior frontal gyrus (IFC)** of the left hemisphere. Specifically, the lesion was located in Brodmann areas 44 and 45 – according to Brodmann's (1909) system of labeling and locating the microanatomy of brain areas. A few years later, German physician Carl Wernicke (1874) elaborated on a patient who appeared to have the opposite language impairments as Broca's patient. Wernicke's patient was able to produce fluent, yet unintelligible, speech but could not comprehend language, including the speech he produced. The postmortem autopsy showed a lesion in the left superior temporal gyrus (Brodmann area 22). This area is now known as **Wernicke's area**. A third place in the brain that is important for language is the region which connects Broca's and Wernicke's areas – the **arcuate fasciculus** (see Chapter 3, Figure 3.6). Lichtheim (1885) found that this language center appears to store conceptual representations. While we will discuss language impairments due to damage to these areas in Chapter 4, it is important to note here that damage to Broca's area will have some effect on language production, damage to Wernicke's area will affect language comprehension abilities, and damage to the arcuate fasciculus will adversely impact word knowledge.

Soon after the seminal works by Broca (1861) and Wernicke (1874), researchers became interested in learning more about whether bilinguals' two languages are represented and subserved by the same key areas as those identified in monolinguals. Scoresby-Jackson (1867) reported on a bilingual patient who suffered selective loss of one language but not the other, leading him to speculate that a bilingual's two languages are represented in different brain areas. This was later rejected by Pitres (1895), who instead favored the idea that the **two languages utilize different circuits of neurons within the same brain areas**. Pitres' explanation was that the loss of one but not both languages in Scoresby-Jackson's patient was due to a functional impairment: The mechanism that regulates the affected language (in that same brain area) was damaged.

Pitres' account that bilinguals' languages were stored in the same language areas but subserved by different neural circuits was widely accepted for several decades. In the 1970s, with the introduction of functional neuroimaging and other methodologies, researchers became even more interested in localization of languages in the bilingual brain. An enduring question within this established paradigm is whether languages are lateralized differently for bilinguals than for monolinguals. Behavioral methods (e.g., dichotic listening tasks, tachistoscopic viewing, and verbal-manual interference) and functional neuroimaging studies have been employed, and while progress has been made toward answering this question, there are quite a few conflicting results. For instance, while some studies have found that **language is left lateralized**, others have shown that **language is bilateralized**. Ongoing work is being conducted to rectify these differential findings.

Meta-analyses of behavioral studies on lateralization of languages in the bilingual brain (Hull & Vaid, 2006; Vaid & Hall, 1991) and commentaries criticizing their experimental validity (Paradis, 1990, 2003) provide explanations that account for some of the inconsistent findings. Paradis (2003), for instance, argues that certain experimental conditions may not have been fulfilled in previous studies. He speculates that in order for **an experiment to be valid**, four conditions must be satisfied: The task should indeed measure cerebral laterality; the aspect of language that is being investigated (e.g., syntax, vocabulary) should be clearly articulated; the stimuli in the task must truly measure the aspect of language under investigation; and the rationale for why this aspect of language is lateralized differently for monolinguals and bilinguals. The importance of empirically valid proficiency data has also been discussed in other works by Paradis (2004), de Bot (2008, 2009), and Abutalebi et al. (2013).

Hull and Vaid's (2006) meta-analysis supported Paradis' (2003) criticism of experimental validity. They found that different behavioral experimental tasks revealed distinct results: Whereas studies using the **dichotic listening task** suggested that languages are lateralized in the left hemisphere for both monolinguals and bilinguals, studies that included **tachistoscopic viewing** and **verbal-manual interference** paradigms favored the view that languages are bilateralized. This indicated that the tasks may not be measuring the same thing. When controlling for the experimental differences, the meta-analysis showed that language in monolinguals is slightly more dominant in the left hemisphere. For bilinguals, Hull and Vaid found considerable variability in participant characteristics. Particularly, the age of acquisition (AoA) of an L2 seems to modulate the laterality of the L1. Early bilinguals, whom they defined as having been exposed to the L2 before the age of six, appeared to have bilateral hemispheric use of their L1, whereas late bilinguals were left dominant. The meta-analysis by Hull and Vaid suggested that there is something about being exposed to an L2 early on that affects neurofunctional organization. However, methodological shortcomings of the behavioral experiments may be too significant to accurately examine language lateralization, at least without further refining and meta-analyses that elucidate what each experiment exactly measured. For this complicated reason, many researchers have turned to functional neuroimaging technologies to study the neural substrate of bilingualism. Methods such as PET and fMRI have been used to explore neural underpinnings and processes of languages and their cerebral organization in bilingual individuals.

A study by Kim et al. (1997) looked at the effects of L2 AoA on the organization of languages in the brain using fMRI. The study showed that both the L1 and L2 were active in the same parts of Broca's area for early bilinguals, but the opposite was true for late bilinguals: Different parts of Broca's areas were recruited for the two languages. The brain imaging did not reveal differences between early and late bilinguals in Wernicke's area, as evidenced by the fact that similar areas were active for both groups. However, Illes et al.'s (1999) study on late English–Spanish proficient bilinguals showed different activated areas. These participants were asked to make semantic decisions (e.g., is the word an abstract or concrete entity?) or nonsemantic decisions (e.g., is the word presented in upper or lower case?) about visually presented L1 and L2 words. Although both languages showed similar areas of activation that were reported by Chee et al. (1999), the degree of this activation was significantly different between semantic and nonsemantic decisions. Illes et al. argued that a bilingual's two languages utilize the same frontal lobe areas for semantic processing and that the two languages activate, access, and share a common semantic system.

Although L2 AoA and relative proficiency are intrinsically inter-twined, and oftentimes, but not always, late bilinguals are less proficient in the L2 than early bilinguals (Johnson & Newport, 1989; Weber-Fox & Neville, 1996), work by Perani et al. (1998) demonstrates just how significant these variables are. In their study, the researchers manipu-lated the L2 AoA variable when maintaining L2 proficiency constant and the results showed that AoA no longer had an effect on L2 rep-resentation in the brain (see also Abutalebi, Cappa, & Perani, 2005). Abutalebi and colleagues have also argued that **L2 proficiency is indeed a stronger predictor of language lateralization in bilinguals than L2 AoA** (Abutalebi, 2008; Abutalebi, Cappa, & Perani, 2001, 2005). They also noted the neurological differences in processing grammar versus seman-tics. Specifically, they speculated that L2 AoA selectively affects the neu-ral representation and organization of grammar, whereas L2 proficiency selectively affects the neural representation and organization of seman-tics (see also Wartenburger et al., 2003).

Xue et al. (2004), however, questioned the validity of this claim and once again reminded researchers of the inconsistent findings regarding understanding the organization of languages in the bilingual brain. In this study, Mandarin-speaking children (aged ten to twelve), who had only been learning their less-proficient L2 English since the age of eight, performed a semantic judgment task. The results showed similar activa-tion patterns for both the L1 and L2, suggesting that the languages share neural substrates for semantic processing even when L2 proficiency was rather weak. Xue et al. argued that **early and extensive exposure to an L2 may affect the pattern of brain activation in the semantic processing** of bilinguals' languages (see also Perani & Abutalebi, 2005; Vingerhoets et al., 2003).

As mentioned earlier in this section, Hull and Vaid (2006) provided meta-analytic insight from behavioral studies. Similarly, Indefrey (2006) conducted a meta-analysis of PET and fMRI research in an attempt to identify reliable neural differences between L1 and L2 processing and organization. The analyses took into account several factors, including task type (word production, semantic decisions, and grammatical/semantic decisions of sentences) and participant characteristics (L2 AoA, L2 proficiency, and the amount of exposure to the L2). The meta-analysis of the 30 included studies showed only 15 differences in activation in the identified 114 brain regions. Importantly, these differences were not associated with the *location* of neural activated but rather the **degree of** *strength* **of activation**. Specifically, in nearly all activation differences, stronger activation was observed for the L2 compared to the L1. The cases of difference in strength were mostly found in the left IFC, which Indefrey argued is evidence for more effortful and less efficient processing for an L2 than for an L1. When testing the effects of participant characteristics, all three variables played a role in the activation differences for word production tasks. But only L2 proficiency affected semantic decision tasks and only L2 AoA predicted grammatical/semantic decisions of sentences (see also Wartenburger et al., 2003). Indefrey's meta-analysis showed that "reliably stronger activation during L2 processing is found (a) only for task-specific subgroups of L2 speakers and (b) within some, but not all regions that are also typically activated in native language processing" (Indefrey, 2006, p. 279).

Sebastian, Laird, and Kiran (2011) provided a meta-analysis of the neural representation of two languages. Their examination included fourteen neuroimaging studies of bilingual language processing and found a consistent effect for L2 proficiency. Whereas low/moderately proficient bilinguals demonstrated smaller and more distributed activation across both hemispheres, highly proficient bilinguals showed similar activation patterns mainly in the left frontal region for both the L1 and L2. The results of their meta-analysis provide additional support for the effects of L2 proficiency. Similar findings for L2 AoA have been reported in another meta-analysis by Liu and Cao (2016) in which the authors showed that the L2 activated several regions (i.e., insula and frontal cortex areas) more strongly than the L1, especially among bilinguals with late AoA.

When studying the neural representation of two languages in one brain, de Groot (2011, p. 435) argues that

many variables need to be taken into account because they all might influence the (strength and/or locus of the) pattern of differential brain activation for L1 and L2: the specific task the participants have to perform while being scanned (comprehension or production; auditory or visual; at the word level or sentence level; one that taps semantic processing, grammatical processing, or both), and participant characteristics such as L2 acquisition age, L2 proficiency, and amount of L2 exposure.

Grosjean's (1989) seminal work suggesting that a **bilingual should not be viewed as two monolinguals in one mind**, along with empirical work on the cerebral organization and lateralization of languages in bilinguals, implies that **the bilingual brain involves a complex neural network that can vary widely across individuals** – a notion which we will continue to explore throughout this book.

Cargnelutti, Tomasino, and Fabbro (2019a) conducted coordinate-based meta-analyses to examine the role of L2 AoA and L2 proficiency with regard to the representation of two languages in one brain. Their analyses investigated specific brain activity associated with each language and compared them within and between groups. Their findings showed that the L2 was more widely represented in the brain than the L1, regardless of AoA (although this was slightly more pronounced for late bilinguals). They noted that the L2 in particular elicited greater activity in brain areas responsible for **executive functions** (EFs) but that early AoA and high proficiency reduced such activity. Overall, this meta-analysis indicates that AoA significantly shapes the bilingual brain and that L2 proficiency can modify the languages' functional representation (see also Fabbro & Cargnelutti, 2018). In Section 2.3, we turn to a discussion on the neural representations and processes involved in the recognition and comprehension of language in bilinguals.

2.3 Language Comprehension among Bilinguals

It is generally accepted that in the brain, language comprehension for bilinguals is flexible and quite variable (Dehaene et al., 1997). Neuroimaging studies of bilinguals have found that individual differences such as L2 AoA, proficiency, exposure, frequency of use, and relative dominance play a significant role in how multiple languages are functionally mapped in the brain (Abutalebi, Cappa, & Perani, 2001). This body of work suggests that there is **considerable plasticity in the network responsible for language comprehension in bilinguals** and that L2 proficiency and exposure seem to modulate functional mappings more than AoA. In fact, findings indicate that attained proficiency in and exposure to an L2 have a larger effect on the cerebral representation of languages in bilinguals than the age at which the L2 was acquired (Perani et al., 1998). For auditory comprehension, highly proficient bilinguals who have acquired their L2 later in life show similar activated neural areas as highly proficient bilinguals who have simultaneously acquired both languages from birth. These similarities are not found when comparing activated neural areas to bilinguals with low L2 proficiency (Perani et al., 1998). In Section 2.3.1 we will discuss two well-researched domains of bilingual language comprehension – namely how bilinguals recognize words in isolation and in sentences. Along the way, we will take a look at some models that explain how these processes function and vary across bilinguals. We also discuss many of these models in more detail in Chapter 6.

2.3.1 Word Recognition in Isolation

Studies that investigate **how bilinguals recognize words** ask important questions such as: Are words in one language active and competing for selection when reading words in the other language? What are the processing differences and cross-language interferences that arise when reading words **in isolation versus in meaningful phrases**? At what point during word recognition does cross-linguistic activation occur and how is this interference overcome? Perhaps the question that has received most attention in the bilingual word recognition literature is whether bilinguals have selective or nonselective access to the mental lexicon. Whereas **language selective access** refers to the exclusive activation of information in the appropriate language, **language nonselective access** implies automatic co-activation of information in both languages (de Groot, 2011).

Imagine that an English–French bilingual is asked to read aloud the word *bonjour*. Do you think that its translation equivalent *hello* is also activated? What about semantically related words such as *goodbye*? Our intuitions may lead us to believe that words in both languages are stored in separate mental lexicons. Likely, this belief is motivated merely by what we can observe from bilinguals' language use: They are able to use one language without massive intrusions from the other (Poulisse & Bongaerts, 1994) and even do more complex things like switch back and forth between both languages with relative ease or simultaneously interpret from one to another (Diamond & Shreve, 2019). However, since around the turn of the century, researchers studying bilingual **word recognition** have argued that bilinguals do not recognize words the same way as their monolingual counterparts, supporting Grosjean's (1989) statement that a bilingual should not be viewed as "two monolinguals in one person" as we mentioned in Section 2.2.

Although there has been empirical evidence from early studies supporting language selective access (Gerard & Scarborough, 1989; Kirsner et al., 1980; Macnamara & Kushnir, 1971; Rodriguez-Fornells et al., 2002; Scarborough, Gerard, & Cortese, 1984), the **nonselective access account has undoubtedly received more support**. Several studies have shown that **both languages are active**, and that they interact with one another when bilinguals are asked to read words aloud in only one of their languages (e.g., Dijkstra, Grainger, & van Heuven, 1999; Duyck, 2005; Van Assche et al., 2009; van Hell & Dijkstra, 2002). In one well-cited study, van Heuven, Dijkstra, and Grainger (1998) conducted a battery of experiments investigating how word recognition is influenced by the **orthographic neighbors** of words in the same language and words in a bilingual's other language. These experiments were performed on Dutch-English bilinguals and English monolinguals. Van Heuven, Dijkstra, and Grainger found that word recognition in both Dutch and English was hindered by orthographic neighbors from the nontarget (irrelevant) language. However, when the orthographic neighbors were presented in the target (relevant) language, they facilitated recognition of target words. These results imply that there is **parallel activation of words in an integrated lexicon.** They also provide evidence for a mechanism of mutual inhibition within an integrated lexicon rather than between two independent lexicons. Based on these findings, the authors put forth a theoretical explanation of how bilinguals recognize words, the **Bilingual Interactive Activation (BIA) Model,** and called for future research examining the possible influence of active phonological representations.

This call was answered four years later by Dijkstra and van Heuven (2002), who tested the BIA Model and proposed several updates to address many of its limitations. These insufficiencies included limited lexical and language representations, the model's handling of context effects, and its lack of an implemented task structure. The revised version of the BIA, the **BIA+,** includes orthographic, phonological, and semantic lexical representations, assigns a new role to **language nodes,** and adds a task/decision component. These additions allowed the model to distinguish between linguistic and nonlinguistic information and their effects on performance. Dijkstra and van Heuven also argued that the model can be applied to other linguistic tasks and modalities. The BIA+ has received support in a number of studies using a variety of experimental methods.

Most of the work reporting on bilingual word recognition is based on nontonal languages. However, a few studies suggest that in **tonal languages** such as Mandarin, lexical tones are considered as important as segments in word recognition (Lee, 2007; Malins & Joanisse, 2010; Schirmer et al., 2005). Even though it is still unclear how tonal information affects word recognition in nontonal languages, one study by Shook and Marian (2016) attempted to address this question. They asked Mandarin speakers of L2 English to select the correct Mandarin translations presented on a computer screen while hearing an English word. The auditory English words were manipulated in pitch contour to either match or mismatch the Mandarin translation. The results showed that the bilinguals were sensitive to the manipulation of pitch contours in English words. Although these effects may have been due to the influence of visually presented Chinese characters, a subsequent study reporting similar findings did not find this (Wang, Wang, & Malins, 2017). It instead revealed that tonal bilinguals require the availability of both tonal and segmental information to induce cross-language lexical competition in word recognition, even when there is no phonological overlap between the two languages. Another study by Wang, Hui, and Chen (2020), however, showed that cross-language lexical competition was only observed with the presence of lexical tones, in addition to segmental overlap.

Although we will discuss word production later in Section 2.4.1, it is relevant at this point to note that the processes by which bilinguals *recognize* words in isolation and *produce* them are not the same. It can be problematic when models such as the BIA+ attempt to account for both processes. To demonstrate this, Mosca and de Bot (2017) examined how bilinguals select words in one of their languages during comprehension and production while minimalizing interference from their other language. Their goal was to find whether these processes could be accounted for by one model alone (e.g., BIA+) or whether claims from additional models (e.g., the Inhibitory Control (IC) Model, Green, 1998) need to be included in the explanation. In the study, a group of Dutch speakers of advanced L2 English participated in a lexical decision task (recognition) and picture naming task (production) involving language switching. The results from the recognition task were in line with the IC Model's predictions, as it was found that the amount of inhibition applied to the nontarget language increased with language dominance. However, for the production task, the results revealed that inhibition of the nontarget language was not due to language dominance but was rather influenced by other unconscious strategies to aid the weaker language. Mosca and de Bot argue that **word recognition and word production use distinct processing mechanisms**, and as such, they claim that no models in their present form can account for both. Mosca and de Bot's study clearly demonstrate that more research is needed to verify whether the recognition and production differences in language control and inhibition are due to different supporting processing mechanisms.

2.3.2 Word Recognition in Context

Whereas most studies have investigated the recognition of isolated words, as we have reviewed, it is well known that words most often appear in meaningful phrases. Consequently, one may speculate that word recognition in isolation and in sentence contexts differ in several ways. Monolingual studies indicate that word recognition in sentences can affect semantic, syntactic, and lexical activation for other words that appear later in the sentence (e.g., Schwanenflugel & LaCount, 1988). These effects are not found when words are presented in isolation. Are these **sentence context effects**, found in word recognition among monolinguals, also used by bilinguals to speed up lexical access through representations of two languages? Is it possible that, for bilinguals, word recognition in sentences is a procedure in which lexical activation can be restricted to words of the target language (i.e., a language selective procedure)? Van Assche, Duyck, and Hartsuiker (2012) offer a synthesis of bilingual visual word recognition both in isolation and sentence contexts, and examine language selectivity. They review eye-tracking studies focused on semantic constraint effects on language nonselective access and discuss the implications of the various patterns of results. The authors argued that the evidence examined did not clearly explain the occurrence of top-down modulation from semantics to the orthographic level during later word recognition stages. They call for the BIA+ and other models to be revised to account for factors influencing linguistic context and lexical variable interactions and how these results could be better generalized (see also Mosca & de Bot, 2017).

Since around 2005 or so, a number of studies have investigated word recognition in sentences (e.g., Duyck et al., 2007; Elston-Güttler, Gunter, & Kotz, 2005; Libben & Titone, 2009; Schwartz & Kroll, 2006; Titone et al., 2011; Van Assche et al., 2011; van Hell & de Groot, 2008). Desmet and Duyck (2007) review bilingual language processing at each level of language representation in order to understand the degree of influence a bilingual's languages have on each other. Their synthesis shows that bilinguals cannot "turn off" a language to process in a monolingual mode and that **both languages are activated at all levels of representation**. Desmet and Duyck also explore in depth the influence of a bilingual's language at the syntactic level. They found that cross-linguistic syntactic priming is present in bilinguals. However, they underscore questions in this area which still need to be answered, such as whether these syntactic structures need to have the same word order in their respective languages, and how L2 proficiency influences interaction between syntactic representations.

As we transition to bilingual language production in Section 2.4, let's take a moment to discuss a study by MacDonald (2013) which used the **production-distribution-comprehension** (PDC) account for how language production shapes language form and comprehension. The PDC hypothesis (MacDonald, 1999) holds that, during language production, memory and planning demands strongly affect the form of speakers' utterances. MacDonald (2013) analyzed verb modification ambiguities and relative clauses and found that production choices influenced these comprehension phenomena. She argued that sentence comprehension phenomena may be better explained through distributional regularities in language and utterance planning processes as proposed in the PDC, rather than by the comprehension system architecture approach. Therefore, she proposes that research in language comprehension must also be studied alongside production processes. MacDonald suggests that the influence language production has on language form and comprehension may support a mechanistic account of language production that includes covert production processes.

2.4 Language Production among Bilinguals

Similar to our discussion on language comprehension, research on language production has also revealed evidence that elements in the nonresponse language are active when bilinguals speak. In both word generation and picture naming tasks, this **cross-linguistic interference persists throughout the stages of lexical access**: The activation of the appropriate concept, selection of the target word from the mental lexicon, phonological encoding, phonetic encoding, and articulation (Levelt et al., 1998). Important theoretical developments in bilingual speech production have come from Costa, Colomé, and Caramazza (2000), Green (1998), and Green and Abutalebi (2013).

Costa, Caramazza, and Sebastián-Gallés (2000) examined various models of monolingual lexical access. They consider whether these models, primarily **cascaded** and **discrete models**, can account for bilingual **lexical access**. They discuss assumptions and proposals surrounding the activation of semantic representations and lexical nodes in bilinguals, particularly theories which suggest that both languages of a bilingual are activated in parallel. From their review, they observed two possibilities: Either bilinguals have a mechanism which inhibits activation of lexical nodes belonging to the irrelevant language, suggesting that lexical selection is language nonspecific, or they possess a lexical selection mechanism which only considers activation of the lexical node of the relevant language, implying that lexical selection is a language-specific operation. Costa, Caramazza, and Sebastián-Gallés conclude that both of a bilingual's lexicons may be activated in parallel by semantic representations and that the semantic system is shared by each language.

Green's (1986, 1998) **IC Model** explains bilingual language control and the underlying mechanisms supporting it during speech production. As Schwieter and Ferreira (2013) describe:

The IC Model argues that the language production system has multiple levels of control and that lexical nodes are marked with language tags which designate them to a specific language. When words in both languages are active and competing to control output, successful selection requires the suppression of competing non-target words. The primary assumption of the IC Model is that language production is a product of inhibition, control schemas, and a supervisory attentional system. Although the model further argues multiple levels of control in the bilingual mind with each level corresponding to a specific schema, IC operates exclusively at the lemma level. [The model] assumes that when bilinguals speak, the language selection and control procedures entail a conceptualizer which builds conceptual representations that are driven by the communicative goal. These both are mediated by the SAS together with components of the language system (i.e., language task schemas). The bilingual mind will turn to language tags to help determine which non-target words (i.e., those competing for selection) will need to be inhibited and subsequently apply IC to those competitors. (p. 246)

Building on some of the facets of Grosjean's (2001) **language mode hypothesis**, which posits that the relative activation level of bilinguals' languages varies along a continuum ranging from monolingual mode to bilingual mode, Green and Abutalebi (2013) proposed a set of neural correlates that underlie eight control processes in bilingual speech production. In their **adaptive control hypothesis**, different language contexts (e.g., monolingual mode vs. code-switching) lead to distinct patterns of language selection. These various situations have differential demands on the cognitive and neural processes for each language. As such, the neural networks supporting bilingual speech production are hypothesized to adapt to utilize these processes as necessitated by the context (see Chapter 7). For example, a frequent code-switcher will engage inhibitory control mechanisms in different ways than bilinguals who rarely switch between their languages. On this theoretical backdrop, we now turn to discuss the most-studied areas of bilingual language production: Word production, picturing naming, and word translation.

2.4.1 Word Production

Neuroimaging studies of word production investigate the cerebral representation of language activity in bilinguals. Typically, tasks that ask bilinguals to generate words may include **rhyme generation** to examine phonological bases or **synonym generation** to study lexical-semantic processing. Regardless of whether bilinguals are engaging in rhyme or synonym generation in either of their languages, there is significant activation in the **brain's frontal areas**. However, there are subtle, yet notable, differences with respect to the exact loci of these processes: Rhyme generation seems to activate the left IFC and the posterior frontal operculum while synonym generation engages anterior frontal regions (Klein et al., 1995).

For highly proficient bilinguals, even when acquiring their L2 later in life, word production appears to activate similar brain areas (Klein et al., 1994). In fact, some studies have shown that both languages recruit the same brain areas regardless of L2 AoA. For instance, Chee, Tan, and Thiel (1999) examined several areas of the left and right hemispheres among early and late Mandarin–English bilinguals who participated in a word generation task. Their results showed that **word generation activated the same areas for the two languages among both early and late bilinguals**. These areas were the dorsolateral prefrontal areas, inferior frontal areas including Broca's area, the supplementary motor area, and occipital and parietal regions in both hemispheres (see also Illes et al., 1999). Chee, Tan, and Thiel argue that L2 proficiency may be a better indicator of modulating the neural organization of a bilingual's languages than L2 AoA.

As with word generation tasks, **word repetition** is common in bilingual production studies. Neuroimaging has shown that repeating words elicits bilateral activation in areas commonly associated with auditory speech processing (Liégeois et al., 2003; McCrory et al., 2000; Price, 2000). Although most studies have used fMRI, PET, MEG, and ERPs to examine the bilingual brain, Sugiura et al. (2011) used fNIRS to monitor changes in brain activation while bilingual children repeated words. Their study included a sample of 484 Japanese children learning L2 English who participated in a word repetition task in their two languages. The variables of interest were language of production (L1 vs. L2), word frequency (high vs. low), and hemisphere (left vs. right). The results showed that L1 words elicited significantly more brain activity than L2 words, regardless of the participants' knowledge of those words. This activity was particularly strong in the superior/middle temporal and inferior parietal regions (angular/supramarginal gyri). The results also demonstrated an effect for frequency such that low-frequency words elicited more activity in the right hemisphere and high-frequency words elicited more activity in the left hemisphere. Sugiura et al. conclude that, for both L1 and L2, there is a shift from right to left laterality in the inferior parietal region as lexical knowledge increases.

2.4.2 Picture Naming

One of the most common experimental tasks in bilingual speech production is the **picture naming task** in which bilinguals simply name pictures. Researchers have been creative with the task, putting forth several experimental variations. For instance, a target picture may be accompanied with a distracter word or phoneme that has some sort of relationship with the picture's name in either the relevant or irrelevant language. Other times, bilinguals may be required to name the pictures in either one of their languages depending on a color cue. We will look at these types of picture naming tasks and discuss what they tell us about bilingual speech production (see also de Groot & Starreveld, 2015, for a review).

2.4.2.1 Simple Picture Naming

Additional evidence that a bilingual's two languages are activated in parallel even when speaking in one language comes from naming lists of pictures. Costa, Caramazza, and Sebastián-Gallés (2000) asked Spanish–Catalan bilinguals to name pictures whose names in the two languages were either cognates or noncognates. The bilinguals were sensitive to a **cognate effect** such that naming pictures with cognate names was slower than those with noncognate names. The authors interpreted this finding as evidence of parallel activation of the bilingual word production system. Furthermore, they argued that this activation cascades through the semantic, lexical, and sublexical levels in a language nonselective manner. When comparing the cognate effect for picture naming in the L1 to the L2, the results showed that the difference between cognate and noncognate words was larger when the bilinguals named pictures in their less dominant language.

Might this cognate effect in picture naming have to do with the orthographic similarities that cognates often have in the two languages in question? Hoshino and Kroll's (2008) findings suggest that the answer to this possibility is a clear *no*. Their study compared the performance of Spanish–English and Japanese–English bilinguals and found a cognate effect for both groups. This indicates that **the cognate is not sensitive to script differences between languages**. This finding has been reported in other studies (Poarch & van Hell, 2012a; Starreveld et al., 2014). From a theoretical standpoint, as noted by de Groot and Starreveld (2015, p. 400):

The different magnitude of the cognate effect in the participants' two languages is attributed to a difference in the strength of the connections between the conceptual, lexical, and sub-lexical phonological nodes in the two language-subsystems, both the links between the conceptual and lexical nodes and those between the lexical and sub-lexical nodes being stronger for dominant L1 than for L2. Stronger links transmit more activation than weaker links. Consequently, when dominant L1 is the response language the targeted sub-lexical nodes receive less activation from the lexical node in the nonresponse language than when weaker L2 is the response language.

2.4.2.2 Picture Naming with Word Distracters

Research using the **picture-word interference task** seeks to explore whether the set of activated words when naming pictures includes the picture's name in the irrelevant language. In addition to manipulating the semantic or orthographic relationship between the distracter item and the target picture, studies have included word distracters that are phonologically related to the picture's name in the irrelevant language. For example, an English–Spanish bilingual who is asked to name a picture of a fish in English would see an accompanying word such as *pest* (phonological-translation distracter) or *book* (unrelated distracter). The English word *pest* has a phonological relationship with *pez*, the word *fish* in Spanish. If the picture of a fish activates both *fish* and *pez*, a bilingual should be slower to name the picture when accompanied by *pest* compared to *book*. This is indeed what has been found in previous studies (Costa et al., 2003; Hermans et al., 1998), suggesting that when naming pictures in one language, words in both languages, and particularly their phonological representations, are activated.

2.4.2.3 Phoneme Monitoring

At first, it was unclear as to whether the cognate effect in picture-word interference tasks was due to shared morphological representations (see Sánchez-Casas & García-Albea, 2005) or semantic representations (van Hell & de Groot, 1998) rather than the parallel activation of two lexical nodes. An interesting modification to the picture naming task is the addition of **phoneme monitoring** as used by Colomé (2001). Catalan–Spanish bilinguals were shown pictures accompanied by phonemes and were asked to press a "yes" response key if the phoneme was found in the picture's Catalan name and "no" if not. Although pictures were not named aloud, the process of retrieving their name in order to internally generate them is the same. Also, since the task does not utilize cognates or words in the irrelevant language, it is able to avoid any potential language mode effects during task performance (see Grosjean, 1998). In Colomé's study, the accompanying phonemes were either part of the Catalan word (i.e., the target utterance), part of its name in Spanish, or neither (i.e., control). The bilinguals rejected phonemes that appeared in Spanish words significantly slower than control phonemes. When modifying the onset of the distracter phonemes such that they appeared prior to pictures (−2000 ms) or after (+200 and +400 ms), the results were the same. The effects, localized at the sublexical level, were interpreted to support the language nonselective hypothesis in which words in both languages are activated in parallel.

Further support for parallel phonological encoding in both languages was found by Rodriguez-Fornells et al. (2005), who used behavioral, ERP, and fMRI methods. Spanish–German bilinguals and monolingual German speakers were asked to press a response button when the name of a picture they saw on a computer screen started with a vowel in German and to not respond if it started with a consonant. Two conditions were examined: A coincidence condition meant that the picture's name in both languages began with a vowel or consonant; and a noncoincidence condition was when the picture's name began with a vowel in one language and with a consonant in the other language. The findings showed that bilinguals were slower in noncoincidence conditions and had different ERPs than in coincidence conditions, implying that there was interference from the activation of the irrelevant language's phonological representation. Compared to the bilinguals, monolinguals did not show these behavioral or neural interference effects from the two conditions. The fMRI data showed that the bilinguals utilized brain areas responsible for the control of behavior in nonverbal tasks. This likely was due to the **need to deal with the interference caused by a language competing for selection**. We will now turn to testing language control in picture naming.

2.4.2.4 Mixed-Language Picture Naming

The picture naming task can also be designed such that bilinguals are required to switch back and forth between the two languages. The language of production is determined by virtue of a color cue (e.g., if pictures appear in blue boxes, they are to be named in Language A and if they are in red boxes, in Language B). These studies often seek to investigate how bilinguals control their two languages. In a seminal study by

Costa and Santesteban (2004), Spanish learners of Catalan and Korean learners of Spanish performed a switching task between their two languages. For these learners, naming a picture that required a language switch was slower than when naming a picture when the preceding example was in the same language. Importantly, when comparing switching from the L1 into L2, the reaction times (RTs) revealed that switching to the L1 was slower than switching to the L2. This **asymmetrical switching cost** was absent when the researchers tested a new group of highly proficient Spanish–Catalan bilinguals. Given that asymmetrical switching costs have been taken to support the IC Model (Meuter & Allport, 1999), Costa and Santesteban were the first to argue that the processes underlying bilingual speech production for less-proficient bilinguals is not the same as for highly proficient bilinguals (see also Schwieter & Sunderman, 2008).

Costa, Santesteban, and Ivanova (2006) replicated the results from Costa and Santesteban such that highly proficient bilinguals (Spanish–Catalan) exhibited symmetrical switching costs when naming pictures in a mixed-language context. These results were found both for bilinguals with early and late L2 AoA. However, in additional experiments, they found that highly proficient bilinguals from this same population who were learning English (L3) and French (L4) showed asymmetric switching costs when switching between these two weak languages. Another group of bilinguals switched between naming pictures in their L1 and in a newly learned (i.e., artificial) language. Once again, the bilinguals showed asymmetric switching costs. Taken together, the authors suggest that although highly proficient bilinguals typically rely on a language-specific selection mechanism during lexical selection, there is evidence that in some conditions (i.e., such as when language switching involves a weak language), these bilinguals must rely on inhibitory control (note, however, that other factors impact on the switching behavior in such studies: (a) participants' inhibitory control abilities; Festman, Rodriguez-Fornells, & Münte, 2010, and (b) preparation time; Festman & Mosca, 2016). This finding was also supported by Schwieter and Sunderman's (2008) study, in which the authors put forth the **Selection by Proficiency Model**. The model proposes a bidirectional move from inhibitory control to a language-specific selective mechanism as the connections between L2 words and the concepts onto which they are mapped strengthen. The authors' analyses demonstrated that a particular aspect of global proficiency, namely lexical robustness, is a modulating factor in these processes. The study also identified a specific threshold of lexical robustness in which language-specific selection was engaged. The Selection by

Proficiency Model, in part, brings together the IC model and the Revised
Hierarchical Model (RHM), which we will discuss in Section 2.4.3.

2.4.3 Word Translation

We have learned a great deal about the bilingual memory and how words
are represented in the mind based on **word translation experiments**.
Early theoretical explanations suggested that L2 words are understood
and produced by retrieving their L1 translation equivalent (Potter et al.,
1984). Subsequent explanations were more developmental in nature. For
instance, Kroll and Stewart's (1994) RHM demonstrates a shift from lexical to conceptual mediation. Specifically, the model posits that as L2
proficiency increases, L2 words no longer need to be associated with
their L1 translation equivalents to access the conceptual store (see also
Schwieter & Sunderman, 2009).

It has been observed that concrete words and cognates are translated faster than abstract words. Several studies (De Groot, 1992, 1993;
De Groot, Dannenburg, & Van Hell, 1994; Kroll & Stewart, 1994) have
shown that while the representations of concrete words and cognates are
shared across languages, abstract words share fewer semantic features.
In Dong, Cui, and MacWhinney's (2005) study, the researchers found
that conceptual representations of translation equivalents are not necessarily fully shared but rather are partially overlapping. They argue that
links between words and concepts are stronger in the L1 compared to the
L2 (Kroll & Stewart, 1994). More recent theoretical accounts have begun
to describe the architecture of the bilingual memory as a dynamic system
involving conceptual restructuring and overlapping (Benati & Schwieter,
2017; Pavlenko, 2009). We will discuss the lexical-conceptual system in
Chapter 6.

Neuroimaging studies have shed light on the brain regions that are activated when bilinguals translate individual words. Price, Green, and von
Studnitz (1999) used PET to examine bilinguals who silently mouthed
translations of visually presented words. The results showed involvement
of the putamen and head of the caudate nucleus, among other areas,
which are outside of the classic "language areas" in the brain. Similarly,
using PET and fMRI, Quaresima et al. (2002) asked bilinguals to orally
translate short sentences. Significant brain activity was found in the anterior portion of the left hemisphere. Other studies have reported that
particularly during L2 to L1 translation, there is activation of the left
putamen (Klein et al., 1995; Lehtonen et al., 2005). It appears that, for
bilinguals, translating between their two languages, in either direction,

activates the anterior cingulate and bilateral subcortical structures (i.e., the putamen and head of caudate nucleus). This pattern is likely because there is a need for greater coordination of mental operations.

2.5 Summary

In this chapter, we have explored neural representations and language processing in the bilingual brain. In Section 2.2, we began by discussing key language areas and lateralization in bilinguals and looked at some of the primary functions of the hemispheres. Although it is a popular generalization to say that left side of the brain is responsible for logic and the right side for creativity, we noted that many brain functions – including bilingual language processing – are distributed across both hemispheres. We then looked at the function of the four lobes of the brain and identified important areas for language, including Broca's and Wernicke's areas, which have been found to support language production and comprehension, respectively. The chapter then addressed how early or late exposure to an L2 affects the cortical representation of the two languages. Although more research is needed, it appears as though both L2 AoA and proficiency play significant roles in modifying the languages' functional representations.

In Section 2.3, we turned to specific processes of how bilinguals comprehend language. We discussed how bilinguals recognize words when presented in isolation and in phrases. In the bilingual word recognition literature, most attention has been placed on whether bilinguals have selective or nonselective access to their mental lexicon. In general, the findings suggest that both languages are active and interactive with one another when bilinguals are asked to read isolated words in only one of their languages. The BIA+ Model was discussed to provide a theoretical account for bilingual word recognition.

Research on bilingual speech production, as we reviewed in Section 2.4, suggests that a bilingual's lexicons may be activated in parallel by semantic representations and that the semantic system is shared by the two languages. We first discussed prominent theories such as the IC Model, which explains how bilinguals control cross-linguistic competition from the irrelevant language in order to successfully produce the other language, and the adaptive control hypothesis, which argues that these control processes adapt to situational demands. We then reviewed tasks in bilingual language production that have been widely used: Word production, picture naming, and word translation. Many of these studies have tested the effects of L2 AoA. For instance, generating words (rhyme vs. synonym) does not seem to be sensitive to AoA. Studies that ask bilinguals to simply repeat words have revealed at least two important findings: Repeating words in the L1 elicits more brain activity than in the L2; and repeating low-frequency words leads to more activity in the right hemisphere, while repeating high-frequency words gives rise to more activity in the left. Some researchers claim that there is a shift from right to left laterality in the inferior parietal region as lexical knowledge increases.

Simple picture naming studies (i.e., without distracters) show that bilinguals are slower to name pictures whose names are cognates in both languages, suggesting that phonological representations of both languages are active. Additional support for parallel phonological encoding has come from research in which bilinguals decide whether an accompanying phoneme is in the name of the picture. Picture naming in a mixed-language context has allowed researchers to test the control processes involved in bilingual speech production. Generally, although there is support that less-proficient bilinguals utilize inhibitory control, it is less clear as to whether inhibitory control and/or language selective mechanisms are involved in speech production among highly-proficient bilinguals. In line with the adaptive control hypothesis, one particular aspect of L2 proficiency, namely lexical robustness, was hypothesized to be a variable that may determine which processes are recruited and executed. Finally, from word translation experiments, we have learned that there is a differential relationship for L1-to-concept and L2-to-concept mapping. Neuroimaging shows that, during word translation, there is a need for greater coordination of mental operations as evidenced by significant neural activity in the anterior cingulate and bilateral subcortical structures. Overall, we have seen that the neural representations and processing of two languages are far from being fully understand. Nonetheless, we are gaining a clearer picture of the dynamic nature of two languages in one brain and the many individual differences, such as L2 AoA and proficiency, which can affect it.

Review Questions

1. What are three key brain areas associated with language? What functions do they have? What evidence supports these functions?
2. Which behavioral tasks and neuroimaging methods have been used to examine language lateralization in the bilingual brain.
3. Discuss evidence supporting the notion that words in both languages are active and competing for selection when reading words in only one of the languages.

4. How does the IC Model explain bilingual speech production?
5. What is the theoretical explanation for why naming pictures whose names are cognates in two languages is slower than doing so for pictures whose names are not cognates?

Further Reading

Costa, A. (2019). *The bilingual brain: And what it tells us about the science of language* (J. W. Schwieter, Trans.). Allen Lane/Penguin Random House.

De Groot, A. (2011). *Language and cognition in bilinguals and multilinguals: An introduction*. Taylor & Francis.

Hernández, A. (2013). *The bilingual brain*. Oxford University Press.

Vaid, J. (Ed.). (2016). *Language processing in bilinguals: Psycholinguistic and neuropsychological perspectives*. Routledge.

CHAPTER THREE

Bilingualism, Language Development, and Brain Plasticity

Learning Objectives

- Compare the notions of mind and brain in order to understand how they are linked to scientific disciplines.
- Distinguish maturational-based changes of the brain from experience-based changes and understand the related processes (e.g., synaptic development) in the brain.
- Develop an understanding of the differences between acquisition and learning, the stages of learning, and the brain areas involved.
- Gain insight into the ability of sound discrimination in nonnative speech.
- Learn about differences between early and late bilinguals, critical and sensitive periods, and influential factors for language acquisition and learning.

3.1 Introduction

As demonstrated in Chapters 1 and 2, researchers have long been interested in language, in particular the acquisition and learning of more than one language. There are several disciplines reporting on these lines of research – on language itself, on the speaker, on mental processes, and on the structures and functions of language-related areas in the brain. To begin, we will clarify the approaches and interests of these different disciplines to show which researchers are focused on linguistic or psychological facets of bilingualism, which use experimental designs to explore language processing in the mind, and which undertake research on the brain. These different disciplines and approaches can give rise to theories and models based on empirical data.

Linguists traditionally investigate the product (e.g., an utterance, a written text, orthography, error analysis, native-like pronunciation, translation) and its linguistic aspects. In naturalistic observations or descriptive research, researchers examine speakers' behavior, such as reading or conversation. **Sociolinguists** are concerned with the conditions of language in society and culture (i.e., language use in a specific context and

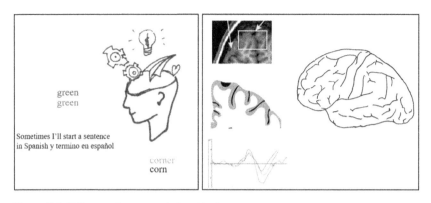

Figure 3.1 Difference between mind and brain
Note: A black and white version of this figure will appear in some formats. For the color version, please refer to the plate section.

language changes), often leading to theories, for example, of languages in contact with other languages (Weinreich, 1953). Bilingual language acquisition at home can be investigated by observing a child's play on the playground and noting/recording verbal utterances. Researchers interested in learning languages in **educational settings** observe and describe motivational and emotional factors (see the influential book by Dewaele, 2010 and Dewaele & Li, 2020, for reviews), the interaction among peers and with the teacher, materials, and degree of immersion.

Psychologists (mainly cognitive and developmental) are more focused on processes in the mind related to language activities (see Figure 3.1). For example, they use the method of eye-tracking to shed light onto how we read; eye-tracking is used to identify the location a reader is looking at in order to formulate assumptions about the reader's focus. Moreover, there is vital interest in babies born into and brought up in a bilingual environment; researchers try to capture the linguistic environment and the way this impacts babies' **linguistic, cognitive, and social development**. Other processes in which psychologists are interested include, for example, how words are learned and stored in memory, and how cognition and language interact. **Experimental scientists (linguists and psychologists alike)** conduct research on speakers' specific behaviors (e.g., reading comprehension, garden-path sentences, tip-of-the-tongue phenomena, code-switching) in experimentally well-designed and controlled studies which may also examine other factors such as working memory (WM) capacity, IQ scores, vocabulary size, and so on (e.g., switching between languages, see Meuter & Allport, 1999). Researchers with a **focus on educational learning** analyze and manipulate measures of SES, quality and quantity of input, level of education, and so on. In particular, **psycholinguists** study how people **learn, use, and comprehend** language. There are a number of models put forward by psycholinguists regarding language production, for example, the seminal model by Levelt (1993) and its bilingual extension by de Bot (2004), or language perception (e.g., Dijkstra & van Heuven, 2002). Psycholinguists are interested in the properties of bilingual language, cognition, and memory; thus, they strive to determine the crucial concepts of language processing, such as the bilingual mental lexicon (e.g., Kroll & Stewart's, 1994, Revised Hierarchical Model, see chapter 2.4.3; for an overview of bilingual models, see de Groot, 2011; Kroll & Tokowicz, 2005; and Chapter 6). They discover and describe phenomena which are of particular interest to the context of bilingualism, such as cognates, interlingual homographs, language transfer, and cross-language interference (see Chapters 5 and 6). Finally, they attempt to clarify patterns by both separating language systems (e.g., nonspecific lexical access) and mixing them (un)intentionally.

Neurolinguists and neurologists are also involved in the study of the bilingual brain (see the influential works by Albert & Obler, 1978; Fabbro, 2001; Paradis, 2004). The seminal paper by Grosjean (1989) entitled "Neurolinguists, beware! The bilingual is not two monolinguals in one person" draws attention again to the fact that an understanding of the complex concept of bilingualism is essential for the study of bilingualism on the neural level. With the advent of neuroimaging techniques, the brain activity of people with two languages can be observed during processing, that is, while performing a task such as picture naming in one or both languages (e.g., Hernandez, Martinez, & Kohnert, 2000; for an overview, see Hernandez, 2013; Schwieter, 2019). What is more, cognitive (neuro)scientists are attentive to processes involved in **managing the challenges on the human mind and brain** to pick up and handle two languages. They are interested in control processes (see Green, 1998), and in representational and organizational questions related to dual language abilities (e.g., Abutalebi, Cappa, & Perani, 2001; Liu & Cao, 2016, for a recent overview). Crucially, **cognitive neuroscientists** have become increasingly aware of the multitude of background factors responsible, to some degree, for the complexity of the concept of bilingualism (see Festman, 2013). Consequently, this chapter also includes much available research regarding, for example, social aspects of language learning and use (e.g., conditions of language use operationalized in the adaptive control hypothesis, Green & Abutalebi, 2013).

In the next sections, we will first define and describe plasticity of the brain (Section 3.2) to increase our understanding of how acquisition and learning take place in the brain (Section 3.3). In Section 3.4, we will reflect on a number of factors that have been found to influence bilin-guals' acquisition and learning. These may include the learning environ-ment (e.g., group dynamics, attitudes, and culture), the input the person receives, and internal factors such as motivation, personality, and emo-tion. Finally, we will elaborate on the critical period hypothesis (CPH) in Section 3.5 to show that the observational evidence that is the basis of this hypothesis provides new light when paired with brain-imaging techniques.

3.2 Brain Plasticity and Learning

The developing brain undergoes changes related to maturational devel-opment as well as to experiences. The former, **developmental-based changes**, are linked and restricted to certain critical time periods and are usually genetically set. They are often related to filtering in sensory areas. For example, only if babies receive adequate stimulation from their environment within the first months of their life can they develop filters in their visual system for perception of orientation and spatial rep-resentation. "Critical period" means that if they do not receive the nec-essary stimulation in time, development is significantly reduced or does not occur (see Section 3.5).

Neurons (see Figure 3.2) are the building units of the brain. Each neu-ron is equipped with a **cell body** and an **axon**. The cell body produces and collects electrical signals. The axon is responsible for transferring infor-mation from the cell body to other neurons. Two (or more) neurons are connected through a terminal located at the end of an axon. Terminals form a **synapse** together with the area onto which they have docked. Thus, they can pass impulses from one neuron to the other(s). Impulses are collected via **dendrites** (often called dendritic trees, due to their shape). According to the famous Hebbian learning principle, **repeated coactivation of neurons** changes the strength of connection among them, which leads to faster and easier activation (Hebb, 1949). Learning is fundamentally based on the coactivation of neurons and learning a new task (rather than continually undertaking an already learned task) causes changes in brain structure (Driemeyer et al., 2008).

After birth, there are major processes involved in neural develop-ment (e.g., Casey et al., 2005), each with its own time course (Banich & Compton, 2018). Brain development in newborns continues several pro-cesses which began after conception, for example, tube formation and development into the ventricular system, the generation of new nerve cells close to the ventricle (i.e., cell proliferation), and cell migration

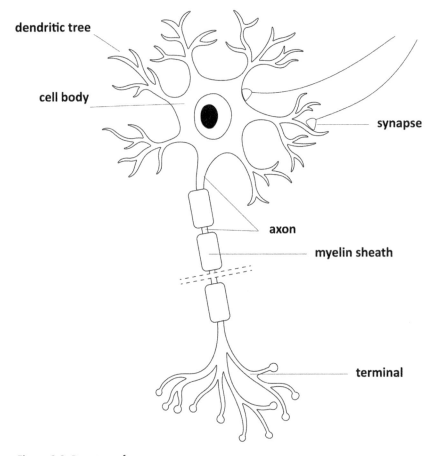

dendritic tree

cell body

synapse

axon

myelin sheath

terminal

Figure 3.2 Prototype of neuron

to build different cortical layers. **Synaptogenesis** (i.e., the creation of new synapses) takes place in which the many neurons already available can start to connect through synapses with dendrites (see Figure 3.3) in cortical areas.

Additionally, the "dramatic increase in synapses, combined with the subsequent paring down of these synapses, is one of the most important mechanisms of plasticity in the developing brain" (Banich & Compton, 2018, p. 458). Importantly, synaptogenesis starts in some brain regions faster and earlier than in others (Huttenlocher, 2009): The primary sensory and motor areas undergo these changes before the parietal and temporal association cortex. The prefrontal cortex (PFC) is the last area. The temporal sequencing of these processes is more or less in line with

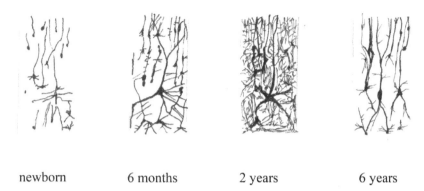

| newborn | 6 months | 2 years | 6 years |

Figure 3.3 Changes of synaptic density through "blooming" and "pruning" processes

newborns' needs for basic sensory and motor skill development followed by abilities that are more complex.

Two processes follow and shape brain development: "**Blooming**" and "**pruning**." The so-called "pruning" follows synaptic proliferation, that is, the abundance of synaptic formation (also known as "blooming"; i.e., the elimination of those synapses). Banich and Compton (2018) state that "synaptic overproduction allows the brain initially to have maximal capacity to respond to the environment. Then, during development, the neurons or connections that do not receive much stimulation wither away. This enables the brain to fine-tune and specialize for its specific environment" (p. 459). Note that, depending on cortical regions, pruning processes differ in their time course; they continue, for example, in the frontal cortex until adolescence and the third decade of life (Huttenlocher, 1979).

The process of **myelination** refers to "the coating of the axons of neurons by **myelin**, a fatty substance [i.e., a lipid layer] that speeds up the conduction of electrical signals" (De Groot, 2011, p. 47). For brain development and processing, this improves, in particular, the speed of neural signal transmission. Also, the process of myelination differs between brain regions. It begins in regions which support basic functions (the spinal cord, and basic sensory and motor systems). Importantly, "brain regions cannot interact quickly in the infant" (Banich & Compton, 2018, p. 459). Only when the child is somewhat older can myelination processes take place to connect integrative systems, for example, the cortical and subcortical areas; around teenage years into the early twenties even longer-range connections between different brain regions are myelinated (e.g., Thompson et al., 2000).

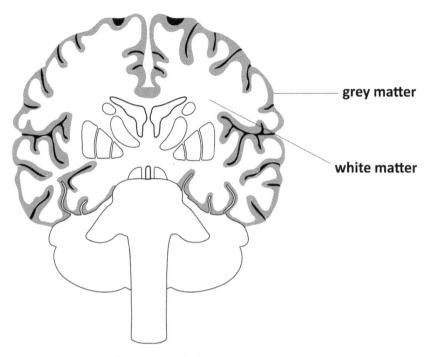

grey matter

white matter

Figure 3.4 Grey and white matter in the brain
Note: A black and white version of this figure will appear in some formats. For the color version, please refer to the plate section.

Tiny blood vessels give the living brain a pinkish appearance. The **grey matter** of the brain (mainly in the brain's surface) is made up of cell bodies. Myelinated axons form **white matter** (see Figure 3.4).

Bundles of axons form **white matter tracts** (for images, see www.neu rosurgicalatlas.com/neuroanatomy/sagittal-view-of-white-matter-tracts), which slowly improve communication between brain regions, allowing for **more integrated perception, cognition, and action in the brain**. The process of myelination continues into adolescence and impacts the functional connectivity between brain areas, that is, the way networks of interacting brain areas coordinate their activities. In sum, the two main processes are the driving forces supporting development and efficiency in the brain: Grey matter volume declines due to synaptic pruning while white matter volume increases due to myelination (Banich & Compton, 2018, p. 460). fMRI and EEG studies reveal age-related changes in inter-regional coordination, showing development from initially local functional coactivation and quite random activity across the child's brain to more long-distance functional coactivation and more ordered patterns of synchronized activity in adults (Kelly et al., 2009; Smit et al., 2012).

In contrast to the developmentally-based changes described, which are often restricted to specific time windows for full development, **experience-based changes are possible throughout a lifetime** (Rösler, 2011). The ability to learn allows for continuous adaptation of the organism to variable changes and demands of the environment (Rösler, 2011). **Brain plasticity** is commonly defined as the capacity of the cortex to reorganize its connections as a reaction to perceptual, cognitive, and/or motor skill learning (Buonomano & Merzenich, 1998). How can the brain implement these changes? This can happen in two ways at the physiological level. Neuronal plasticity is implemented by (a) developing new nerve cells and (b) by flexibly and adaptively changing synaptic connections (Rösler, 2011). The concept of **lifelong learning** refers to this overall neuronal plasticity enabling the brain to structurally change in all phases of life. Crucially, these changes are commonly experience-based (Rösler, 2011). Learning a new skill involves repeated exposure and experiencing, for example, a new activity. Consequently, to support the new activity, the related neural substrate tunes and changes, either by synaptogenesis or by "rewiring" the brain.

Famous examples for this type of experience-based learning are functional changes and often structural enlargement of a specific area, commonly associated with learning a new skill (e.g., Gaser & Schlaug, 2003), for example, see the famous hippocampus study with taxi drivers in London (Maguire et al., 2000). Also, in a study comparing the entire brain of musicians to nonmusicians, structural differences were found in terms of grey matter volume in motor, auditory, and visual-spatial regions. The authors suggest that these differences are mainly due to structural adaptations necessary for the acquisition of the new, complex skills of mastering an instrument and as consequence of the repetitive rehearsal of those skills (Gaser & Schlaug, 2003). Chapter 4 on aphasia in the bilingual brain will describe in more detail functional changes following disease or damage to parts of the brain.

3.3 Language Acquisition and Language Learning in the Brain

In Sections 3.1 and 3.2, we looked closely at cells, their makeup, and why they are fundamental to learning and processing. We followed their developmental path (cell proliferation, synaptogenesis, blooming and pruning, myelination, and long-range connections) and discovered that plasticity in the brain is at work throughout a lifetime. These basic principles and components are involved in the brain when learning any skill. But how do we **acquire** (in an informal context) and **learn** (in a

Table 3.1 Differences between acquisition and learning

Acquisition	Learning
Subconscious process	Conscious process
Informal, natural situation	Formal situation
Very personal and individual process	Formalized process
At home	In classroom, group of learners
Individual rule discovery, statistical learning	Language analysis, deductive teaching (rule-driven)
No explicit instruction	Learning explicit vocabulary and phrases
	Learning explicit grammatical rules
	Focus on form
Guided by own capability/maturation of brain	Order of acquisition structured according to (mainly) preset learning material (curriculum, books, …)
Guided by interest, learner-centered activities, room for improvisation	Little room for individuality in learning
"Feeling for one's own language"	Knowledge about language (rules)
Focus on spoken language	Focus on spoken and written language
Language in use for real communication, authentic, meaningful interaction	Language used mainly for communication and tasks in learning environment
Activities in the language	Activities in and about the language

formal context; for a distinction, see Krashen, 1976) a language or two? Note that this distinction between acquisition and learning is usually made in fields of linguistics when focusing on context (see Table 3.1). These two concepts, as characterized in Table 3.1, reflect the end points of a continuum in modern teaching approaches since many of them rely on mixing aspects of acquisition into learning settings to various degrees.

However, in cognitive neuroscience, a discipline focused on explaining learning mechanisms on the neuronal level and their synaptic changes and on determining underlying brain structures related to the specific domain of skill, the term **learning** is more common and more generally used. Anatomical changes in the brain likewise rely on neuroplasticity to accommodate language learning (for a review on neuroplasticity in L2 learning, see Li, Legault, & Litcofsky, 2014).

3.3.1 Learning Languages

Language learning always proceeds stepwise and involves **multiple memory and learning systems**, because memories are stored in various parts of the brain, not only in one. We will first describe the different steps involved in learning and then dive into the multiple memory and learning systems.

Encoding (medial temporal lobe and PFC): In brain terms, initially learning a language (e.g., a new word) is considered to be a "complex cortical pattern of activation and deactivation that takes place in the initial word learning process on the same day" (Leminen et al., 2016, p. 2). These immediate plastic changes have been observed in fMRI investigations in a hippocampally centered system (Takashima et al., 2019) and the amount of hippocampal activity at the time of first encounter and encoding is predictive of how well it will be remembered (Brewer et al., 1998). The ventrolateral and dorsolateral PFC are mainly involved in the encoding stages. During memory encoding, they help with focusing and organizing, that is, arranging relevant information and inhibiting irrelevant issues.

Storing (anterior parts of hippocampus and associated medial temporal lobe structures): Learning a new word entails that the brain automatically builds representations for the word and its constituents (morphemes, grammar units) in terms of new cortical memory circuits (Yue, Bastiaanse, & Alter, 2014), which are then stored. These representation-building processes take place in the medial temporal lobe, and in particular in the hippocampus (Breitenstein et al., 2005).

Consolidation: The next stage often linked to the storing of information is commonly called consolidation, a sort of strengthening over time taking minutes or days (for a review, see Dudai, Karni, & Born, 2015). Initial learning processes can be consolidated by overnight sleep (Bakker et al., 2015; Leminen et al., 2016; see also Banich & Compton, 2018). Consolidation of memory circuits has been found to profit from associative learning opportunities (see Merkx, Rastle, & Davis, 2011, for morphological learning, e.g., when learning both the form and the semantic content of a new word). This process of **connecting related information** is well known in language learning (cf. Skeide, 2019), for example, when linking the form of a word to its meaning, or the visual representation of a word to its form, or when building up connections between the phonological form of a verb, its meaning of the action, and its movement (Pulvermüller, 1999). The **frequent coactivation of this information** changes the cell assembly representing the word itself and the different elements of representation of a word end up being strongly connected (Pulvermüller, 1999).

The transformation of earlier episodic memories of words (during first encounters which allow only for recognition of newly learned words) into lexical representations is attributed to lexical integration processes in the left posterior middle temporal cortex (Takashima et al., 2019), a region of the brain which is thought of as a memory area for word representation (Hickok & Poeppel, 2004).

Retrieval (posterior parts of hippocampus and prefrontal and parietal cortex): The hippocampus is involved in reactivating long-term memories. With frequent exposure to newly learned words, as well as their repetition and use, these robust representations can be quickly recognized (during comprehension) and easily retrieved (during production). One reason for speedy and efficient processing is that even when only part of a complex representation (e.g., the form, meaning, action, or motion of a verb) is being activated, the entirety of the complex representation is activated (Pulvermüller, 1999; see also Squire, Stark, & Clark, 2004). The PFC is involved in organizational, selection, monitoring, and evaluation processes during retrieval (e.g., it has been found that left posterior PFC is activated during word generation, classification, and memorization, see McDermott et al., 1999). The parietal cortex is important for attentional and integrative aspects of memory.

Before presenting the different memory systems, it is important to stress again one crucial point: Studies involving fMRI and multivoxel pattern activity report that the same brain structures are involved both for initial processing of perceptual information and its recall. For example, when participants are presented with words (either in auditory or visual form) and are asked to recall in which form these appeared, fusiform activation for visual form and auditory regions of the superior temporal gyrus are activated (Polyn et al., 2005; Wheeler, Petersen, & Buckner, 2000). This means that different cortical processors involved in vision, language audition, and so on "also store the outcomes of their processing. Memory of visual elements of the experience is stored in visual processing areas, memory for linguistic elements is stored in language processing areas" so "that different portions of a given event are processed and stored in separate regions of the cortex" (Banich & Compton, 2018, pp. 272–273).

The different memory and learning systems are summarized in Figure 3.5a, b, and Table 3.2. Note that there is disagreement in the field on how best to describe the differences between the different memory systems (Banich & Compton, 2018).

In this chapter, we have already learned that learning is composed of distinct stages and that different memory and learning systems are involved, depending on the type of information to be retained and the

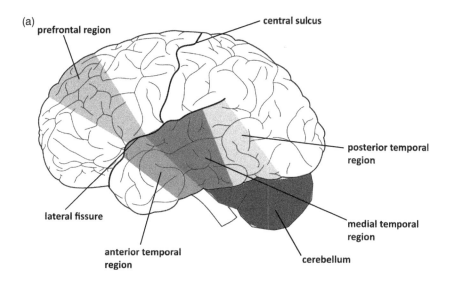

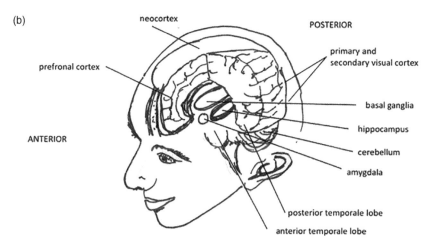

Figure 3.5 Localizing multiple memory and learning systems in the brain: View from the surface (a) and inside (b)
Note: A black and white version of this figure will appear in some formats. For the color version, please refer to the plate section.

quality of the representation. For a focus on language, we need to move away from earlier, traditional models of language in the brain, which assumed that certain regions of the brain were associated with specific aspects of language processing. Today, neuroimaging studies suggest more integrated and therefore more complicated language networks in the brain (Banich & Compton, 2018; see e.g., Lindell, 2006, for a review

Table 3.2 Multiple memory and learning systems in the brain

THEORIES OF MEMORY SYSTEMS: Dichotomies

Explicit vs. implicit (e.g., Schacter, 1987)	• **Explicit** (hippocampus, neocortex, and amygdala): Conscious recall of information, prior experiences, and facts • **Implicit**: Unconscious recall
Declarative vs. procedural memory (e.g., Cohen & Squire, 1980)	• **Declarative** (hippocampal regions): Knowledge about information which can be used flexibly, not linked to specific situations, remembering relations between different elements of an experience or event • **Procedural** (independent of hippocampus): Acquisition and expression of skill through gradual incremental learning, integration of information across events
Episodic vs. semantic memory (Tulving, 1972)	Two types of declarative/explicit memory: • **Episodic memory**: Autobiographical memories specific to one's own unique experience, including context, time, space, and circumstances relating to a specific episode • **Semantic memory**: Knowledge of how to form and retain facts, concepts, categories about the world/people, not linked to specific episodes
Long-term vs. working memory	• **Long-term memory**: Creates enduring records of experience and facts for later use; maintains information for longer times • **Working memory**: A buffer to maintain only a **limited amount of information online for a short time** (associated with retrieval from posterior brain regions); to access relevant information to put into the buffer and to **manipulate the contents of the buffer** (associated with prefrontal regions)
Various working memory capacities (e.g., Baddeley, 1986; Caramazza et al., 1985)	• **Auditory-verbal/phonological store** (e.g., for repeating verbal utterances) • **Visual-verbal** (e.g., reading) • **Visuospatial** (nonverbal visual information)

Table 3.2 (cont.)

MEMORY SYSTEMS: Explicit memory

Hippocampus and prefrontal regions	• Encoding new information (i.e., creating new memories) • **Hippocampus**: Binds together different attributes of an event • **Prefrontal regions**: Support in terms of focusing and organizing encoding processes
Hippocampus and neocortex	• For some time, information is stored in the hippocampus; it is also indexed in the **neocortex** (=largest part of the cortex, the wrinkled outside surface of the brain), where discrete aspects of an event are stored (e.g., sounds, feelings, images) for later access, i.e., over time information is transferred from the hippocampus to the neocortex as general knowledge (probably during sleep) • This index allows memory retrieval via pattern completion of information accessed from interactions with neocortical areas • Associations across a variety of different neocortical processors (e.g., visual system, language, etc.)
Anterior temporal regions: **Semantic memory**	• Reflects **general knowledge about the world** = facts, concepts, categories • Integrates sensory input from modality-specific regions with regards to specific episodes
Posterior temporal regions	• Long-term storage of phonological and semantic knowledge
Amygdala	• Almond-shaped structure in temporal lobe • Role in learning **stimulus-reward** associations • Memories that are emotional in nature • Attaches emotional significance to memories • **Fear** conditioning: Linking events and stimuli to fearful experience, forms new memories related to fear
Prefrontal regions	• Front part of the brain • Involved in short-term memory tasks: Left side more for verbal working memory, right side for spatial working memory

Table 3.2 (cont.)

	• **Help to select the information** relevant for current working memory demands
	• **Point to the information** in posterior cortex that needs to be activated
	• **Assist in retrieval** by aiding in the search process for relevant information stored in memory
	• **Selection of most important information** for the current context after relevant options have been retrieved
	• **Short-term maintenance and strategic control** over phonological and semantic information (Banich & Compton, 2018)
	• **Lateral prefrontal regions** help to **implement domain-general executive processes** that allow information in working memory to be reordered, manipulated, or considered in relation to other relevant information
MEMORY SYSTEMS: Implicit memory	
Basal ganglia	• Structures deep within the brain
	• Role in implicit/procedural learning ("**skill learning**" = gradual, **incremental learning** through repetition of motor, perceptual, and cognitive operations → improve performance)
	• Involved in emotion, learning, reward processing, habit formation, movement
	• Particularly important for coordinating sequences of motor activity
	• Aid in the linkage of sensory information to the motor outputs, actions, and required choices
	• Associations between stimulus and response
	• Activity of dopaminergic cells within basal ganglia may serve to support **error-driven** learning (learning is driven by mismatch between expected and real outcome; trial and error)
Cerebellum	• Structure in rear base of the brain
	• Most important in **fine motor control**
	• Procedural memory

Source: Banich and Compton (2018, pp. 224–295).

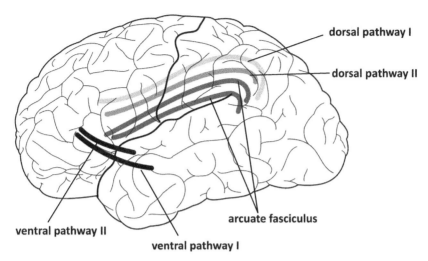

Figure 3.6 Arcuate fasciculus and ventral and dorsal pathways
Note: A black and white version of this figure will appear in some formats. For the color version, please refer to the plate section.

of right-hemisphere involvement). For example, the white matter pathway, which connects anterior and posterior language regions, called the **arcuate fasciculus** (see Figure 3.6 and Section 2.2), is thought to be crucial for language processing in the brain (Rilling et al., 2008). What is more, it has been suggested that different **ventral and dorsal pathways** (see Figure 3.6) are involved in language processing at specific linguistic levels, for example, one ventral pathway links phonology to semantics and meaning, while one of the dorsal pathways connects sound to action and articulation (e.g., see Brauer et al., 2013, for a review).

But how about **learning two languages?** Based on modern neuroimaging techniques, the current view (following Del Maschio & Abutalebi, 2019) holds that there is a **common neural mechanism by which all languages learned are supported** (for reviews, see Higby, Kim, & Obler, 2013; Mouthon, Annoni, & Khateb, 2013). Moreover, L2 representations are thought to converge with an already-specified L1 network (Abutalebi & Green, 2007; Green, 2003). This idea of **convergence** summarizes the state-of-the-art of how a new additional language is learned: For example, on the lexical level, an L2 is attached to already existing structures of an earlier learned L1 to build up an integrated lexical system. To give just one specific example: The concept and word "dog" has already been learned in the L1; when learning the respective word in an additional language, it is attached to the conceptual representation of the word in the L1 (**concepts** refer to the nonverbal knowledge about things, actions,

Table 3.3 Speech perception development

Time range	Abilities
Up until 6 months	• Able to discriminate phonetic contrasts of all languages
From 6 months onwards	• Language-specific perception of vowels increases greatly
From 8 months onwards	• Able to detect typical stress patterns in words
From 11 months onwards	• Consonant perception in their L1 increases greatly
At around 7 to 11 months of age	• Possible reduced ability to discriminate nonnative speech sounds, but de Groot (2011, p. 23) suggests that "the longevity of the ability to perceive non-native contrasts" has been underestimated (see also Best & McRoberts, 2003).

Note: See de Groot (2011) for an overview.

etc.). The findings of a brain imaging study by Isel et al. (2010) showed that early as well as late bilinguals share a common space of conceptual representations for L1 and L2 concepts. **New language information is like an extension of an already existing language knowledge system**. More support for this claim comes from another brain imaging study in which eleven late bilinguals with L1 Portuguese and L2 English were asked to silently read concrete nouns (either in Portuguese or English, assessed on two different days) from two semantic categories (tools and dwellings). At the neural level, the semantic properties of words in both languages were similarly represented in proficient late bilinguals (Buchweitz et al., 2012).

3.3.2 On (Variability in) the Ability to Discriminate Nonnative Contrasts

Language development in newborns and infants is impressive, in particular with regard to both speech perception and production (see Table 3.3).

Up until recently, the reduced ability to discriminate nonnative speech sounds has been treated as if it were set in stone. A closer look at the literature reveals that there is **interindividual variation in the loss of the**

ability to discriminate nonnative contrasts and, even more importantly, a "residual sensitivity to non-native contrasts" (De Groot, 2011, p. 24). Using ERPs has allowed for a more detailed look at individual data, revealing two subgroups with group-specific and significantly different brain responses: One subgroup of eleven-month-old participants had not yet lost the ability to perceive nonnative contrasts in Spanish (Rivera-Gaxiola, Silva-Pereyra, & Kuhl, 2005). It has been reported that this sensitivity can be restored (cf. Bijeljac-Babic et al., 2009; Höhle, Bijeljac-Babic, & Nazzi, 2020). De Groot (2011) explained that "the later the onset of second language exposure, and therefore the further advanced native language phonetic development and neural commitment, the more effort it will take to restore the perceptual abilities required of proper perception and production of the new language" (p. 25). See Kuhl, Tsao, and Liu (2003) for the efficacy of social interaction in the context of reversal of the decline of foreign-language speech perception.

This shows that language acquisition is characterized by high interindividual variation from early on (cf. Kidd, Donnelly, & Christiansen, 2018, for a review). **Stability research in language acquisition** has been, until recently, a rather overlooked line of research (but see, e.g., Bornstein, Hahn, & Putnick, 2016). To give an example, Paradis (2016) showed that developments for young children are divided by language domain per length of exposure. She argues that:

variability in outcomes across linguistic sub-domains and individuals could be seen as a natural outcome of the complexity of dual language learning; therefore, early L2 learners could end up with mostly similar linguistic abilities as monolinguals but still have some subtle differences, e.g., their precision with morphology might be less tight. This would be the "bilingual difference" interpretation, which is the view I espouse and the one I think is appropriate in our increasingly multilingual societies. (pp. 23f.)

3.3.3 Early (Simultaneous and Sequential) and Late Bilinguals

In Chapter 1, we discussed the definitional difficulties with early bilinguals given the various cut-offs periods. But this issue is more complex than at first glance. The notion of **early bilinguals** is usually split into two subcategories.

As can be seen from Table 3.4, terminology, in particular for early bilinguals, diverges according to their age of exposure to an L2. Irrespective of the details of the exact timeframe, the assumption is that **it makes a difference whether and how much knowledge and processing routines**

Table 3.4 Types of early bilinguals

Type of bilingual	Characteristics
Early simultaneous bilingualism or BFLA	• Newborns • Simultaneous development of two languages from birth (e.g., de Houwer, 1990; Meisel, 1989; Swain, 1976).
Early consecutive/sequential/successive bilingualism	• Infants and toddlers who start to acquire the L2 sometime after birth • Still during early childhood – for the upper age limit there are various suggestions, ranging from right after birth to age 2 (De Houwer, 2009) • L2 acquisition takes place when the infants/toddlers have already acquired some of the properties of their L1 in a naturalistic environment, i.e., in immersive, informal settings at home → linguistically slightly more advanced
Early L2 acquisition	• Age of L2 onset between the age 2 and 4 (cf. Schulz & Grimm, 2019; Schulz & Tracy, 2011) • Children who are exposed to L2 after the age of 24 months have already developed **substantial lexical and grammatical knowledge** in L1, so they cannot be considered "simultaneous learners anymore" (Schulz & Grimm, 2019, p. 2) • Exposed to L2 in daycare or preschool (de Houwer, 2021)
L2 acquisition, late bilingualism/late L2 learners/sequential bilingualism	• Exposure to L2 after entering school • A "general agreement that the acquisition of a second language after age seven qualitatively differs from first language acquisition" (Schulz & Grimm, 2019, p. 2) • One language is already well established before learning another one • Cognitive capacities (e.g., verbal memory and analytic reasoning) improve with age (see Berk, 2015, for an overview) → sequential L2 children have access to superior cognitive mechanisms for uptake of the language input compared to early bilinguals

are at disposal for learning the new L2. It is understood that L2 learning should be easier with some L1 structures in place and experience in acquiring a language. For example, child L2 learners were found to show higher rates of acquisition in the lexical domain, accuracy in verb morphology, and use of complex sentences compared to children who had started to acquire their L2 before the age of five (e.g., Golberg, Paradis, & Crago, 2008; Paradis, 2011; Paradis et al., 2017).

When learning an L2 starts somewhat later, it is mainly (but not necessarily) linked to learning an L2 in institutionalized, more formal settings (e.g., in kindergarten, in other forms of day care, or in preschool) (see again our distinction between acquisition and learning in Table 3.4). It should not be overlooked that institutionalized learning, including language use and exposure in this new context, is dependent on national educational policies and varies across cultures; for children with an L1 that differs from the majority language, language exposure to their L2 often coincides with their attendance of day care and other formal education settings. Importantly, there is a teacher in the room who influences learning to a great extent, in particular in terms of feedback, instructional quality, teaching knowledge and style, and classroom environment (Hattie, 2008). For this reason, we will describe research findings on bilingualism in relation to various factors found to influence language acquisition, learning, and processing in Section 3.4.

3.4 Factors Interacting with Acquisition and Learning

An individual acquiring/learning a language at any age, is not seen as isolated during this process. Rather, **the environment in which the acquisition/learning process takes place is of crucial importance**, be it within the family, in childcare, at school, in an adults' learning class, in another country where the target language is the language of the majority. Note that "one's unique genetic make-up mediates how environmental factors affect one's mind and body" (Diamond, 2007, p. 1; see Mamiy et al., 2016; Vaughn & Hernandez, 2018, for examples of studies which show detailed genetic influences on language learning).

Apart from the environment, it is decisive for later language success and attained language proficiency if the language has **only been overheard** (i.e., mere exposure), or if the person was **in interaction and communication** with speakers of this language (e.g., within the family, with peers, etc.). We will describe the characteristics of this perceived verbal input in some detail below (see Section 3.4.2). Finally, it is not only what happens around the language learner but also (or even more) what happens inside them that modulates learning. Several learner characteristics, often termed **internal factors**, which influence the acquisition and learning process, have been identified (see Section 3.4.3).

In other words, language acquisition and language learning can be influenced in a number of ways. To give an example: While acquiring a language in a family setting at home is often considered to be taking place in a warm, supportive environment, this might not be the case for all children. Some children are deprived in many ways, they are neglected, ignored, and spend many hours on electronic devices. There are numerous studies on the effect of childhood neglect and orphanage settings on children's neural development (e.g., Sheridan & McLaughlin, 2014; Sheridan et al., 2012; Teicher & Samson, 2016; Teicher et al., 2016, for a review). What this example attempts to show is that early language acquisition is often contrasted in a black-and-white fashion to learning languages later on, such as at school. Importantly, schools as institutions – the pedagogy, teacher training, and even learning materials – have changed. There are still some teachers who prefer learning by heart, or who criticize and correct their pupils in an unsupportive way, creating a classroom filled with anxiety. These teachers might care little about whether what the pupils learn has any relevance to them or whether they are interested. They hardly ever offer choices to learners, they do not care whether their teaching input is comprehensible and accessible to the pupils, and they do not allow collaborative learning. But there are many others who differ. Let us now look more closely at the learning environment and begin with newborns.

3.4.1 Learning Environment, Interaction, and Culture

A newborn, born into a "dynamic world full of sights, sounds, smells, tastes, and tactile sensations" (Banich & Compton, 2018, p. 464), starts to explore the environment first sensually, then more and more visually, and finally motorically (Böttger, 2016). Hence, a newborn's brain is strongly dependent on its natural, social, and cultural environment. A commonly held view is that "[e]nriched environments are generally better for cognitive and brain development than impoverished ones" (Banich & Compton, 2018, p. 464). But what is the specific effect of enriched environments on the brain? They positively influence the structure of neurons such that they create more robust dendrites and increase the number of synapses per neuron. Hence, more and varied synaptic connectivity can increase "the brain's computational power so that it can effectively deal with a more cognitively demanding and complicated environment" (Banich & Compton, 2018, p. 464).

As language development takes place in an environment, early exposure to two languages could be seen as an enriched environment per se. Findings from linguistic research additionally show that "L2 acquisition can be advanced by a richer L2 environment" (Paradis, 2019, p. 23). When observing infants' behavior in detail, D'Souza et al. (2020) report on enhanced information-seeking behavior, because "varied, less predictable (language) environments have been suggested to make bilingual infants explore more" (Festman, 2021, p. 2). The findings from an eye-tracking study of 51 monolingual and 51 bilingual infants (aged seven to nine months)

revealed a heightened exploration behavior in the bilingual group: They disengaged attention faster from an already familiar visual stimulus in order to shift their attention to another, new stimulus; moreover, they switched attention more frequently between these two visual stimuli. The authors suggested that this reflects the bilingual infants' adaptation to the specific language circumstances in their bilingual homes: The study shows that it was more important for the bilingual infants to collect more samples of novel information from their environment than for monolingual infants. (Festman, 2021, p. 3)

Language interaction between parents and newborns is highly important for the latter's neural and cognitive development (see Filippa et al., 2021, for an investigation of early vocal contact of mothers with preterm infants). Reports on feral children, that is, those lacking crucial aspects of human interaction and communication (e.g., Curtiss, 1977; Pinker, 1994), underscore the fact that their development suffered due to extreme, combined linguistic and social deprivation (Jones, 1995). What is more, affection and tenderness promote the distribution of oxytocin, which in turn plays a central role for establishing a social bond, as between child and parent (Böttger, 2016, p. 63). In Diamond's (2007, p. 2) words, we are "social creatures and […] can suffer if we lack fulfilling, caring relationships and/or meaningful connections to a larger social group." On top of that, parental care increases the boost of synapses and has a positive effect on the development of synaptic networks (Böttger, 2016).

"Social interaction appears to be fundamental and necessary for language acquisition" (Kuhl, 2010, p. 716) and social factors seem to play a far more significant role than previously thought for human learning both across domains and throughout an individual's life span (Meltzoff et al., 2009). Kuhl's (2010) **social gating hypothesis** suggests that "social interaction creates a vastly different learning situation, one in which additional factors introduced by a social context influence learning. Gating could operate by increasing: (1) attention and/or arousal, (2) information, (3) a sense of relationship, and/or (4) activation of brain mechanisms linking perception and action" (p. 720). Infants' degree of social engagement has been indeed found to predict phonetic and word learning, such that more socially engaged infants demonstrated greater learning (see Kuhl, 2010, for a review), and infants' gaze following the speaker's gaze significantly predicted receptive word learning (e.g., Brooks & Meltzoff, 2005; Pfenninger, Festman, & Singleton, 2023). What is more, it is claimed that "cultural knowledge" is transferred via collaborative learning (Goswami, 2008) and shared reading (e.g., Gapany et al., 2022; Garcia-Alvarado, Arreguin, & Ruiz-Escalante, 2022; Jiménez, Filippini, & Gerber, 2006).

Moreover, Diamond (2007) stresses the **impact of culture** on the developing brain: "Cognition, perception, and emotion are shaped by and filtered through one's current cultural context and cultural background" (p. 1). Similarly, Hinton, Miyamoto, and Della-Chiesa (2008) claim that **culture plays a pervasive role in shaping our experiences (and therefore our brains)**. Values, expectations, and aspirations, as well as common practices and traditions in the family and societal group, can be subsumed under the umbrella term of culture. Culture may influence how much time children spend in out-of-home childcare or with family members, it may also determine adults' reaction to mistakes or what is openly discussed and what is unacceptable. In relation to language acquisition and learning, culture has a crucial influence, but it should not be overlooked that language socialization practices, developmental goals, and ways how to support children's development may vary across cultures and communities (cf. Farah, 2018; Keels, 2009; Ochs & Schieffelin, 2011). Consequently, "already for early language acquisition, there is an abundance of aspects which are influenced by the cultural setting in which a child grows up as well as by the circumstances in which a child is exposed to language(s), including whether a certain language is socially valued or devalued" (Pfenninger, Festman, & Singleton, 2023, p. 25). Early childhood is the phase of life in which "linguistic and cultural affiliation to the family's culture or assimilation to a host country and its speaker community are rooted" (Pfenninger, Festman, & Singleton, 2023, p. 25). This means that from early on, children create their first identity (a "sense of self") and expectations – how others function in relation to them and what is expected from them (Yusuf & Enesi, 2012).

3.4.2 Focus on Input

The **impact of quantity and quality of input** on children's language development has been researched extensively (see e.g., Anderson et al., 2021, for a review of L1 development; Rowe, 2012, for a longitudinal investigation; Hoff & Core, 2013, for early bilingual language development; and Unsworth, 2016, for bilingual language development of children between two and ten).

Quantity of language input refers to the number of words/tokens/utterances a child could theoretically listen to. A recently published study with 1,001 infants (two to forty-eight months old) from six continents (Bergelson et al., 2022) shows that the **amount of adult talk and infants' speech production correlate**. Those children who heard more adult talk produced considerably higher rates of spontaneous speech: "For every 100 adult vocalizations per hour, children produced 27 more vocalizations" (Bergelson et al., 2022, p. 10). In this study, quality of input was not measured.

Quality of language input refers to vocabulary diversity (Hirsh-Pasek et al., 2015; Jones & Rowland, 2017) and influences language development and output. For example, Coffey et al.'s (2022) study with adopted children (aged fifteen to seventy-three months) showed that characteristics of the input are taken up in child speech. Crucially, not every type of input is equally supportive of language development in child-directed speech. To name but a few **supportive characteristics**: Vocabulary and syntactic structure vary and multiple speakers provide input. Other important features are exchanges during communication (rather than just monologues), appropriate verbal responses to the children's verbal utterances, or shared book reading (see de Cat, 2021, for a review; de Houwer, 2011; Hoff & Core, 2013; see McCabe et al., 2013, for a review).

Language acquisition is a slow process, as it relies on large amounts of input over time (Dörnyei, 2009) or years of learning an L2. Input may fit to the continuously increasing learning capability of a newborn, infant, toddler, and child at their respective ages, with parental practices (e.g., cognitive stimulation) mediating the relation between SES and language outcome in preschoolers (Raviv, Kessenich, & Morrison, 2004). Importantly,

our environment is also more conducive to language learning earlier in life. In many cultures and in many families, young children experience a very rich language environment during the first years of life. They hear language in attention-grabbing, digestible bundles that are targeted skillfully at their developmental level (Fernald & Simon, 1984). Caregivers typically speak in ways that are neither too simple nor too complex, and children receive hours and hours of practice with language every day. This high-quality and high-quantity experience with language – a special feature of how people communicate with young children – often results in successful language learning. It gives children rich, diverse, and engaging opportunities to learn about the sounds, syllables, words, phrases, and sentences that comprise their native language. (Byers-Heinlein & Lew-Williams, 2013, p. 7)

Note that **child-directed speech shows great variation, depending on the speaker's level of proficiency in that language**, and can thus strongly influence how rich a database for acquisition it provides for the child (Dąbrowska, 2012; Hoff, Core, & Shanks, 2020). **SES** is assumed to influence the quality of language input at home (Masek et al., 2021) as well as the length of conversations (e.g., Hoff, 2003) and is often related to book-reading practices. More specifically, children from low-SES families receive in general substantially less input overall, and this input is often characterized by less diversity in vocabulary and less child-directed speech than for children from high-SES families (Dailey & Bergelson, 2022). Beyond direct influences on language development, SES has been found to predict brain development and cognitive achievement (see Hackman & Farah, 2009, for a review). All these factors have been consistently shown to influence language development (e.g., see de Cat, 2021, for a review; also Fernald, Marchman, & Weisleder, 2013; cf. Fernald & Weisleder, 2015, for a concise review of the strong impact of this factor, pointing to variability of behavior, in particular with regard to verbal engagement, within groups with high and low SES). It has been suggested that higher SES is linked to the "opportunity for larger amounts of high-quality input, interaction, and education in the target language" (Singleton & Leśniewska, 2021, p. 6), whereas poverty has strong effects on the cognitive (and social) development of children. This relation is mediated by family factors (such as parental stress, parenting practices) as well as material deprivation and accumulative experience in childcare, with peers, and in a child's neighborhood (Huston & Bentley, 2010).

3.4.3 Toward a More Holistic View of Child-Internal Factors

Next, we consider **child-internal factors, which influence language acquisition rates and success**, as reported in numerous linguistic studies. These child-level factors have been found to **modulate access to, and uptake of, language-level properties**. For example, children vary with respect to the cognitive development of their attentional and verbal memory abilities (see e.g., the impressive compilation on five-year-olds' cognitive status in the UK by Cattan et al., 2022). This has an impact on their cognitive capacities for learning language, thus influencing acquisition rates (see Paradis, 2011, for a review). Additionally, both the resources and the mechanisms for children's language development have been found to vary individually (Paradis, 2019).

Typical child-level factors include:

- age at time of testing
- age of onset of exposure to an L2
- chronological age, that is, cognitive maturity linked to a specific age
- cognitive capacities
- gender
- language aptitude (comprised of various components, i.e., verbal memory skills, analytic reasoning)
- language proficiency in both languages (in different language domains)
- length of L2 exposure (see Unsworth, 2013, for cumulative vs. current exposure).

Diamond (2007) goes beyond these factors by speculating that noncognitive qualities may be

even more critical to a child's success. Motivation, determination, drive, a positive self-image, belief in oneself, a sense of security, excellent social skills, and/or 'emotional intelligence' can be far greater determinants of success than intellectual brilliance [...]. We learn what is relevant for our actions and we learn best when we must actively use what we learn (p. 3).

Importantly, early work on the psychological aspects of L2 learning has revealed the intriguing role of **language learning motivation** (see Al-Hoorie & MacIntyre, 2019, for an overview; also Dörnyei, 2019), **learner characteristics** (Dörnyei, 2005; Dörnyei & Ryan, 2015), and **self-conception** (see Csizér & Magid, 2014, for an overview). **Emotion, self-regulation, and a sense of belonging to the learner group can strongly influence a child's readiness to learn**. Dewaele has produced an in-depth look into foreign classroom anxiety – and enjoyment – (see Botes, Dewaele, & Greiff, 2020) and into emotion in L2 learning (e.g., Dewaele & Li, 2020, for a recent review).

It has become apparent that personal and largely affective factors, alongside cognitive capacities, are critical for language learning success and are therefore increasingly the focus of (early childhood) studies on language development (cf. Weissberg et al., 2015).

3.5 Critical and Sensitive Periods

The CPH is certainly one of the most longstanding hypotheses in language learning research and is still under debate. It suggests that there is a clear-cut point in time (originally linked to puberty) before which a young child can automatically acquire a language with ease and attain "native" language proficiency, and that once this window closes, language learning success is constrained and "native" language proficiency can no longer be achieved.

- On the one hand, it is assumed that L1 acquisition is effortless; this assumption has been extended to the acquisition of two languages in parallel. Later language learning has been linked to effortful learning (e.g., Meisel, 2011).
- On the other hand, it has been suggested that learning an L2 at an older and more mature age makes the process easier, as the individual is already familiar with learning a language, having acquired an L1 already. Language acquisition experiences may help facilitate L2 learning, and slightly older learners might profit from extended, more mature cognitive abilities (see also Table 3.4 for the same argumentation in the context of early bilingualism).

Age of onset of L2 exposure has long been considered the most decisive factor for success in language learning (cf. Lenneberg, 1967; Penfield & Roberts, 1959; see Hu, 2016, for a review). In Chapter 2, we noted that the brain adapts to changing experiences. Throughout its development, it is affected by experience (social and cultural experience included) (e.g., Schlaug et al., 2005). This means that: (a) new input leads to the growth of new fiber connections in the brain; (b) the nervous system encodes our experience; and (c) there needs to be individual variation because personal, unique experience-dependent connections make "each brain subtly different" (Goswami, 2008, p. 383). This also implies that **experiences modify the brain more than age-related maturation**.

Goswami (2008, p. 387) holds that the "growth of interconnected networks of simple cells distributed across the entire brain eventually results in complex cognitive structures such as *language*." In the previous paragraph, we explained that fiber connections that are most active are stabilized and strengthened, while less active connections are weakened or eliminated (following a "use it or lose it" rule). Gradually, these modifications lead to significant changes in brain structure and function (Hinton, Miyamoto, & Della-Chiesa, 2008). These stronger fiber connections appear to not be easily reorganized (Goswami, 2008, p. 388). This observation has been used to explain the apparent difficulty of learning an L2 later in life (Goswami, 2008). According to de Groot (2011), this account of age of acquisition effects in terms of gradually increasing neural commitment can, on its own, explain age effects over the whole age spectrum. It holds that the brain resources of young language learners are still largely uncommitted and can therefore be easily recruited for the learning task. The older the learner, the more neural tissue is already committed to other knowledge and processes and recruiting neurons to subserve new knowledge and tasks becomes increasingly difficult.

Presenting an opposing view, DeLuca et al. (2019a) claim that there is "no evidence to suggest that there is a loss of language-related neural plasticity and/or that language areas of the brain recruited for particular linguistic functions are any different between monolinguals and adult L2 learners" (p. 176), rather that both L2 acquisition and learning "occur via the same neural substrates [...] suggesting that biological maturation does not affect the brain's capacity to deal with/adapt to the task of novel language learning" (p. 180).

But what about **puberty**? It is well known that experience-dependent processes of synapse formation and dendritic arborization are ongoing until around the age of sixteen, in particular in the PFC (Banich & Compton, 2018). The PFC, the "cognitive control system" responsible for controlling lower brain areas and crucial for goal-oriented behavior, decision-making, planning, and problem-solving as well as controlling impulses, and so on (Blakemore & Choudhury, 2006) develops rather late (see Steinberg, 2005, for a review). Brain development does not stop when adolescence or puberty begin – on the contrary (see Casey, 2013, for an overview) myelination continues into the twenties, and the "dramatic increase in synapses, combined with the subsequent paring down of those synapses, is one of the most important mechanisms of plasticity in the developing brain" (Banich & Compton, 2018, p. 458). Thus, **there is obvious cognitive development and increasing sophistication in adolescence, yielding cognitive abilities superior to those available in childhood**. During adolescence, the PFC is remodeled, as unnecessary synaptic connections, which also consume energy, are eliminated (at a rate of 30,000 per second, see Böttger & Sambanis, 2017). This process may take until the age of thirty (Dow-Edwards et al., 2019) and is done in order to increase effective functioning and to better fulfill specific environmental needs (Crews, He, & Hodge, 2007).

Importantly, in fMRI scans, "adolescents displayed a unique pattern, not seen in either children or adults, of elevated limbic response in combination with relatively lower prefrontal response" (Banich & Compton, 2018, p. 463). The increasing need for control is related to learning to maintain the highly active, more mature limbic system in check; in other words, the amygdala and the hippocampus are two key areas for controlling the emotional regulatory centers (Colver & Longwell, 2013). For example, longitudinal fMRI studies have provided information about the changing activity of the ventral striatum, with its peaks in mid-adolescence, followed by a decrease (see Shulman et al., 2016, for a review). Adolescents strive for social acceptance and for belonging to peer groups. Adolescence is a crucial time for the maturation of brain areas to be linked to social cognition, emotion regulation, and complex decision-making processes (see Somerville, 2013), and for adolescents to gain regulation of their emotions and self-control (Casey & Caudle, 2013). They can then move from spontaneous emotional responses, excitation, reward-seeking behavior and riskier choices to more calculated, logical, thought-through responses and actions (Heller & Casey, 2016; see Steinberg, 2005, for a review).

3.6 Summary

In this chapter, we have explored bilingualism, language development, and brain plasticity. In Section 3.1, we began by distinguishing studies on the mind from studies investigating the brain and by describing the linguistic, psychological, and cognitive neuroscience approaches to these issues from different domains of research. In this broad universe of research on bilingualism, some aspects which have been found to be relevant for bilingualism have been studied only in linguistic terms, leaving open whether certain findings are limited to the mind level only or whether there is correspondence on the brain level. Other aspects, well researched in linguistic or psychological studies, have not yet been taken up and included in neuroscientific studies, leaving the question of whether certain variables would change the results or explain variance unanswered.

In Section 3.2, we then looked at details of learning in the brain and in particular at brain plasticity, a lifelong available characteristic of the brain. We familiarized ourselves with the building blocks of the brain (i.e., neurons) and how they work, with typical processes of synaptogenesis and the paring down of unused synapses, myelination, and longer-range connections between brain areas. We saw how the brain reacts to new information and experiences and how it increases in efficiency. We also realized that more and more aspects in the mind are connected due to more integrated perception, action, and cognition.

The chapter then addressed the point that, in linguistics, acquisition and learning are not the same given that the former takes environment and factors such as input quality and quantity into account (Section 3.3).

In brain terms, there is only learning; we took a close look at how the brain learns language in different consecutive stages and discussed the different memory systems, both in theory and with brain areas found to be involved in different aspects for memory and learning. The example of the ability to discriminate nonnative contrasts, usually set around the age of seven to eleven months shows that – when considered carefully – there is individual variability among children and that the time is ripe to consider this individual variability in language acquisition and learning more seriously. We also tried to elucidate the terminological difficulty with early and late language acquisition and learning, and the assumptions and findings related to these subgroups of bilinguals.

In Section 3.4, we shed light on different factors influencing language acquisition and learning and revealed that individual differences can be found to a great extent: Language acquisition at home, often thought of as a perfect environment in which to acquire languages, was long considered superior to language learning in an educational setting. However, while earlier research findings may have been influenced by the societal level of families selected to participate in these studies and the often negatively described formal education hand in hand with the fiercely defended CPH, newer research shows that there are many different factors, including culture, richness of stimulation in learning environment, and many aspects of social interaction, which are relevant both for home and school. Today, it is not only parents who use information on how to best communicate with their child, but teachers may also learn about teacher–student communicative interaction, building self-concept through feedback, and how to reduce language anxiety in the classroom. Learners themselves are more the focus of language learning today, and our understanding of the processes taking place during adolescence both in cognitive and socioemotional terms has helped in the realization that the brain of an adolescent is not incapable of learning an L2, but that learners at this age and older probably have not been provided with ideal learning conditions and support for optimal L2 learning.

Review Questions

1. Which disciplines are predominantly interested in studying the mind and which ones focus on the brain?
2. Why and how do experiences alter the brain?
3. In which contexts are the terms acquisition and learning used? What is our current knowledge about how the brain learns?

4. Discuss the intriguing observations about nonnative speech sound discrimination in infants.
5. Compare the notions of early and late bilinguals, as well as critical and sensitive periods, and how additional factors that come into play change the earlier simple view of dichotomous bilingualism.

Further Reading

Bialystok, E. (2001). *Bilingualism in development: Language, literacy, and cognition*. Cambridge University Press.

Fuchs, E., & Flügge, G. (2014). Adult neuroplasticity: More than 40 years of research. *Neural Plasticity*, 541870. https://doi.org/10.1155/2014/541870.

Garraffa, M., Sorace, A., & Vender, M., with Schwieter, J. W. (2023). *Bilingualism matters: Language learning across the lifespan*. Cambridge University Press.

Gregersen, T., & Mercer, S. (2022). *The Routledge handbook of the psychology of language learning and teaching*. Routledge.

Osterhout, L., Poliakov, A., Inoue, K., McLaughlin, J., Valentine, G., Pitkanen, I., … & Hirschensohn, J. (2008). Second-language learning and changes in the brain. *Journal of Neurolinguistics*, *21*(6), 509–521.

Pfenninger, S., Festman, J., & Singleton, D. (2023). *Second language acquisition and lifelong learning*. Routledge.

CHAPTER FOUR

Aphasia and the Bilingual Brain

Learning Objectives

- Learn about the causes of bilingual aphasiology and theoretical approaches to understanding it.
- Become familiar with the clinical manifestations of lesion sites in the brain.
- Gain an understanding of various premorbid factors that influence language impairment in bilinguals, such as frequency of L1 and L2 use, L2 proficiency, and AoA.
- Compare ways in which aphasia is assessed and rehabilitated in bilingual patients.
- Explore typical recovery patterns of language(s) in bilingual aphasics.

4.1 Introduction

Just as studies using behavioral and neuroimaging methods have elucidated our knowledge of the healthy bilingual brain and what specific neural areas are responsible for various language activities, research investigating bilinguals who suffer from language impairments due to sudden trauma in the brain or developmental degeneration of neurons has also revealed a wealth of findings. In this chapter, we will review research on neurological aspects of aphasia in bilinguals. **Aphasia** is an impairment that affects the production and/or comprehension of language. The most common cause of aphasia is a stroke but it can also be caused by tumors, traumatic injury, and neurological diseases such as forms of dementia. The area of study which looks at language impairments that result from disease or damage to the parts of the brain that are vital to language is called **bilingual aphasiology** and is the focus of this chapter.

Around one third of individuals will have some form of aphasia after having a stroke, although this prevalence can range from 15 to 42 percent. Interestingly, however, most people are not familiar with the term **aphasia**. In a survey conducted by the National Aphasia Association

(2020), it was reported that only 14 percent of their respondents in the United States had heard of the term aphasia and only half of these individuals (7 percent of all respondents) could identify it as a **language disorder**. This is somewhat surprising given that there are an estimated 180,000 new cases of aphasia per year in the country (National Institute on Deafness and Other Communication Disorders, 2015) and around one million people in North America living with some form of aphasia. Of these new cases of aphasia in the United States, Paradis (2001) estimated more than 45,000 each year will be bilingual patients, although this number is likely to have increased since the analysis. Similarly, we can expect more cases of bilingual aphasia in countries that have more than one official language or where the population uses two or more languages on a regular basis.

For an aphasia patient who spoke two languages in the **premorbid** (i.e., healthy) state, one may ask whether one language, the other language, or both suffer from aphasia. As you probably guessed, all three of these possibilities can occur, as we will see in this chapter. However, we will learn that these impairments, along with their recovery patterns, are affected by several factors. In Section 4.2, we will present the two main theoretical accounts for bilingual aphasia, the localizationalist and dynamic accounts. In Section 4.3, we examine the specific lesion sites that cause several different types of aphasia, both fluent and nonfluent in nature. We then look at the premorbid factors that influence language impairment in Section 4.4, including frequency of use of the languages, L2 proficiency, AoA, and modes of learning. The topic of Section 4.5 is the clinical assessment of aphasia, and in Section 4.6 we discuss the rehabilitation and treatment plans for bilinguals with aphasia. Following this, in Section 4.7, we discuss the recovery patterns that have been observed in bilingual aphasia. In Section 4.8, we review other types of aphasia that emerge as a consequence of a progressive neurological disease rather than from sudden trauma. Finally, Section 4.9 concludes the chapter.

4.2 Theoretical Approaches of Bilingual Aphasia

Our theoretical understanding of bilingual aphasia is informed by our knowledge of language lateralization and overlapping language processes in bilinguals. As we discussed in Chapter 2, it is believed that for most right-handed people, language is lateralized in the left hemisphere, as it is mainly in this hemisphere that primary language functions occur. One theoretical view of bilingual aphasia takes a **localizationalist approach**, which holds that if a bilingual's languages are represented in different neural areas, a patient may suffer from aphasia in only one of their languages. Indeed, there have been cases in which only one language was affected, supporting this traditional localizationalist approach (see Albert & Obler, 1978). However, as we also saw in Chapter 2, more recent neuroimaging studies reveal that the two languages can share the same brain regions, particularly when there is early L2 AoA (Paradis, 2000; Wartenburger et al., 2003) or when the bilingual has a relatively high L2 proficiency (Chee et al., 1999; Klein et al., 1999; Perani et al., 2003). Although there is still an ongoing debate with respect to language localization in bilinguals, what it can explain about bilingual aphasia impairment, and how it can inform assessment and rehabilitation, there is considerable evidence indicating that two languages in the brain overlap.

This overlap has been found in studies investigating bilingual language processing and has largely informed a **dynamic approach** to bilingual aphasia. According to Abutalebi and Green (2007), "a dynamic view leads to a focus on how the system is controlled and on the connectivity of different neural regions during the performance of different language tasks" (p. 268). This approach sees language control and representation as being compromised as a result of brain damage to critical language areas (Green & Abutalebi, 2008). Since Zatorre's (1989) call for neurocognitive research examining language behaviors specific to bilinguals, such as language switching and translation, a number of studies have revealed interesting results. For instance, when switching between the two languages, there is increased activity in the dorsolateral PFC, anterior cingulate gyrus, and supramarginal gyrus (Hernandez, Martinez, & Kohnert, 2000; Wang et al., 2007). When bilinguals translate between the two languages, there is increased activation in the anterior cingulate gyrus and basal ganglia (Price, Green, & von Studnitz, 1999). Abutalebi and Green (2007) argue for a **neurocognitive dynamic approach to study bilingual aphasia** which emphasizes questions that arise when examining these bilingual processes. They articulate that an understanding of the **dynamic inhibitory and excitatory resources** required to perform language tasks can help to inform bilingual aphasiology and the treatments used during rehabilitation.

4.3 Lesion Sites and the Classification of Aphasia Subtypes

Damage to a brain area is referred to as a **lesion**. Aphasia will most likely occur when there is a lesion in certain areas in the left hemisphere of the brain. When a lesion is located in the right hemisphere and yet there are observable impairments to language, these typically are not

Table 4.1 Types of aphasia and their clinical characteristics

Type	Clinical manifestation			
	Comprehension	Production	Grammar	Repetition
Nonfluent (Broca)	Relatively preserved	Poor up to telegraphic speech	Agrammatism	Poor
Fluent (Wernicke)	Poor	Fluent but mostly meaningless	Mostly normal sentence structure	Poor
Global	Poor	Poor	Poor	Poor
Amnestic (anomic, nominal)	Relatively preserved	Poor object naming, word-finding difficulties	Good	Good
Conduction	Good	Fluent, but with paraphasias	Good, mostly complex sentences	Poor
Transcortical sensor	Poor	Fluent but meaningless speech with many semantic paraphasias	Sentences with normal structure	Preserved up to echolalia
Transcortical motor	Relatively preserved	Poor	Agrammatism is uncommon	Relatively preserved
Mixed transcortical (isolation)	Poor	Poor	Poor, also due to poor production	Relatively preserved

Source: From Khachatryan et al. (2016).

forms of aphasia, but rather the result of cognitive components important to language processing, such as WM (Silveri et al., 1998). In the case of bilingual aphasia, the **exact site of lesion is the best predictor of what type of language impairment will result from damage** to that area (although we will look at language-related predictors in Section 4.4). Most of these impairments can be classified as either fluent or nonfluent in nature (see Table 4.1 for more detail), meaning that language impairments are primarily in production or comprehension, respectively, although there are several other types. For nonfluent aphasics, speaking is effortful and telegraphic and usually does not contain normal intonation or stress patterns. Often, they have problems accessing words and structuring word order. On the other hand, for types of **fluent aphasias, speech production is mostly preserved** and usually has normal intonation or stress patterns, however, **what they produce makes little sense**. Because these patients have impairment with language comprehension, this affects their ability to monitor their own speech.

4.3.1 Lesion Sites and Their Clinical Manifestations

The **Boston Aphasia Classification** is perhaps the most widely used method to identify which type of aphasia a patient has. This classification technique is based on the clinical characteristics observed in each language and has identified seven different types of aphasia. The clinical characteristics of these aphasias can be seen in Table 4.1.

There may be a combination of one or more damaged brain areas that result in aphasia, with more affected areas increasing the severity of the symptoms. Informed by Fabbro (1999) and Schoenberg and Scott (2011), in Figure 4.1 we provide illustrations of approximate lesion locations that can cause the eight types of aphasias listed in Table 4.1.

In **Broca's aphasia**, affected areas can include the IFC, left opercula, insula, and subjacent white matter. In **Wernicke's aphasia**, the lesion can be traced to the posterior part of superior temporal gyrus and middle and inferior temporal gyri. In **global aphasia**, the lesion location covers a large area in the perisylvian region. In **amnestic (anomic) aphasia**, the affected brain areas are not clearly defined, although they likely include the angular gyrus, middle temporal gyrus, and parietotemporal junction. In **conduction aphasia**, affected areas can include the temporoparietal junction, insula, primary auditory cortex, and supramarginal gyrus. In **sensory aphasia**, the middle and inferior temporal gyri and inferior occipital-temporal regions can be affected. In **motor aphasia**, lesion sites can include a dorsolateral frontal area that extends into the deep frontal white matter. Finally, **mixed transcortical aphasia**, also known as isolation aphasia, arises when a combination of lesions is found in motor and sensor aphasias. In this form of aphasia, key language areas in the brain, namely, Broca's and Wernicke's areas and the arcuate fasciculus, are isolated from the rest of the brain.

4.3.2 Tasks that Explore Lesion Sites and Impairment

Experimental tasks that attribute lesion sites to specific impairments include lexical decisions (Zahn et al., 2004), word repetitions (Abo et al.,

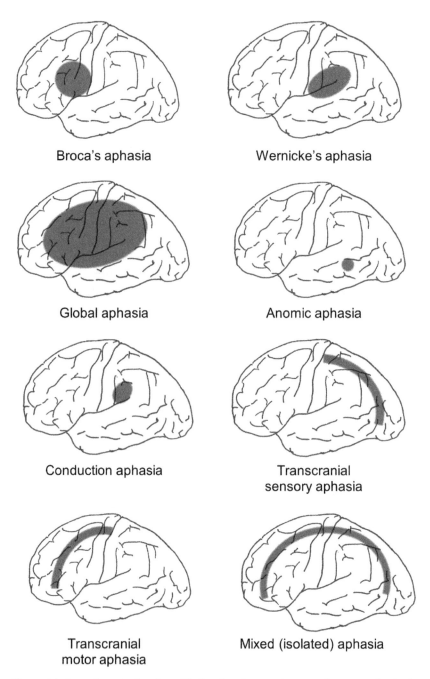

Broca's aphasia   Wernicke's aphasia

Global aphasia   Anomic aphasia

Conduction aphasia   Transcranial
                                   sensory aphasia

Transcranial   Mixed (isolated) aphasia
motor aphasia

Figure 4.1 Example approximations of lesion sites that correlate to various types of aphasia
Note: A black and white version of this figure will appear in some formats. For the color
version, please refer to the plate section.

2004; Karbe et al., 1998), word generation (Miura et al., 1999; Weiller et al., 1995), semantic judgments (Fernandez et al., 2004), sentence comprehension (Thulborn, Carpenter, & Just, 1999), and picture naming (Postman-Caucheteux et al., 2010; see Sebastian, 2010, for a review). Neural activity is recorded while bilingual aphasics perform tasks which each place different demands on the language-processing system. For instance, lesion studies using the lexical decision task have revealed an association between lesions in the left temporoparietal regions, particularly in the angular gyrus, and impairment of word recognition (Black & Behrmann, 1994; Hillis, Wityk, & Tuffiash, 2001). From semantic judgment tasks, we have learned that when a bilingual aphasic has a lesion in the posterior region of the left IFC, there is difficulty generating the verb forms of concrete high-frequent nouns but not low-frequent nouns (Thompson-Schill et al., 1998). Finally, studies of picture naming tasks have shown that if a lesion is located in the classical language areas – the left inferior parietal and temporoparietal regions – a bilingual aphasic will be unable to generate the names of pictures (Damasio et al., 2004).

4.3.3 Impairments Specific to Reading and Writing

Two types of aphasia where impairments only affect reading and writing are alexia and agraphia, respectively. There are several types of **alexia**, with the most common being **pure alexia**. In this case, patients have normal to near-normal expressive and receptive abilities across all language modalities but have severe reading problems. Pure alexia occurs when there is a lesion in the posterior part of the corpus callosum and primary visual cortex. Because this type of aphasia affects visual processing and not auditory comprehension, patients are able to write coherently, but they are not able to process what they (or anyone for that matter) have just written.

Other types of alexia include surface dyslexia, phonological dyslexia, and deep dyslexia. In **surface dyslexia**, patients are unable to recognize words as a whole but instead must "sound them out." This impairment arises when there is a lesion in the temporoparietal region of the left hemisphere. The opposite can also occur, as is the case in **phonological dyslexia**, in which there is a selective impairment to pronounce new words while the ability to recognize whole words remains intact. This language impairment is often observed when there is damage to the superior temporal lobe, although the specific location can vary among patients. An even more severe form of phonological dyslexia is **deep dyslexia**. In addition to being unable to recognize nonwords (or new words), individuals suffering from deep dyslexia make frequent semantic errors when reading. For instance, when reading aloud, they may substitute synonyms, antonyms, or other semantic-related words in place of the target words. The lesion site for deep dyslexia also varies but usually includes most of the left frontal lobe.

In the case of **bilinguals suffering from types of alexia**, Goral (2019) reviewed orthography effects in previous studies and argued that traditional models of reading may not account for reading impairments in a variety of languages with differing orthographies. From her review, Goral stated:

Evidence from bilingual and biscriptal individuals who acquire alexia suggests that whereas most researchers report possible orthographic effects in the manifestation of reading impairment they found, the majority of bilinguals who experience reading impairment as a result of an acquired brain lesion demonstrate relatively comparable-impairments in their two languages. Orthography-specific characteristics may affect the errors that individuals who acquire alexia produce during reading, and therefore may lead to differential diagnosis of alexia type in each language. Yet, the majority of cases reported in the literature demonstrate fewer differences than similarities in the reading impairment observed in the two languages and are thus consistent with the assumption of a shared representation of different languages and their reading systems in the brain. (p. 604)

Whereas alexia impairs reading, **agraphia** affects writing abilities. Depending on whether the lesion is located in motor or language areas, one of two different types of agraphia will result. **Peripheral agraphia** happens when there is damage to the motor system. It is considered a nonaphasic agraphia because language abilities are not affected. These patients produce distorted letters when writing such that their writing is almost illegible. Although their writing is incomplete and effortful to produce, their spelling is unaffected. In **central agraphia**, an aphasic form of agraphia, there is damage in the left parietal lobe, affecting both language and motor skills. Depending on the exact location of the lesion, different types of language problems in writing will emerge, ranging from lexical, phonological, and semantic impairments. For instance, a patient may have difficulties with sound-to-spelling rules or with orthographic memory, which impair their ability to correctly spell words. For bilinguals with agraphia, the symptoms in both languages are relatively similar, especially in the case where only motor skills are impaired.

To sum up, the severity and type of language impairments are modulated by the location and distribution of the lesion. This has been found using a number of language production and comprehension tasks that we have described. However, there are several premorbid language-related factors that affect language impairment. Some of these considerations include how many languages an individual speaks, the order in which they were acquired, the person's relative proficiency levels, how frequently the languages were used prior to impairment, in what context they were learned (e.g., formal vs. informal), and the localization of language functions as shaped by the bilingual's specific language development and experiences. In Section 4.4 we will discuss some of these factors in more detail.

4.4 Factors That Influence Language Impairment

As we saw in Section 4.3, the size and location of a brain lesion are two of the main predictors of the type and severity of the resulting language impairment(s). However, since a bilingual's languages only partially overlap in the brain, lesions do not always affect the two languages equally (Lucas, McKhann, & Ojemann, 2004). Furthermore, language lateralization and the localization of language processes can vary among bilinguals, making it challenging to generalize or predict the type of language impairments that arise from a given lesion site. To complicate matters further, premorbid language-related factors affect the severity of and recovery from language impairment. Interest in the effects of language-related factors on impairment and recovery in bilingual aphasia is not new. For instance, with respect to AoA, **Ribot's law** (1892) suggests that language impairment and recovery is related to the order in which the two languages are acquired. Similar interest can be seen with respect to frequency of language use as shown by **Pitre's law** (1895), which argues that language impairment and recovery are determined by how frequently the languages were used in the premorbid state. Both of these hypotheses have received support as we will see in Section 4.4.1.

4.4.1 Frequency of Language Use, L2 Proficiency, and AoA

The frequency of use of a bilingual's two languages prior to brain damage has been shown to be one of several determining factors relating to the severity of and recovery from impairment (Goral et al., 2012; Goral, Naghibolhosseini, & Conner, 2013; Knoph, Simonsen, & Lind, 2017). In a recent meta-analysis by Kuzmina et al. (2019), the authors reviewed 130 cases of bilingual aphasics from 65 studies. Their analyses showed that patients who **more frequently used their L1** performed better postinsult in their L1 than L2. Contrarily, patients who had used their L2 as frequently or more frequently than their L1 performed better in both languages. When considering the AoA of these patients, however, those with an early L2 AoA, but who also reported more frequently using their L1 prior to impairment, showed comparable performance. These findings suggest that "language use affected the magnitude of L1 advantage when L2 became the most frequently used language. Thus, … language use has a moderating role on [impairment], which does not seem to be independent of AoA" (Kuzmina et al., 2019, p. 17).

Kuzmina et al.'s (2019) meta-analysis also investigated how **AoA and premorbid language proficiency influence poststroke language impairment**. The results of their analyses showed that bilinguals with aphasia almost always performed better in the L1 than in the L2, although a small number of cases demonstrated better L2 performance. The authors found that L2 AoA moderated these performance differences and higher premorbid language proficiency resulted in higher levels of language preservation poststroke. Kuzmina et al. argue that patients' language background should be thoroughly recorded and reported in a consistent manner. They propose that additional examination of the influence of AoA on language performance should be conducted and that studies should also investigate the variables of impairment type and prestroke mastery as they apply to bilingual aphasia.

In a study by Kiran and Iakupova (2011), the authors investigated how **language proficiency, language impairment, and rehabilitation** relate to each other in two Russian–English bilinguals suffering from aphasia. The first part of their test assessed premorbid language proficiency and abilities of the patients using a questionnaire and the Bilingual Aphasia Test (BAT), an assessment method that we will discuss in Section 4.5.1. After measuring the language abilities of the patients poststroke, the authors found that both languages had been similarly impaired. One of the patients was then placed in a semantic therapy program for ten weeks. Following this, the patient's proficiency in both languages was measured again. Kiran and Iakupova found that the semantic treatment had similar results as previous studies, showing that treatment for naming abilities in one language improves naming abilities in the other. They discuss the limits of the BAT for measuring posttherapy language abilities for both languages and suggest that it should be more standardized and have its effectiveness assessed using psychometric measures. The authors emphasize that understanding prestroke language abilities and proficiency is essential to develop further treatment, and that assessment methods must be improved.

A study by Peñaloza, Barrett, and Kiran (2020) examined how prestroke proficiency in both the L1 and L2 affected poststroke lexical-semantic performance. The authors drew on the notion that **language proficiency is a multifactorial construct** (van Hell & Tanner, 2012). L1 proficiency was determined based on daily use of the language, educational background, exposure throughout the lifetime, and a language ability rating. L2 proficiency was determined by these same factors in addition to AoA, lifetime confidence, and family proficiency. The results demonstrated that premorbid L1 proficiency predicted poststroke performance in the L1. These within-language effects were also found for premorbid L2 proficiency and performance. Interestingly, prestroke proficiency was more predictive of poststroke lexical-semantic performance for the L2 than for the L1. The authors argued that this finding could be due to the fact that the acquisition of and experience with an L2 are distinct from that of the L1. Relatedly, a study by Miikkulainen and Kiran (2009) put forth a computational model of bilingual lexical access instantiated by AoA and proficiency, which demonstrated the close relationship between premorbid proficiency and the resulting naming impairment observed in patients' behavioral data. These studies underscore the importance of using sensitive measures of L1 and L2 proficiency rather than only employing self-reported measures, as these may not fully capture the multifaceted nature of language proficiency.

In addition to frequency of use, proficiency, and AoA, another individual difference to consider in bilingual aphasiology relates to **educational and socioeconomic factors**. Research has shown that low educational attainment and low SES are related to the likelihood of succumbing to diseases, including Alzheimer's. Connor et al. (2001) analyzed the effect of SES on aphasia severity and recovery by evaluating 39 aphasic patients at 4 months and 103 months postonset. Their analysis showed that the initial severity of aphasia was significantly greater for patients from lower educational and occupational groups. However, the rate of recovery was the same for all (see also Lazar et al., 2008). It is not yet understood as to why SES had different effects on the severity and recovery of language impairments in Connor et al.'s study.

One final nonlesion factor affecting the outcome of language impairment is that **bilingualism itself may give rise to a protective effect**. When compared to monolingual aphasic patients, bilingual patients appear to have a better recovery. Alladi et al. (2015) examined over 600 patients with ischemic stroke and tested the role of bilingualism in predicting their poststroke cognitive impairment. The results showed that a larger proportion of bilinguals (41 percent) had normal cognition compared to monolinguals (20 percent). The authors argued that **being bilingual doubles the chances of recovering from poststroke cognitive impairment** due to bilinguals' higher cognitive reserve compared to monolinguals (Bialystok et al., 2014). **Cognitive reserve** refers to the long-term benefit of maintaining cognitive functioning and protecting against its normal decline with healthy aging (Bialystok & Craik, 2015). Interestingly, among the patients in Alladi et al.'s review, stroke-induced aphasia was similar for monolinguals (12 percent of cases) and bilinguals (11 percent cases), suggesting that bilingualism didn't protect from a stroke, but rather from the severity of cognitive impairment poststroke. The authors argue that "the mechanism underlying the protective effect of bilingualism is not because of better linguistic but executive functions acquired through a lifelong practice of language switching" (Alladi et al., 2015, p. 260).

Taken together, it is clear that there are a number of lesion and nonlesion factors that affect the severity and type of language impairment. As we will see in Section 4.5, this is why it is essential to gather as much information about an aphasic's language history and demographic information as possible. Remarkably, when the effects of these language-related factors are combined to generate a more complete linguistic profile of a bilingual aphasic, researchers are able to predict the recovery patterns that will likely be observed (Paradis, 1977). We will return to recovery patterns in Section 4.7.

4.5 Assessment of Bilingual Aphasia

After a neurological insult, bilinguals who suffer from aphasia pass through three stages: An **acute, subacute, and chronic stage** (Paradis, 2004). Patients typically undergo initial assessment for aphasia within two days of being admitted to a hospital (Vogel, Maruff, & Morgan, 2010), at which time they are in the acute stage. Treatment is often performed in both the lesion and late phases, with both phases showing that improvement can be made (Faroqi-Shah et al., 2010; Kohnert, 2009). Cargnelutti, Tomasino, and Fabbro (2019b) offer the following description of these three stages:

The **acute phase**, lasting a few weeks after the insult, is often characterized by initial temporary mutism, followed by unstable improvements in one or more languages. In the subsequent **lesion phase** [also called the subacute phase], some language functions are more stably regained and it is possible to define the extent and type of impairment of each language. The regain of language functions in this post-onset period is usually indicated as spontaneous recovery. In the last stage, named **late phase** [also called the chronic phase], the pattern of deficits is in fact steady and there is almost no margin for spontaneous improvements. Nevertheless, further recovery is still possible. (p. 538)

The premorbid factors that affect language impairment which we discussed in Section 4.4 are considered when assessing bilingual aphasics. The individual who gathers and utilizes this information is often a **speech pathologist**, a specialist who evaluates, diagnosis, and treats communication disorders, among other speech and voice disorders. In the case of screening for bilingual aphasia, speech pathologists typically have a very limited amount of time, often around thirty minutes, in which to conduct their clinical examination (LaPointe, 2011). As such, these clinicians need to make very quick and effective decisions or "run the risk of patients being missed and lost post discharge" (Rohde et al., 2018, p. 3; see also Johnson, Valachovic, & George, 1998).

Rohde et al. (2018) offer a review of **language assessments** for aphasic patients, although the authors do not specifically discuss how these assessments are adapted (if necessary) to assess aphasia in bilinguals. Nonetheless, these tasks are typically separately administered to bilinguals in each of their languages. The objective of these language assessments is to assist the clinician in evaluating the patient's language skills, and strengths and weaknesses of communication, along with planning for a treatment program (Spreen & Risser, 2003). The assessments range from informal measures, tests developed by healthcare institutions, and commercially published tests that can be purchased in kits. While there are a wide range of assessments available, some are more widely used than others. For instance, common measures for poststroke patients include the European Stroke Scale, the Canadian Neurological Scale, and the National Institutes of Health Stroke Scale (see El Hachioui et al., 2017, for a review). All of these assessments evaluate the severity of the stroke and include subtests that measure acute language functioning.

There are also brief aphasia assessments that are designed for nonspecialists. These may or may not be conducted in the absence of a speech pathologist and are often used to provide prompt referral to a specialist. For instance, the Frenchay Aphasia Screening Test (Enderby et al., 1987) and the Language Screening Test (Flamand-Roze et al., 2011) have been used to evaluate poststroke language performance. However, these tests are not sensitive to nor directly test more narrow linguistic abilities such as reading and writing, and, as such, they should not be considered suitable when used in isolation for diagnosis. This said, they do offer an excellent *preliminary* screening for aphasia, which can subsequently be used by a specialist.

4.5.1 The Bilingual Aphasia Test

One particular assessment for aphasia that is important for our purposes here is the **Bilingual Aphasia Test** (BAT). The BAT is a battery of assessments developed by Paradis (1987) and Paradis and Libben (1987) and is now available in over 70 languages (see Paradis, 2011, for an overview). Since 2011, it can be accessed online for free at www.mcgill.ca/linguistics/research/bat. The BAT consists of three sections and a total of 32 tasks that "assess comprehension and production of implicit linguistic competence and metalinguistic knowledge (which provide indications for apposite rehabilitation strategies)" (Paradis, 2011, p. 427).

The first section of the test gathers information related to language history. The second section measures competences in each language at the word, sentence, and discourse levels across all language modalities (i.e., speaking, listening, reading, and writing). The last section is unique in that it tests the patient's residual abilities with regard to the specific languages they speak. More specifically, this last section evaluates translation abilities and critical aspects such as reversible contrastive features. These are obligatory elements of one language that are unacceptable in the other and whose exact translation is therefore considered to be an error (e.g., obligatory use of the future tense in French vs. use of the present tense in English). This is particularly useful when investigating language dominance, given that patients may recognize as incorrect only sentences in the strongest language containing features of the weakest, but not vice versa (Cargnelutti, Tomasino, & Fabbro, 2019b, p. 534).

The validity of the BAT has been widely supported. For example, Peristeri and Tsapkini (2011) directly compared the BAT to the short version of the Boston Diagnostic Aphasia Examination. Their results found that the BAT provided a more comprehensive examination and finer-grained characterization of language impairment in bilinguals. Peristeri and Tsapkini also found that the BAT reliably discriminated between different types of aphasia. Other researchers have demonstrated the BAT's **ability to distinguish between aphasia and other clinical conditions such as Alzheimer's disease, mild cognitive impairment, and normal aging** (Gómez-Ruiz & Aguilar-Alonso, 2011). Another noteworthy feature of the BAT is that its versions in the available languages are *adaptations* of the original version, rather than *translations*, taking into account the **unique structure and cultural characteristics of**

languages. For speakers of more than one language, the BAT is, to date, the most systematic and congruent evaluation of aphasia in each of the bilingual's languages. In Section 4.6, we will review how assessments of aphasia help to inform treatment and rehabilitation programs among bilingual aphasics.

4.6 Rehabilitation of Languages in Bilingual Aphasia

The premorbid factors and the exact nature of language impairment that we have discussed thus far also provide insight on how to best treat aphasia. However, the timing of treatment and language therapy regimen (intensity, dosage, and duration) in bilingual aphasia unfortunately has not been studied in detail (Peñaloza & Kiran, 2019). Furthermore, unlike the monolingual aphasia literature, in the bilingual literature it remains unclear as to whether treatment programs delivered at high intensity, high dose, and over an extended period of time are optimal for bilingual aphasics (Brady et al., 2016). As can be imagined, there are many challenges that clinicians face when establishing the **optimal treatment plan for bilingual aphasics**. These difficulties are partially due to the fact that lesions do not always affect a patient's two languages equally (Lucas, McKhann, & Ojemann, 2004). Furthermore, healthcare professionals face the complex task of deciding in which language or languages to provide treatment, although this may be determined by the languages spoken by the healthcare individuals performing the speech and language interventions. Clinicians must also identify which types of language exercises provide optimal results, predict the different outcomes that arise when providing treatment during different stages of recovery, and determine whether there will be observable improvement within and across the bilingual's languages (Peñaloz & Kiran, 2019). None of these are easy tasks. Each patient responds differently to the treatment plans established by healthcare professionals and, thus, their recovery patterns vary. We will discuss these recovery patterns in Section 4.7, but first let us consider some of the complexities we have just mentioned that arise during the treatment of bilingual aphasia.

4.6.1 The Language(s) in Which Treatment Is Provided

For the most part, research shows that **rehabilitation targeting either the L1 or L2 will improve language abilities (receptive and/or expressive) in that same language** (Peñaloza & Kiran, 2019). Faroqi-Shah et al. (2010) conducted a meta-analysis on prior work, examining the outcomes of treatment when delivered in the L2. Their analyses showed consistent improvement across the studies, such that treatment in the L2 led to improved L2 receptive language skills (Abutalebi et al., 2009; Faroqi & Chengappa, 1996; Gil & Goral, 2004; Khamis, Venkert-Olenik, & Gil, 1996; Miertsch, Meisel, & Isel, 2009). The meta-analysis also found similar patterns for L2 expressive skills when treatment was provided in the L2. This was observed for word retrieval (Abutalebi et al., 2009; Edmonds & Kiran, 2006; Gil & Goral, 2004; Khamis, Venkert-Olenik, & Gil, 1996; Laganaro, Di Pietro, & Schnider, 2003; Maragnolo et al., 2009) and morphosyntactic and syntactic skills (Faroqi & Chengappa, 1996; Goral, Levy, & Kastl, 2009).

4.6.2 Cross-Language Generalization

Another consideration in the treatment of bilingual aphasia is whether there is cross-language generalization when treatment is provided in only one language. In other words, **does improvement in the language of treatment extend to the language not treated?** The findings on this issue are mixed, with some studies showing no transfer effects to the untreated language (Galvez & Hinckley, 2003; Hinckley, 2003; Meinzer et al., 2007; Miller Amberber, 2012; Radman et al., 2016) and others, which we will look at in this section, demonstrating evidence for cross-language improvement, albeit dependent on several factors.

Faroqi-Shah et al.'s (2010) meta-analysis reviewed studies which provided treatment in the L2 or L1 and examined the pre-to-post treatment effects on receptive and expressive abilities in the untrained language (L1 or L2, respectively). With respect to *receptive language abilities*, their analyses revealed that cross-language improvement occurred from L2 to L1 in some studies (Faroqi & Chengappa, 1996; Gil & Goral, 2004; Khamis, Venkert-Olenik, & Gil, 1996), while it actually worsened in another study (Miertsch, Meisel, & Isel, 2009). When treatment was provided in the L1, both of the studies they reviewed reported positive cross-language generalization (Gil & Goral, 2004; Junqué, Vendrell & Vendrell-Brucet, 1989). For *expressive abilities*, Faroqi-Shah et al. (2010) identified 11 studies in which treatment was given in the L2 and four where treatment was provided in the L1. While all four studies examining cross-generalization from L1 to L2 demonstrated positive effects (Ansaldo, Ghazi Saidi, & Ruiz, 2009; Edmonds & Kiran, 2006; Gil & Goral, 2004; Junqué, Vendrell & Vendrell-Brucet, 1989), these effects were more variable when treatment was provided in the L2. Of these 11 studies, only 4 reported cross-language improvement from L2 to

L1 (Faroqi & Chengappa, 1996; Khamis, Venkert-Olenik, & Gil, 1996; Maragnolo et al., 2009; Miertsch, Meisel, & Isel, 2009). A study subsequent to the meta-analysis also reported that treatment in the L1 led to cross-language improvement in L2 verb production (Knoph, Simonsen, and Lind, 2017).

These mixed findings are likely "due to a plethora of factors such as difference between treatment approaches, focus on different language domains such as lexical retrieval or syntax, structural differences between languages, and patient-related variables such as pre-morbid language proficiency, type of aphasia, relative severity of impairment in each language, and extent/size of the neurological lesion" (Faroqi-Shah et al., 2010, pp. 336–337). This is echoed by Peñaloza and Kiran (2019), who identified a number of factors that could determine whether cross-language generalization from unilingual treatment is observed. Their review suggests that the primary factors seem to be the type of treatment and the type of items utilized in therapy. For instance, many studies have shown that cross-language effects are more likely to occur from semantic treatment approaches (Croft et al., 2010; Edmonds & Kiran, 2006; Kiran & Iakupova, 2011; Kiran & Roberts, 2010; Kiran et al., 2013), but less so from phonological treatment (Abutalebi et al., 2009; Croft et al., 2011). Furthermore, cross-language effects are reported more often when treatment items are similar in structure (Miertsch, Meisel, & Isel, 2009) or semantically related (Edmonds & Kiran, 2006) across the two languages (see Kohnert, 2009, for a discussion).

In one study by Kohnert (2004), the author presented a case study in which a bilingual with nonfluent aphasia received two consecutive treatments. The first treatment was cognitive-based, in which non-linguistic abilities, such as visual scanning, categorizing, and simple arithmetic were trained. The second treatment was a lexically-based treatment, which focused on cognates and noncognates across the bilingual's languages. The results showed that the patient demonstrated between-language generalization for cognates but not for noncognates. This is perhaps not surprising given their phonological and semantic overlap between the two languages. Nonetheless, Kohnert's study demonstrates that using cognates in the rehabilitation of bilingual aphasia has clinical benefits.

While more research is clearly needed, these findings together suggest that **cross-language generalization can occur** during treatment of bilingual aphasia, for both expressive and receptive abilities. However, the extent to which positive outcomes occur is **sensitive to treatment factors**. The clinical implications for this variability are important. Peñaloza and

Table 4.2 Patterns of recovery in bilingual aphasia

Parallel recovery	Both languages recovery at a similar rate
Differential recovery	Both languages improve, but one language improves more than the other
Selective recovery	One language is recovered while the other remains impaired
Antagonistic recovery	One language initially improves but gets worse with the recovery of the other
Alternate antagonistic recovery	One language improves while the other is affected during alternating periods
Successive recovery	One language improves before the other
Blended recovery	Both languages are mixed together, involuntarily interfering in the recovery process

Kiran (2019) argue that "treating the weaker and less-proficient language, targeting cognates in language therapy, and using a semantic feature analysis approach are valid considerations for clinical practice to enhance therapy effects in bilinguals with aphasia" (p. 536) (see also Ansaldo & Saidi, 2014; Faroqi-Shah et al., 2010). In Section 4.7 we will consider the various patterns of recovery that arise during treatment.

4.7 Patterns of Language Recovery in Bilingual Aphasia

While, for the most part, there is agreement that bilingual aphasics proceed through an acute, chronic, and late stage, there is more variability in the **patterns of recovery** in the two languages. Recovery patterns refer to the rate of and extent to which one or both languages improve post-neurological insult. Unfortunately, the recovery patterns for both languages vary considerably and are unpredictable (Ansaldo et al., 2008). As shown in Paradis' (1977) synthesis of over 100 bilingual aphasics, some bilinguals may recover their languages simultaneously, others may recover one language only after the other has recovered, and others recover one language while the other regresses or never improves at all. Paradis' (1977, 2004) classification of these recovery patterns can be seen in Table 4.2.

The **most common of these recovery patterns** is that of **parallel recovery**. Paradis' (2001) review of cases of bilingual aphasia between

1990 and 2000 showed that 61 percent of cases showed parallel recovery, 18 percent a **differential recovery**, 9 percent a **blended recovery** pattern, 7 percent **selective recovery**, and 5 percent **successive recovery**. From bilingual aphasics whose language recovery occurs in parallel, we know that the areas involved in processing language may be the same, suggesting that the languages' neural representations might overlap. However, in cases where only one language recovers, it begs the question as to whether cortical representations merely partially overlap or do not overlap at all. This continues to be an ongoing investigative endeavor.

4.7.1 Lesion Factors Affecting Recovery

In the monolingual literature, Watila and Balarabe (2015) presented a review of studies reporting factors that predicted poststroke aphasia recovery among monolingual patients (see also Kiran & Thompson, 2019). Many of the variables that we have discussed in this chapter predicting the severity, assessment, and treatment of aphasia are once again relevant for its recovery patterns. From their review, Watila and Balarabe (2015) found that the most important factors that determine recovery are the size and location of the lesion, the resulting type of aphasia, the nature of early reperfusion (to some extent), and the type of treatment received. For instance, all of the studies in their review (with the exception of one study by Lazar et al., 2008) found that **larger lesions predicted poorer aphasia recovery**. The location of the lesion also predicted recovery patterns in several studies, such that damage to the superior temporal gyrus predicted poorer recovery (e.g., Parkinson et al., 2009). This suggests that there are certain brain areas whose functions may never be replaced and other areas for which the brain is able to "rewire" itself over time (and with rehabilitation) to overcome language impairment.

4.7.2 Nonlesion Factors Affecting Recovery

Nonlesion factors were also analyzed in Watila and Balarabe's (2015) review of monolingual studies to examine whether variables such as gender, age, handedness, and educational level were indicative of observed recovery patterns. Unlike the lesion-related factors, the findings from previous studies have been more inconclusive. Although Watila and Balarabe found that none of these factors were robust enough to predict recovery patterns, a number of studies did report an effect. For instance, there is some evidence that **gender** modulates recovery patterns, such that females may recover oral expression and comprehension better than males (Basso, Capitani, & Moraschini, 1982; Pizzamiglio, Mammucari, & Razzano, 1985). Other studies reported no effects for gender (e.g., Pedersen et al., 1995). With respect to the **age of the patient**, there is some evidence that older aphasics have poorer recovery than younger aphasics (Laska et al., 2001) while other studies failed to find age effects (e.g., Holland et al., 2014). Variability in recovery patterns was also found to be related to effects of educational attainment, some supporting modulating effects (Jacobs, Schall, & Scheibel, 1993) and others report- ing no effect (Seniów, Litwin, & Leśniak, 2009). There is one factor, **handedness**, which, across the studies examined by Watila and Balarabe, consistently did not predict recovery.

For bilingual patients, the same factors that modulate the severity and assessment of language impairment also affect recovery patterns. For instance, L2 AoA modulates the degree of recovery of stroke patients due to differences in language mapping and the amount of grey matter developed from an early age, among other things. Stroke patients who have acquired an L2 early on have a higher chance of recovery than those who acquired the language later in life. Some studies have reported evidence that early AoA and premorbid language dominance significantly contribute to language recovery and should thus inform rehabilitation (Conner et al., 2018; Faroqi-Shah et al., 2010; Knoph, 2013; Lorenzen & Murray, 2008). As we mentioned, the frequency of premorbid language use can determine the degree of impairment and recovery from aphasia (Goral et al., 2012, 2013; Knoph, Simonsen, & Lind, 2017). This is particularly true for individuals who live in a monolingual L2 environment (e.g., following immigration, working abroad, etc.).

4.8 Primary Progressive Aphasias

The types of nonfluent and fluent aphasias we have discussed so far are due to sudden trauma and damage in one or more areas of the brain. However, the progressive loss of neurons in the frontal, temporal, and/or parietal regions due to **degenerative diseases** such as dementia can also negatively affect language. These impairments are classified as **primary progressive aphasias** (PPA). Unlike sudden-onset aphasias, there is no defined lesion. Instead, there is atrophy which is initially in a confined area of the brain but progressively gets larger, as revealed in studies using PET (Sinnatamby et al., 1996) and fMRI (Gorno-Tempini et al., 2004). However, neuronal destruction never fully happens; instead, the remaining neurons continue to facilitate language function but with dif- ferent patterns of brain network connectivity (Mesulam et al., 2014). The majority of PPA patients will have increasing difficulties in language production and expressing themselves even though their memory may (or may not) remain unaffected.

Typically, researchers have elaborated three variants: PPA-nonfluent, PPA-semantic, or PPA-logopenic. **PPA-nonfluent**, also known as PPA-agrammatic, occurs when there is cortical atrophy in the left inferior frontoinsular area (Gorno-Tempini et al., 2011) or middle temporal areas secondary to the inferior frontal area (Grossman, 2010). The clinical manifestations include difficulty pronouncing words or producing speech fluidly, poor syntactic structure, and speech sound errors. As this progressively gets worse, patients use shorter sentences, are more telegraphic, and eventually may use very little language at all.

When there is cortical atrophy in the anterior and inferolateral temporal areas, either bilaterally (Mion et al., 2010) or slighter greater on the left side than on the right (Rogalski et al., 2011), the result is **PPA-semantic**. The observed language impairments in PPA-semantic are seen in both expressive and receptive abilities because of the deficit in semantic memory. Patients will have trouble remembering the names of people, objects, words, and facts, among other things. With the progression of PPA-semantic, word meaning becomes more impaired and patients have trouble comprehending auditory discourse.

The third type of progressive aphasia is **PPA-logopenic** in which there is atrophy in the left posterior temporoparietal region (Gorno-Tempini et al., 2011). Patients will have increasing problems with word retrieval, phonemic paraphasias, and sentence repetition. This creates pauses in their speech, making their discourse much slower. As PPA-logopenic worsens, patients are eventually unable to retain complex or long sentences or information.

The location of the atrophy and resulting impairments in all forms of PPA appear to be the same for monolinguals and bilinguals (Malcolm et al., 2019). In Malcolm et al.'s review of 13 published case studies of bilinguals with PPA, the authors found that the rate of decline can be parallel or differential in the two languages. This is true regardless of the variant of PPA. Of the studies reviewed, five (38 percent) reported that both languages declined in parallel and eight (62 percent) reported a differential rate of decline. They also found no effects of AoA, frequency of language use, or L2 proficiency on decline. Interesting, in all cases of differential decline, the L1 was better preserved than the L2. Upon further examination, Malcolm et al. found that as the PPA worsened, there was a shift toward parallel decline overall, suggesting that "the degenerative nature of PPA, likely resulting in compensation for declining language abilities over the progressive decline, at least in the early stages, may explain why the two patterns of language decline converge to parallel decline over time" (p. 587).

4.9 Summary

In this chapter, we have reviewed work on a range of bilingual aphasias, the language impairments that occur due to a lesion or atrophy in the brain. We began the chapter by discussing two theoretical approaches that account for the extent to which one or both languages are affected (Section 4.2). The localizationist account holds that if a bilingual's languages are located in different areas of the brain, a patient may suffer from aphasia in only one of their languages. The dynamic account, drawing on evidence that there is significant overlap of two languages in the brain, views bilingual aphasia in the context of highly controlled and connected neural regions. On this theoretical backdrop, in Section 4.3 we discussed several types of aphasia (global, Broca's, Wernicke's, conduction, amnestic, sensory, motor, and mixed), their corresponding lesion sites, and their clinical manifestations. We also identified two aphasias, namely alexia and agraphia, that only affect reading and writing abilities, respectively. We saw that the severity and type of aphasia that results from a lesion depends on its size and location.

A number of other nonlesion factors can affect the severity of the resulting aphasia. In Section 4.4, we reviewed the premorbid variables that have been most studied: Frequency of language use, AoA, and L2 proficiency. Many studies have found that bilingual aphasics who used the L1 more frequently prior to impairment had better post-impairment performance in their L1 compared to the L2, whereas aphasics who used the L2 as often as or more than the L1 performed better in both languages. These effects, however, appear to be modulated by AoA: For bilingual aphasics with an early AoA but who used the L1 more frequently prior to impairment, there was improvement in both languages. Thus, it is essential for clinicians to gather as much language background information from the patient (and often from their family and friends) as possible, as this can help inform assessment and optimal treatment of bilingual aphasia.

In Section 4.5, we looked at how bilinguals are assessed for aphasia. Speech pathologists use a variety of language assessments to evaluate the patient's strengths and weaknesses with language skills across all modalities and help plan for a treatment program. There are also brief versions of these assessments that are specifically designed for nonspecialists. For bilingual patients, the most common assessment is the BAT, which is freely available online in over 70 languages. In Section 4.6, we turned to the treatment methods of bilingual aphasia. Important questions were addressed, such as: In which language(s) should treatment be provided and what are the differential outcomes? and Is there cross-language generalization to the language not treated? While it is believed that treatment in either the L1 or L2 improves receptive and/or expressive abilities in that same language, there are mixed findings with respect to cross-language improvement. Some findings do not report transfer benefits from one language to the other, while other studies have shown that treatment in the L2 may help the L1. However, this effect is sensitive to the type of treatment and items used in therapy.

In Section 4.7, we reviewed the patterns of recovery and impairment in bilingual aphasia, noting that the most common is parallel recovery in which both languages improve at a similar rate. These recovery patterns, as we noted, are affected by many of the same modulating factors we discussed throughout the chapter. Finally, in Section 4.8, we reviewed types of PPAs that, instead of resulting from a sudden lesion, emerge due to atrophy in the brain, which progressively gets worse. PPAs are usually caused by degenerative diseases affecting brain and cognition such as forms of dementia.

Overall, in this chapter, we have seen that our understanding of bilingual aphasia still has a long way to go. Although we have learned a great deal about the relationship between lesion sites and the language impairments that arise, researchers continue to find themselves at the mercy of several factors that modulate these effects, including differential language lateralization and localization of language processes among bilinguals and whether these overlap or partially overlap in the brain. Furthermore, the exact nature of the effects of premorbid, nonlesion factors on the severity, assessment, treatment, and recovery of bilingual aphasia is still unclear, although our understanding is improving as more and more research and meta-analyses are conducted.

Review Questions

1. List and describe the main types of aphasia and their clinical characteristics.
2. What causes aphasia and the severity of language impairments in bilingual aphasics?
3. Describe some of the tasks that can be used to diagnose aphasia in bilinguals.

4. How is bilingual aphasia clinically treated?
5. Discuss the recovery patterns often observed in bilingual aphasia and some factors that affect them.

Further Reading

Paradis, M. (1995). *Aspects of bilingual aphasia*. Emerald.
Paradis, M., & Libben, G. (1987). *The assessment of bilingual aphasia*. Psychology Press.
Weeks, B. (2010). Issues in bilingual aphasia [Special issue], *Aphasiology, 24*(2).

CHAPTER FIVE

Cross-Linguistic Effects of Bilingualism

Learning Objectives

- Learn about linguistic influence and transfer effects that occur in bilinguals.
- Explore different domains of cross-linguistic transfer, including phonological, lexical, morphological, syntactic, discursive, pragmatic, and sociolinguistic.
- Become familiar with various factors that affect cross-linguistic transfer, including language dominance and proficiency, input frequency, and typological similarity.
- Learn about code-switching, the theoretical models that explain code-switching, and what happens in the brain when bilinguals switch between their languages.
- Examine the language in which bilinguals dream and what determines this.

5.1 Introduction

As mentioned in Chapter 3, Grosjean (1989) famously stated, "Neurolinguists beware! A bilingual is not two monolinguals in one person" (p. 3). This quote speaks to the heart of the fact that languages do not exist separately, but rather mutually coexist and interact in one mind/brain. There is strong evidence that this coexistence affects several linguistic domains. For instance, having a "foreign accent" in one's L2 reflects the influence of their L1 sound system. Consequently, a careful listener may be able to identify what the speaker's L1 is. In this chapter, we will review studies that investigate the cross-linguistic effects of knowing and using more than one language. Given that much research in this area has examined language production, we will mostly focus our discussion on this area. In Section 5.2, we start by taking a broad view of how languages interact in one mind and the notion of cross-linguistic transfer. Following this, we outline work that has specifically investigated transfer across linguistic domains along with how factors such as cognate status, language dominance, and input frequency can further modulate these effects (Sections 5.3 to 5.8). We then transition in Section 5.9 to examine a unique skill that bilinguals have: The ability to switch back and forth between two different language systems – often with seemingly little effort. In Section 5.10, we address dreaming in one or more languages and what appears to determine the language of dreams. We conclude the chapter in Section 5.11.

5.2 Cross-Linguistic Influence and Transfer

Interest in how bilinguals' knowledge and use of one language affects their other language is not new. In fact, as Jarvis and Pavlenko (2008) note, even as far back as Homer's *Odyssey,* we find mention of **cross-linguistic influence (CLI)** (e.g., when Odysseus tells Penelope about the use of "mixed languages" in Crete). In early research, the terms *transfer* and *interference* were used interchangeably to refer to this phenomenon. However, since the late 1980s, CLI has gained popularity (Kellerman & Sharwood Smith, 1986; cf. Cook, 2002), and while the term *interference* may be more common, it is often still acceptable to use the term *transfer* (Jarvis & Pavlenko, 2008).

Research on CLI gained traction during the middle of the twentieth century. Oldin (1989) offers a review of the major findings of research on CLI from the 1960s to the 1980s (see Table 5.1).

Table 5.1 Major research findings on CLI (cross-linguistic influence) from the 1960s to the 1980s

---

Errors are not the only outcome of CLI. On the contrary, there can be positive outcomes. Rate and ultimate attainment of an L2 are both affected by CLI.

Differences between the L1 and L2/L3 do not necessarily lead to learning difficulties or to CLI. Instead, salient differences often make target-language structures easier to acquire, contrary to the contrastive analysis hypothesis.

CLI does not decrease as proficiency in a less-dominant language increases. In fact, it is only at later stages of L2 acquisition that learners have sufficient proficiency to recognize similarities and differences between more complex aspects of the two languages.

Transfer can occur from an L1 to an L2 (forward transfer), from an L2 to an L3 (lateral transfer), and from an L2 to an L1 (reverse transfer).

Table 5.1 (cont.)

The likelihood of transfer is determined by several factors, including age and typological relatedness of the two languages.

Transfer is not limited to structure and language form. In addition to phonological, morphological, and syntactic transfer, CLI can extend to meaning and pragmatics.

Individual differences (e.g., anxiety and aptitude) among language users lead to different types and extents of CLI.

Table 5.2 CLI (cross-linguistic influence) across ten dimensions

Cognitive Level
- linguistic
- conceptual

Knowledge Type
- implicit
- explicit

Directionality
- forward
- reverse
- lateral
- bi- or multi-directional

Linguistic Area
- discursive
- lexical
- morphological
- orthographic
- phonological
- pragmatic
- semantic
- sociolinguistic
- syntactic

Intentionality
- intentional
- unintentional

Mode
- productive
- receptive

Manifestation
- overt
- covert

Channel
- oral
- visual

Form
- verbal
- nonverbal

Outcome
- positive
- negative

Since the 1990s, researchers have elaborated on additional types of and constraints on transfer. For instance, Jarvis and Pavlenko (2008) have characterized transfer across several dimensions, as summarized in Table 5.2. In Sections 5.3 to 5.7, we will focus on some of the types of transfer within these linguistic domains along with various factors that affect CLI (Section 5.8). We will discuss conceptual transfer (and restructuring) in Chapter 6 in our discussion of the bilingual memory and the mental lexicon.

5.3 Phonological Transfer

Studies in phonological transfer have examined sound at the individual, syllabic, and suprasegmental levels. With respect to the perception of sounds, the most apparent effect of phonological transfer is the difficulty in distinguishing between two sounds in a language that are not phonemically contrastive in the other language (Aoyama, 2003; Escudero & Boersma, 2004). Other research in sound perception has identified transfer effects for segmental duration (Flege, Bohn, & Jang, 1997) and voicing contrasts (Pisoni et al., 1982).

Research on phonological transfer and the *production* of segments has been more robust compared to sound *perception*. Some of the work examining transfer in production has demonstrated that sounds in the L2 can be substituted for other L2 sounds due to the influence of the L1 phonological system. For instance, Japanese speakers of English in a study by Riney, Takata, and Ota (2000) consistently produced the Japanese flap /ɾ/ in place of the English /r/ and /l/. And perhaps the most obvious evidence of transfer in the sound domain is having a "foreign accent." Keys (2002) found that Brazilian Portuguese speakers of English palatalized the English /d/ and /t/ in phonetic environments where this would happen in Brazilian Portuguese but not in English. Because of these and other findings, researchers have asked whether bilinguals have separate or integrated phonological systems. In a pioneering study by Paradis (2001), two-year-old monolingual French-speaking children, monolingual English-speaking children, and bilingual French–English-speaking children participated in nonsense-word repetition tasks. The data was then analyzed for patterns of syllable omissions/truncations specific to French and English and the three groups were compared. The results from these analyses suggested that there are language-specific prosodic sensitivities in phonological production among bilingual children, suggesting that there are differentiated phonological systems. However, the measurements of truncation patterns among bilinguals were not identical to monolinguals, implying that bilinguals' phonological systems are not entirely autonomous. Interestingly, these effects emerged when there was interlanguage structural ambiguity.

Table 5.3 Phonemic and syllabic CLI (cross-linguistic influence) effects

Age	Phonemic CLI occurrences	Syllabic CLI occurrences	Number of opportunities for CLI	Occurrences
5;0	3 narratives	1 conversation	379	0.8%
6;2	2 conversations 1 single word	0	512	0.6%
7;0	1 narrative	0	378	0.3%

Source: Fabiano-Smith and Goldstein (2010).

Paradis argued that between-language asymmetries in word stress variety and/or language dominance may further influence phonological CLI, and that the restrictive nature of these CLI effects "further supports the claim that the children indeed have two phonological representations, as more random interference would be expected from a unified store" (Paradis, 2001, p. 35). Paradis put forth the **Interactional Dual Systems Model** of language representation, which holds that bilingual children have two separate phonological systems that mutually influence one another.

While Paradis (2001) elucidated our understanding of the not-so-autonomous nature of the bilingual phonological systems at the age of two, a study by Fabiano-Smith and Goldstein (2010) provides quasi-longitudinal evidence that further supports Paradis' Interactional Dual Systems Model. However, unlike Paradis' study, Fabiano-Smith and Goldstein specifically examined the frequency and types of phonological CLI effects that occurred over time in three Spanish–English bilingual children, ages five, six, and seven. The researchers investigated the phonological makeup of individual words, conversations, and narrative samples using two analyses of phonemic and syllabic CLI effects. The data revealed very few phonemic CLI effects and only one syllabic; however, these patterns diminished with age, as reflected by the number of occurrences observed divided by the opportunities for CLI (see Table 5.3).

Overall, the results from Fabiano-Smith and Goldstein's (2010) study found that although the frequency of CLI effects was low, bilingual children exhibited phonological differentiation and transferred elements from one language to the other. The study offers further support for the notion that bilingual children's two phonological systems are separate, but not autonomous. Unfortunately, due to the small sample size and the very few occurrences of CLI effects, it is difficult to determine whether the frequency of occurrence truly decreases as children get older or whether they remain more or less stable.

5.4 Lexical Transfer

Lexical transfer refers to the influence of word knowledge in one language on the knowledge or use of words in another language. Much of the research conducted on this concerns how lexical representations are linked across languages and how these links affect the ways in which words are retrieved from the mental lexicon. We will look at this in more detail in our discussion on the architecture of the mental lexicon in Chapter 6. Another line of inquiry within the lexical transfer research is **word choice transfer**. Studies examining this issue are interested in how a person's knowledge of one language affects their choice of words used in another language. For example, Hohenstein, Eisenberg, and Naigles (2006) found that when given several options, Spanish–English bilinguals were more likely to choose L2 English verbs that imply path information (e.g., go, come, cross) compared to monolingual English speakers, who preferred verbs that carry manner information (e.g., run, walk, jump) in the same contexts. These same effects have been found when examining the choice of one-part versus phrasal verbs (Laufer & Eliasson, 1993; Sjöholm, 1995), determiner phrases and compound nouns (Bongartz, 2002), grammatical categories (Pavlenko & Driagina, 2007), and lexical collocations (Hasselgren, 1994).

A more recent study by Agustín-Llach (2019) examined the impact of bilingualism on lexical knowledge, lexical fluency, and lexical CLI. Spanish–Basque bilinguals and Spanish monolinguals, both of whom had a B1 level of English proficiency participated in a lexical availability task. The task required the participants to write down as many words belonging to four semantic categories – hobbies, town, countryside, and food and drink – as they could within two minutes per category. Analyses on the written responses explored instances of lexical transfer (from L1) and cross-lexical interactions. The results suggested that the two groups were too similar for definite conclusions to be drawn, although there was a marginally significant advantage for bilinguals learning an L3 versus monolinguals learning an L2. Specifically, the monolinguals produced more examples but also showed more instances of CLI. Agustín-Llach explained that schooling (bilingual education vs. single-language) and English language learning experiences may be "strong enough to discard any possible advantages gained from bilingualism" (p. 898).

5.5 Morphological Transfer

Although quite a bit of attention has been paid to phonological and lexical CLI, fewer studies have been conducted on morphological influences.

Nonetheless, there is growing interest with respect to the transfer of inflectional and bound morphemes and morphological awareness. Concerning inflectional morphology, it was once assumed that inflection did not transfer even though other aspects of language do (Eubank, 1993). A few years later, Eubank et al. (1997) further elaborated that it was overt morphology, in particular, that does not generally transfer. However, subsequent studies provided contrary evidence to this claim. For instance, De Angelis and Selinker (2001) found that English–Spanish and French–Spanish bilinguals often transferred inflectional morphology from their L2 Spanish to L3 Italian, and Jarvis (2002) reported that Finnish speakers were able to transfer their knowledge of L2 Swedish to acquire articles in their L3 English. The results in Jarvis' study were strengthened further when he compared the Finnish–Swedish–English speakers who had six years of instruction in Swedish and two years in English to another group of Finnish–English–Swedish speakers who had six years of instruction in English and two years in Swedish. The group with only two years of English instruction outperformed the group with six years of English instruction. Jarvis argued that the former group was able to transfer their knowledge of L2 Swedish articles to acquire L3 articles – a process that was faster than for those who were learning another language (i.e., L2 English) for the first time.

While it is most common to observe morphological transfer effects from a more dominant language to a lesser dominant language (although language relatedness and other factors can modulate these effects), there are a few studies that provide indications of transfer in the opposite direction (e.g., L2 transfer to L1, often referred to as **reverse transfer**). Evidence for these effects comes from Pavlenko and Jarvis (2002) and Zhang et al. (2010), among others. In the study by Pavlenko and Jarvis, a Russian speaker's pronominal case-marking errors in the L1 were traced to their knowledge of L2 English's pronominal case system. Zhang et al. provided fifth-grade L1 Chinese children learning L2 English with intensive training in either English or Chinese compound morphology. The post-training tests revealed that compared to control groups, both Chinese and English intervention groups improved in their knowledge of English compound morphology. This indicated that their training and knowledge of L1 compound morphology was transferred to the L2. Reverse transfer effects also trended toward significance ($p < .09$), such that when receiving training in L2 compounds, knowledge of L1 compound morphology improved. However, when further analyzing this finding, Zhang et al. found that participants with higher L2 proficiency were able to transfer from L1, whereas those with lower proficiency were not.

Morphological awareness transfer has also become an emerging theme in CLI research (Chen & Schwartz, 2018). **Morphological awareness** is "the ability to reflect upon and manipulate morphemes and employ word formation rules in one's language" (Kuo & Anderson, 2006, p. 161). With respect to CLI and morphological awareness, Koda's (2005, 2008) **Transfer Facilitation Model** predicts that transferred competence of one language offers top-down assistance for reading development and other related skills in another language. Expanding this model, Chung, Chen, and Geva (2019) proposed an interactive framework that specified key factors that affect transfer in both directions among bilingual learners at different proficiency levels. To test these theoretical claims, in a study by Zhang (2013), sixth-grade Chinese children learning L2 English participated in paper-and-pencil tests measuring their morphological awareness and lexical inference in Chinese and English. The results, in line with Zhang et al. (2010), showed that Chinese morphological awareness transferred to English. Particularly interesting, though, was the finding that this awareness was greater for compounds than for derived words. To read more about cross-linguistic transfer of morphological awareness – in addition to phonological awareness, decoding skills, and vocabulary – specifically between Chinese and English, refer to the meta-analysis by Yang, Cooc, and Sheng (2017).

To sum up, although transfer of inflectional morphemes in either direction is quite restricted, it does occur relatively frequently, particularly when the two languages share lexical and morphological similarities. There also seems to be no restriction on the directionality of transfer, although L2 proficiency (and other factors) may determine whether reverse transfer effects are observed (Zhang et al., 2010). Finally, while most of the literature has examined L1 to L2 transfer, there is also evidence for L2 to L3 and L2 to L1 transfer, as briefly discussed. However, while these effects are highly salient when involving overt morphology, they are either absent or difficult to detect when involving subtle nuances of morphology without using carefully designed analyses (Jarvis & Pavlenko, 2008).

5.6 Syntactic Transfer

Prior to the 1990s, CLI from L1 syntax (like morphology) was believed to be immune to transfer (see Kellerman, 1995, for a discussion). However, many studies once again suggest that this linguistic domain is also venerable to transfer effects in both directions. For instance, there have been investigations on how L1 syntax affects grammatical judgments in the L2.

Among the first of these studies was conducted by Zobl (1992), who found that language learners from different L1 backgrounds show differential patterns of grammatical acceptance in the nonnative language. For some of the participants, this language was their L2 and for others, it was their L3. The study revealed that learners who already knew an L2, and thus were making grammatical judgments in their L3, were less likely to reject ungrammatical sentences. Zobl argued that the finding is a representation of "an inverse relationship between the conservatism of the learning procedure and the pool of linguistic knowledge available" (Zobl, 1992, p. 193). Similar findings were found in the reverse direction in a study by Köpke (2002), in which L2 learners were more tolerant of ungrammatical constructions in their L1 compared to monolinguals (see also Jarvis, 2003).

Erdocia and Laka (2018) compared word order preferences among L1 Spanish speakers learning L2 Basque and L1 Basque speakers proficient in Spanish. The study used EEG to examine electrical patterns in the brain when processing noncanonical sentences in Basque. Object–verb–subject (OVS) orders are noncanonical in both Spanish and Basque but subject–verb–object (SVO) orders are canonical in Spanish but noncanonical in Basque. Erdocia and Laka were interested in seeing if L1 Spanish canonical order affected how L2 Basque SVO and OVS noncanonical sentences were processed. The results indeed provided evidence for this effect, even among participants who were highly proficient and/or had acquired the L2 from an early age. Increased left anterior negativity was observed when comparing S and O in sentence-initial position and a **P600 effect** (i.e., an ERP component often reflecting the processing of grammatical anomalies/incongruities) was found when comparing S and O in word-final position. The authors argued that these findings align with the Competition Model (Bates & MacWhinney, 1989), given that the model predicts differences when processing dissimilar features in the L1 and L2.

Reverse transfer effects have also been reported in research on syntactic transfer. Many of these studies have also been framed in the context of the Competition Model. One example is by Su (2001), in which L1 Chinese learners of English at three proficiency levels and L1 English learners of Chinese, also at three levels, completed a sentence interpretation experiment (based on MacWhinney, Bates, & Kligel, 1984). As expected, the results showed that when interpreting L2 sentences, L1-based cue preferences were utilized, but these preferences diminished as L2 proficiency increased. However, the same effects were also found in the reverse direction: When interpreting L1 sentences, the participants increasingly relied on L2-based cues as their L2 proficiency increased. Interestingly, the reliance was not a complete shift to L2 strategies, but rather a mixture of L1 and L2 processing, a finding also reported by Cook et al. (2003), among others.

Eye-tracking technology has also played a significant role in experimental designs looking at CLI in the domain of syntax. Dussias (2004) recorded and analyzed the eye movements of Spanish–English bilinguals while reading temporarily ambiguous sentences in Spanish. The sentences had complex noun phrases followed by a relative clause, as in (1).

(1)   Peter fell in love with the daughter of the psychologist who studied in California (Dussias, 2004, p. 355).

Prior studies (e.g., Mitchell, Cuetos, & Corley, 1992), suggest that whereas monolingual Spanish speakers attach relative clauses to the first noun in a complex noun phrase, English speakers prefer to attach the relative clause to the noun immediately preceding the relative clause. The findings from Dussias' (2004) study provide additional support for this observation. The Spanish–English bilinguals favored local over nonlocal attachment when reading sentences in Spanish, even though this is a typical parsing strategy in English. The author argued that these results support exposure-based and parallel interactive models of sentence parsing as put forth by Brysbaert and Mitchell (1996) and Mitchell et al. (1995), as these models hold that frequency-based exposure affects syntactic parsing.

Finally, researchers have also examined L2 to L3 syntactic transfer. In a study by Bardel and Falk (2007), learners with different L1 and L2 backgrounds were placed in two groups: One that was beginning to learn L3 Swedish and the other L3 Dutch. When analyzing production of negation in the L3, the results showed that "syntactic structures are more easily transferred from L2 than from L1 in the initial state of L3 acquisition" (Bardel & Falk, 2007, p. 459) and are attributable to both L2 proficiency along with the typological relationship between the L2 and L3. The surge in research in this area is evidenced by an edited volume by Angelovska and Hahn (2017), which includes thirteen papers reporting on L3 syntactic transfer.

5.7 Discursive, Pragmatic, and Sociolinguistic Transfer

Due to space limitations, we are not able to explore transfer across *all linguistic domains*, but we should point out some key issues concerning discursive, pragmatic, and sociolinguistic transfer. **Discursive transfer** concerns "the ways thoughts are introduced, organized, and contextualized within an oral or written discourse, and also relates to the conversational strategies that are used to maintain a conversation" (Jarvis & Pavlenko, 2008, p. 102). The contrastive rhetoric framework, originally conceived by Kaplan (1966), suggests that languages have unique rhetorical conventions – including how discourse is organized and contextualized and how main ideas are conveyed – that can negatively affect writing in another language. Discursive transfer has been reported in both language production and reception (e.g., Thatcher, 2000), and in both directions, that is, from L1 to L2 and vice versa (Shi, 2002). Karim and Nassaji (2013) provide a review of studies on discursive transfer. To our knowledge, there have been few studies investigating discursive transfer effects between two nonnative languages.

The illocutionary and sociolinguistic competence that is carried over from one language to another is referred to as **pragmatic transfer**. It is generally accepted that L2 speech forms are acquired before pragmatic competence that regulates contextually-appropriate speech (Jung, 2005). Indeed, pragmatic competence is acquired very late in L2 learning and even many highly proficient learners struggle to use their L2 in pragmatically appropriate ways. In a study by Takahashi (1996), L1 Japanese leaners of English at low and high proficiency levels judged the contextual appropriateness of indirect English request strategies. The results showed that for both low- and high-proficient learners, responses were in accordance with the request strategies that are conventionally used in their L1. For a more recent review on the negative effects of L1 pragmatic transfer to L2 (particularly L2 English), refer to Meznah (2018).

Finally, transfer can also be attributed to purely social factors involving language. **Sociolinguistic transfer** refers to how the social variables that account for linguistic variation in one language system affect the use and knowledge of another language system. Much of this research has taken a variationist perspective, showing how sociolinguistic transfer from the L1 affects various speech acts in the L2. Variables of interest have included social distance, status relationships, and gender, among others. For instance, some studies have shown that L1 Chinese and L1 Korean speakers learning English vary their ways of apologizing, complaining, and responding to complaints according to the tradition of social distance and hierarchies of their L1 culture (Lee, 2000; Yu, 2004). Other studies have reported that L1 Japanese speakers learning English utilize compliment response patterns and topic development in English discourse that concord with gender-specific patterns in Japanese (Itakura, 2002).

Thus far, we have mostly focused on the various types of transfer, although we have also alluded to the fact that transfer can be influenced by factors such as the typological relatedness of the languages and the L2 level of proficiency. In Section 5.8, we will explore some of these factors.

5.8 Factors Affecting Transfer

CLI effects are notoriously hard to predict. This is clearly reflected in the many studies that identify various factors which either modulate the degree of transfer across languages or whether CLI will emerge at all. Following Jarvis and Pavlenko (2008), Table 5.4 provides some of the variables that have been investigated and organizes them into five categories. In the following subsections, we limit our discussion to language dominance and proficiency, input frequency, cross-linguistic similarity, and cognate status.

Table 5.4 Factors interacting with CLI organized across five categories

Linguistic and psycholinguistic factors
Cross-linguistic similarity and cognate status*
Linguistic domain and use
Markedness and prototypicality
Linguistic context

Cognitive, attentional, and developmental factors
Level of cognitive maturity
Developmental and universal processes of language acquisition
Cognitive language learning abilities
Attention to and awareness of language

Cumulative language experience and knowledge
Age
Frequency of language input*
Intensity and length of language exposure
Length of residence
Language dominance and proficiency*
Number and order of acquired languages

Factors related to the learning environment
Formal vs. naturalistic exposure, learner is focused on form vs. meaning and
    communication, etc.

Factors related to language use
Level of formality, language task, etc.

* Elaborated in Sections 5.8.1–5.8.3

5.8.1 Language Dominance and Proficiency

Without a doubt, language proficiency affects the nature and occurrence of CLI (Odlin & Jarvis, 2004). This is particularly true in the case of source language proficiency. Guion et al. (2000) found that performance-related forward transfer grew as L1 knowledge increased. Other studies on forward transfer have reported that L2 proficiency has performance-related effects on L3 use (Ringbom, 2001). However, the effects of recipient language proficiency on CLI are less clear, perhaps due to inconsistences regarding how proficiency is measured and what specific proficiency ranges are examined. It is often the case that the recipient language is the L1 in which participants have full proficiency and thus, when reverse transfer is observed, it is unclear "whether L2 effects on the L1 are the cause or consequence of eroding L1 proficiency" (Jarvis & Pavlenko, 2008, p. 203).

In a study by Argyri and Sorace (2007), the researchers sought to explore three issues: (a) Whether language dominance plays a role in the occurrence and magnitude of transfer; (b) in which direction(s) CLI occurs; and (c) what syntactic structures account for these effects. Eight-year-old English–Greek early bilinguals living in Greece and Greek–English early bilinguals living in the UK were asked to participate in a battery of elicited production and grammatical judgment tasks. The results suggested that CLI can persist over time and can have unidirectional effects on both narrow syntax and syntax–pragmatics interface structures. However, these effects only emerged in the performance of the English-dominant bilinguals, suggesting that "the actual occurrence of CLI seems to be at least partially affected by the amount of input received, since it is manifested only in English-dominant children" (Argyri & Sorace, 2007, p. 97). We discuss these frequency effects further in Section 5.8.2.

Transfer effects in vocabulary acquisition also appear to be sensitive to proficiency. Pham et al. (2018) examined whether training in L1 vocabulary transfers to L2 vocabulary development. In the study, first- and second-grade children participated in learning sessions in which they were intensively taught vocabulary in their L1 through narrative-based, mediated learning experiences. The participants consisted of three groups according to their L1 proficiency: Low Spanish–English, Low Vietnamese–English, and High Spanish–English. As expected, the results showed that all three groups improved in learning target words and their definitions in the L1. However, only the group with high L1 proficiency improved in the L2. Pham et al. argue that these findings reveal a degree of spontaneous cross-language transfer to an L2 that is determined by L1 proficiency.

With regard to phonetic behavior, there is a growing body of studies that suggest that **language proficiency is a robust predictor of CLI** (Amengual & Chamorro, 2015; Tomé Lourido & Evans, 2019). However, less is known about how language-specific phonological processes are implemented and transferred and whether they are sensitive to language dominance. In a study by Amengual and Simonet (2020), adult Catalan–Spanish and Spanish–Catalan bilinguals participated in picture naming tasks. The sound processes of interest were the reduction of /a/ to /ə/ and the mid-vowel contrasts /e/-/ɛ/ and /o/-/ɔ/. These two processes are found in Catalan but not in Spanish (i.e., Spanish does not reduce /a/ to /ə/ in unstressed environments as Catalan does, nor do the sounds /e/-/ɛ/ and /o/-/ɔ/ yield phonemic differences in Spanish). The results from the acoustic analyses suggested that language dominance did not affect vowel reduction; however, mid-vowel contrasts were sensitive to language dominance. The authors argued that phonemic contrasts with a low functional load may be more difficult to acquire than other phonological processes such as vowel reduction that are more frequent and predictable. In all, the study demonstrates that the language dominance effects consistently observed in the literature (see Tomé Lourido & Evans, 2019) do not necessarily imply that the same effects will apply to phonological processes. On the contrary, language dominance appears to differentially affect CLI depending on the phonological processes in question (i.e., phonological contrasts vs. phonological alternations).

5.8.2 Input Frequency

Among the first researchers to suggest that CLI is affected by frequency of input was Selinker (1969), who argued that L2 learners often transfer frequency tendencies from their L1 to L2. A later study by Poulisse (1999) provided further evidence for this claim when analyzing Dutch–English bilinguals' slips of tongue in English. The analyses showed that 30 percent of the slips of tongue reflected L1 transfer and that nearly all of them were accidental insertions of highly frequent L1 words. Poulisse elaborated that the lexical selection processes for frequent words in the L1 are automatized and difficult to suppress when using an L2.

There is criticism for input frequency effects in CLI. For example, Hauser-Grüdl et al.'s (2010) systematic review concluded, contrary to previous findings suggesting that frequency of L1 input affects L2 acquisition in simultaneous bilingual children (e.g., Paradis & Navarro, 2003), that this "contact-variety approach cannot account for cross-linguistic influence in early bilingualism. The effects of cross-linguistic influence depend on language complexity and on the bilingual's fluency" (Hauser-Grüdl et al., 2010, p. 2638). Hauser-Grüdl et al.'s view of CLI is that it is a competence-based, grammar-driven phenomenon.

Paquot (2017) explored L2 learners' preference for three-word lexical bundles in their L2 writing. In the study, L2 word combinations were extracted from argumentative essays written by French–English and Spanish–English learners. The frequency of their L1 equivalent was calculated based on L1 French and Spanish corpora. The results showed a strong relationship between L2 lexical bundles and the frequency of their L1 equivalents. Furthermore, differential patterns emerged for L1 French versus L1 Spanish participants that reflected the relative differences in frequency in each of the languages. Paquot argued that future research should consider operationalizing the construct *input* by including both L1 and L2 input that have measurable degrees of frequency.

5.8.3 Cross-Linguistic Similarity and Cognates

Among the issues investigated in research on CLI is how the typological relationship between the two languages influences transfer effects. The **contrastive analysis hypothesis** (Lado, 1957) argues that differences and similarities in the structure of the two languages can predict whether such structure is more difficult or easier to acquire, respectively. Furthermore, it posits **positive transfer** from L1 to L2 when these similarities exist and **negative transfer** when they differ (see also Melby-Lervag & Lervag, 2011). While there is evidence that CLI occurs between languages that are objectively different (Yang, Cooc, & Sheng, 2017), the extent of transfer seems to be greatest when the languages are perceived to be very similar by the user (Ringbom, 2007). However, these perceived similarities can lead to overgeneralization and cause errors in the target language that are grammatical in the source language but are ungrammatical in the target language (Ringbom, 1987).

Lowie and Verspoor (2004) tested L1 Dutch learners of L2 English at four levels to see if input frequency or L1/L2 similarity affect the acquisition of English prepositions. The results from a cloze test (i.e., a task in which a participant must supply missing words from a written passage) demonstrated main effects for both language similarity and frequency among beginners and intermediate L2 learners, but not for highly proficient learners. Interestingly, an interaction was reported between frequency and similarity, demonstrating that the effects of the similarity of L2 prepositions with the L1 depended on the relative frequency in which they appear in L2 input: Language similarity only affected infrequent L2 prepositions, not those that frequently occur in the L2. Furthermore, these effects only held for beginners and intermediate learners. The authors argued that at lower levels of L2 proficiency, learners tend to rely more on their L1 to understand unfamiliar prepositions.

Amengual (2016) explored cognate effects in production and processing of the Catalan back mid-vowel contrast /o/-/ɔ/. In the study, two groups of highly proficient Spanish–Catalan and Catalan–Spanish bilinguals participated in picture naming and lexical decision tasks containing cognates and noncognates. The acoustic analyses on the production data from picture naming showed that both groups maintained the vowel contrast in Catalan; however, the lexical decision data suggested that both had difficulties distinguishing between real words and nonwords based on the identification of the Catalan mid-vowel. Finally, both groups' performance was sensitive to cognate effects in the two tasks, such that the realization of /ɔ/ was closer to the acoustic properties of /o/. In all, the study offers evidence that past experience with cognate and noncognate words creates lexically specific expectations that determine where these words fall in their acoustic space.

5.9 Code-Switching

We have spent most of the chapter looking at how the knowledge and use of one language affects another across several linguistic domains. However, another important issue that is relevant to our exploration of the interaction of two languages in one mind is how bilinguals are able to shift back and forth between the two. **Code-switching** is the alternation between the use of one language and another within the same context. We use the terms code-switching and language switching interchangeably to encompass both switching within or between single utterances (Kutas, Moreno, & Wicha, 2009). **Speakers do not switch back and forth between languages at random**. Instead, they (unconsciously) adhere to a rule-governed system that allows English–Spanish bilinguals, for example, to accept sentences such as (2) and reject those as in (3).

(2)   Los clientes have bought a new service.
      "The clients have bought a new service."

(3)   * Los clientes han bought a new service.
      "The clients have bought a new service."

Muysken (2000) distinguished three types of code-switching: Alternation, insertion, and congruent lexicalization. **Alternation** refers to code-switching instances in which strings of words in one language alternate with words in another language within a conversational turn, as in (4). **Insertion** refers to instances where words or constituents in one language are placed into a syntactic frame in another language, as in (5). And **congruent lexicalization** refers to code-switching when there is a shared, or largely overlapping, structure between the two languages that can be lexicalized by elements from either language, as in (6).

(4) Spanish/English
     Ándale pues, and do come again.
     "All right then, and do come again."
     (Muysken, 2000, p. 5)

(5) Bolivian Quechua/Spanish
     chay-ta las dos de la noche-ta chaya-mu-yku
     that-AC the two of the night-AC arrive-CIS-1PL
     "There, at two in the morning we arrive."
     (Muysken, 2000, p. 63)

(6) Sranan/Dutch
     wan heri gedeelte de ondro beheer fu gewapende machten
     one whole part COP under control of armed forces
     "One whole part is under control of the armed forces."
     (Muysken, 2000, p. 139)

On the premise that there are different types of code switches, we will now further explore code-switching as a cognitive phenomenon that is commonly observed across various types of bilingual situations. With respect to the social aspects of code-switching, including the negative stigma that is often associated with it, we refer the reader to Yim and Clément (2021). In Section 5.9.1, we will first look at how code-switching is theoretically modeled and then proceed with a discussion of what happens in the brain when bilinguals switch between their two languages (Section 5.9.2).

5.9.1 Modeling Language Switching and Control

Significant theoretical contributions to the understanding of code-switching and language control in bilinguals have come from Green and colleagues. Green's (1998) **IC Model**, which we briefly discussed in Chapter 2, provided an initial framework for current models. Recall that this model holds that cognitive control processes assist in preventing the language not in use from interfering with the target language. Evidence for this comes from consistent findings that it takes longer to switch into (i.e., bring out of suppression) a more dominant language compared to a weaker language. However, the control system is adaptable to contextual needs (Blanco-Elorrieta & Pylkkänen, 2017; Green & Abutalebi, 2013). Green and Abutalebi argue that bilingual speakers use their languages in different ways depending on the context in which they find themselves, implying that language control mechanisms must be able to facilitate various patterns of language use. Building on this backdrop, Green and Wei (2014) elaborated a **control process model of code-switching**, which proposed that the mechanism for speech planning is mediated by various cognitive processes that are determined to be best suited according to the type of code switch. According to the model, access to speech planning is restricted by language task schemas external to the language network. In code-switching, these schemas operate in a cooperative manner, permissive of alternations and insertions, or in an open control mode, required for situations of dense code-switching in which there are rapid changes of language within a clause during a single conversation. Returning to the three types of code switches exemplified in (4)–(6), Green and Wei argue that alternation (4) and insertion (5) can both be realized by coupled control in which the matrix language temporarily gives control to the other language long enough to allow for the insertion or alternation before control is returned. However, code switches involving congruent lexicalization (6) are realized by open control in which the items or constructions from both languages with the highest activation levels determine whether they enter into speech planning. Further support for Green and Wei's model came from Beatty-Martínez and Dussias (2017); they argued that bilinguals who reported various degrees of code-switching in their daily lives were differentially sensitive to code-switched stimuli. Given that the differences were directly attributed to their previous language experiences with code-switching, the authors argued that, for bilinguals, **language comprehension becomes optimally attuned to variation in the input**.

Goldrick, Putnam, and Schwartz (2016) proposed an alternative explanation for code-switching that draws on the **gradient symbolic computation framework** (Smolensky, Goldrick, & Mathis, 2014). According to Goldrick, Putnam, and Schwartz, the mapping of communicative intent into speech output is captured by weighting grammatical constraints, with activation values serving as the medium for such weighting. Furthermore, the authors argue that code-switching in many ways is no different from noncode-switched utterances: "the grammatical principles we use to account for code mixing are the same principles that underlie non-code-mixed utterances. Our account therefore does not assume that bilingualism in general or code mixing specifically represents atypical, exceptional circumstances" (Goldrick, Putnam, & Schwartz, 2016, p. 872). However, this account fails to take into consideration the role of language control mechanisms in code-switching that are essential in doing things such as constructing speech in one language and switching to another.

In a critical review of the gradient symbolic computation approach to code-switching, Green and Wei (2016) further identified some shortcomings. For instance, they noted that Goldrick, Putnam, and Schwartz's (2016) proposal does not consider differences in activation in competitive language control and cooperative language control. Nor does it consider different attention states and, consequently, the different types of possible speech outputs. On applying the gradient symbolic computation framework to code-switching, Green and Wei (2016) state:

[Goldrick, Putnam, and Schwartz's (2016)] proposal may capture input-output mappings and so achieve weak equivalence, but it does not provide the causal machinery necessary to achieve strong equivalence. In particular, it lacks an explicit account of the mechanisms of language control required to account for the varieties of bilingual language use. Such mechanisms are required for monolingual speakers too who can elect to speak with greater or lesser focus on grammatical correctness and spend more or less time searching for the *mot juste*. (p. 883)

Further refinement to Green and Wei's (2014) control process model of code-switching was undertaken by Green (2018) in the **Extended Control Process Model**. This updated version adds speech input as an explicit component and elaborates the process of mapping a speech act onto the utterance planning procedure. The model accounts for the neurocomputational bases of the construction and execution of code-switching in speech production. It also posits that different control states mediate distinct patterns of language use and that the frequency of code-switching is a key factor in determining control states. Finally, according to Green, using a single language network within a conversation requires more effort and computational focus, while dense code-switching requires the use of more resources and active neural regions.

5.9.2 Code-Switching and the Brain

In Section 5.9.1, we addressed the mental processes that facilitate language switching. In this section, we will now look at what exactly happens in the brain when bilinguals switch between their languages. Kutas, Moreno, and Wicha (2009), in perhaps the first synthesis of studies on the neuroanatomy of code-switching, reviewed studies that have led to inferences in the neurocognitive mechanisms of language processing. The authors note that inhibition applied during language switching to the nontarget language is evidenced by involvement of the left basal ganglia (Mariën et al., 2005), and/or attentional/executive control mechanisms involving the anterior cingulate, prefrontal, and frontal cortices (Fabbro, Skrap, & Aglioti, 2000), or bilateral supramarginal gyri and Broca's area (Price, Green, & von Studnitz, 1999). Furthermore, given that damage to the **dorsolateral PFC** often causes uncontrollable language switching, this particular brain area has been hypothesized to be a **key pathway for code-switching** (Holtzheimer et al., 2005). Unfortunately, as stated by Kutas, Moreno, and Wicha, it is difficult to compare results across studies because often the effects are reported in and confined to one study, demonstrating high sensitivity to the inconsistent experimental designs and populations tested.

A pioneering study by Moreno, Federmeier, and Kutas (2002) revealed that code-switched words are processed differently from within-language lexical switches. Using an EEG, the authors asked English–Spanish bilinguals to read sentences in English while ERPs were recoded. The sentences, which consisted of both regular sentences as in (7) and highly constrained idioms as in (8), included a final word that was either a code-switch into the L2 (7a, 8a), a lexical switch (7b, 8b), or no switch (7c, 8c).

(7)   a.   Each night the campers built a fuego ["fire"].
      b.   Each night the campers built a blaze.
      c.   Each night the campers built a fire.

(8)   a.   Out of sight, out of mente ["mind"].
      b.   Out of sight, out of brain.
      c.   Out of sight, out of mind.

The results showed that regular and idiomatic sentences resulted in an **N400 effect** (i.e., an ERP component often reflecting semantic processing) at lexical switches (7b, 8b). For sentences with code switches (7a, 8a), however, the N400 effect only emerged in regular but not idiomatic sentences. Finally, proficiency was found to modulate these effects differentially in both sentence types, such that higher L2 proficiency was associated with earlier peak latency and smaller amplitude of the late positive component to code-switches, whereas L1-dominant individuals showed greater N400 amplitudes and earlier onsets for lexical switches. Moreno, Federmeier, and Kutas argued that the N400 modulation in code-switched versus nonswitched sentences implies that switching does not incur a cost in the lexical-semantic integration of the switched word into the sentence but that code-switches are treated as an unexpected event at a nonlinguistic level. This implies that "language switching costs arise from outside the bilingual lexico-semantic system, and originate from competition between task schemas that coordinate the output of the lexico-semantic system with the response task" (Van Hell, Litcofsky, & Ting, 2015, p. 466). Similar results were later reported in Liao and Chan (2016).

Among the many subcortical structures that are responsive to a change in language is the caudate. Evidence of this comes from studies (e.g., Abutalebi, Miozzi, & Cappa, 2000) which demonstrate that damage to the caudate results in inappropriate code-switching, as was seen in (3). Based on these and other results, Abutalebi and Green (2008) elaborated on **five brain regions that are involved in language switching** – each of which have distinct and complementary functions in negotiating the cognitive demands of language control. These are: the left dorsolateral PFC, anterior cingulate cortex (ACC), caudate nucleus (a subcortical structure belonging to the basal ganglia), and bilateral supramarginal gyri. Luk et al. (2012) conducted a meta-analysis to evaluate Abutalebi and Green's hypotheses of the bilingual subcortical-cortical control network. The analysis included ten fMRI or PET studies examining a total of 106 bilinguals. The results identified ten key brain areas, that were largely left lateralized and frontal, which were involved in language switching across the studies. Although there was no significant engagement of the ACC or the supramarginal gyri (Abutalebi & Green, 2008), the results were consistent with Abutalebi and Green's account that there is a frontal-subcortical circuit involved in language switching (see also Green & Abutalebi, 2013, for a proposed set of neural correlates that underlie eight control processes in bilingual speech production).

Further support for Abutalebi and Green's (2008) proposal was provided by Lei, Akama, and Murphy (2014). In this study, Korean–Chinese early bilinguals participated in two production tasks: A conventional switching task in which either the L1 or L2 is used in each trial, but randomly changes from trial to trial; and a novel experimental design in which language switching occurs within each trials, alternating in either L1-L2 or L2-L1 translation directions. The results from the trial-to-trial switching experiment showed that key brain areas included the bilateral occipital lobe, temporal lobe, and some discrete regions. However, the results from the within-trial switching showed more activity along the connecting regions around the left fusiform, left and right lingual, and left supramarginal gyri. The study demonstrates the effects of task difficulty: In the case of focused simultaneous word translation (i.e., in which switching occurred within trials), bilinguals need more attentive control, as reflected by more intense and regulated activations of the corresponding brain areas.

As we have mentioned, **language switching involves, among other things, the disengagement from one language and engagement with another language**. In a unique study by Blanco-Elorrieta, Emmorey, and Pylkkänen (2018), the researchers were able to dissociate the issue of engagement and disengagement by examining American Sign Language (ASL)–English bilinguals who often sign and speak simultaneously. The individuals participated in two production tasks while MEG was recorded. In the first task, individuals named pictures that required them to switch back and forth between ASL and English. In the second picture naming task, no switching was required: The stimuli were presented in solid blocks of English, ASL, and both (code-blends). The two experiments, respectively, allow for a characterization for both switch-related and sustained control components of language control. The analyses on the MEG data showed that switching from simultaneous to single language production – what the authors referred to as "turning off a language" – caused increased brain activity in the ACC and dorsolateral PFC. However, the reverse (i.e., switching from a single to two simultaneous languages, i.e., "turning on a language") did not. Further analyses investigating the connectivity patterns between these regions showed that "turning off" a language necessitated stronger connectivity between the left and right dorsolateral PFC. The dorsolateral PFC also was found to predict ACC activity. Blanco-Elorrieta, Emmorey, and Pylkkänen argue that "the burden of language switching lies in disengagement from the previous language as opposed to engaging a new language and that, in the absence of motor constraints, producing two languages simultaneously is not necessarily more cognitively costly than producing one" (p. 9708).

Further evidence that **the brain differentially reacts to various types of code switches** comes from a recent study by Zeller (2020). Russian–German learners were asked to listen to sentences in Russian that included code switches in German. The code switches were either whole prepositional phrases or only their head noun. ERPs revealed different patterns for switches at nouns versus prepositions at time windows 100–200 ms, 200–500 ms, and 500–800 ms. For noun switches, there was a late positive component, whereas switches at prepositions resulted in a broad early negativity immediately followed by an anterior negativity with a posterior positivity. In the latest time window analyzed (800–100 ms), however, switches at prepositions resulted in broad positivity in line with switches at nouns. Zeller interpreted this as an indication that the late positive component is either independent from or less sensitive to structural aspects of switching. In all, the results of Zeller's study demonstrate that the psycholinguistic processes that underpin code-switching appear to be more heterogeneous and complex than previously thought.

5.10 Dreaming

If you are a bilingual, you may have been asked in what language you think and dream. This likely stems from the **belief that dreaming in another language is a sign of proficiency**. While this claim is unsubstantiated by scientific research (and in fact, is partially rejected in an empirical study by Sicard & de Bot, 2013, which we will discuss in Section 5.10.2), it does imply that even in the sleep state, both languages are available and active among bilinguals. In general, people are interested in dreams and what they mean but, surprisingly, there has not been much research on bilingualism and dreaming. As is the case with language in conscious thought – what scholars such as Pinker (1994) have called prelinguistic mentalese – dreaming can also be independent of language. However, when language *is* involved in a dream, most bilinguals (64 percent) have reported that they dream in both languages (Grosjean, 2010). The language used in the dream appears to be determined by the situation and context. For instance, an English–French bilingual who lives in the United States may dream in French when dreaming about a visit to the small village in the south of France where they studied years before. It would be very odd for them to speak in English to the villagers in the dream when they are aware that the villagers do not speak English and that they used to speak (only) French while studying there. The few studies that have examined bilingualism and dreaming have focused on which language(s) are used while dreaming and what factors determine this unconscious selection. We will discuss these next.

5.10.1 What Determines the Language in Which Bilinguals Dream?

While awake, bilinguals exercise excellent control over their languages, as we saw in Chapter 2 and Section 5.9. If the intention is to speak in one language versus the other, this is easily accomplished. And if they find themselves in situations in which using both languages is appropriate, this is perfectly feasible. However, when sleeping, there seems to be much less control not only over the topic of a dream, but also the language in which bilinguals dream. Although there is little research on dreaming and bilingualism, we know that there are several factors that influence the language in which bilinguals dream.

One of the earliest studies on language selection and dreaming was conducted by Foulkes et al. (1993). In this study, eight German–English and eight English–German bilinguals were examined for four nonconsecutive nights in a sleep laboratory. The native speakers of English lived in Zurich and the German L1 speakers lived in Atlanta. The participants completed a language questionnaire in which they described their AoA, oral competence, and usage by age and context, along with self-ratings of their proficiency in English and German. Prior to going to sleep, the participants were interviewed and had conversations in either English or German. Pre-sleep thought and rapid eye movement (REM) dream reports were collected each night in which participants were asked to judge the appropriateness of the waking sources of their dream imagery. The results showed that the language in which the pre-sleep interviews were conducted significantly affected the language in which they dreamed. Furthermore, although the dominant language spoken at the research site (i.e., English in Atlanta; German in Zurich) significantly correlated with the language mostly used in waking thought, this correlation was much weaker in dreams. The main findings from Foulkes et al. are summarized below:

- Bilingualism does not impede dreaming or the contextual appropriateness of language phenomena within dreams. Furthermore, bilingualism does not disrupt the construction of grammatically accurate language in dreams (see also Heynick, 1983). This implies that the high-level processing systems which serve different languages are most likely shared and not separate.
- Language selection in dreaming is modulated most by the contextual relevance of an immediate imagined situation. And it is in line with the notion that information integrates during REM sleep.
- Pre-sleep priming in a language can influence language selection and use in dreams. There is a predictable pattern of language selection and dreaming but some may be more related to language proficiency while others may be dependent on the site or immediate linguistic context.

In a study by Vaid and Menon (2000), the researchers tested variables that may determine the language in which bilinguals compute mental arithmetic, think, and dream. The predictor variables that were examined included: (a) the language used in elementary school; (b) the length of residence in the L2 environment; (c) the age of onset of bilingualism; and (d) the current dominant language. The results revealed that all four variables correlated with the language in which bilinguals do mental math, with (a) and (b) being the strongest predictors. Only (a) and (b) significantly predicted the language used when bilinguals think. Finally, among the four variables, only (c) did not significantly predict the language in which bilinguals dreamed. Furthermore, when comparing the predictive power of (a), (b), and (d) on the language of dreaming, (d) was the best predicator variable. Overall, the findings suggest that various variables influence, to different degrees, the language in which bilinguals dream, but that language dominance appears to be most correlated, followed by length of residence in the L2 environment. Similar results were later reported by Schrauf (2009), who examined language use among Puerto Ricans living in Spanish-speaking neighborhoods in central Chicago. The participants were grouped according to their English proficiency levels: Fluent, high-intermediate, and low-intermediate. These findings revealed that fluent individuals reported dreaming, thinking, and swearing in English more than low-intermediate speakers but only marginally more than high-intermediate speakers.

5.10.2 Dreaming in a Second Language among Less-Proficient Bilinguals

Returning to the natural intrigue surrounding dreaming in an L2 and the belief that it may be evidence of proficiency in an L2, a more recent study disputed this belief. Sicard and de Bot (2013) tested the following hypotheses: (a) a high level of L2 proficiency is not a requirement for L2 dreaming; and (b) L2 environments are contributing factors in L2 dreaming. In the study, 209 international students enrolled in programs at a university in the Netherlands were asked to self-assess their L2 proficiency according to the Common European Framework of Reference for Language (CEFR), to state their duration in the L2 environment, and to report how often they dream in their L2. Dreaming in an L2 was broadly defined and included anything from one word to full-length, fluent conversations. The findings demonstrated that participants at all proficiency levels reported dreaming in an L2. Furthermore, correlational analyses showed a strong positive correlation between L2 proficiency and L2 dream occurrences, such that higher proficiency levels correlated with more L2 dreams. When analyzing the effect of duration in the L2 environment on dreaming in an L2, the findings again showed a significant correlation: **The more time spent in the L2 environment, the more occurrences of dreams in the L2**.

Together, the results suggest that both duration in the L2 environment and L2 proficiency correlate to how often a bilingual will dream in an L2. They also show that regardless of L2 proficiency level, bilinguals – at least those living abroad – dream in their L2. Sicard and de Bot (2013) conducted further analyses to see whether it is in fact a combination of these factors that influence L2 dream occurrences. Linear regression modelling showed that while the environment has some influence on L2 dream frequency, **L2 proficiency was a much better predicator variable**. Finally, comparisons were made between the number of dreams in the L2 in the home country versus living in the L2 environment. In their home countries, 78 percent of the participants reported having dreamt in their L2. However, during the experimental period in which they were living in the L2 environment, this increased to 93 percent, suggesting that living in an immersive setting increases the amount of dreams in the L2.

A final note to mention is that making inferences based on participants' recollection of what languages they were speaking in their dreams can be challenging. For instance, a Czech–Slovak bilingual from an early study (Vildomec, 1963) who also spoke a little Russian, believed that he was speaking in fluent Russian during the dream only to realize upon waking up that he was actually speaking in a mixture of Czech and Slovak with a few Russian words here and there. Other bilinguals in the study reported making cross-linguistic errors in their dreams even when they normally do not experience interference effects while awake. This implies that the **control mechanisms that underpin language during consciousness may be weakened when languages are present in dreams**.

5.11 Summary

For bilinguals, the use and knowledge of one language affects how they process the other. As we have seen throughout this chapter, various CLI effects can be observed in both language production and comprehension across all domains of linguistics. In Section 5.2, we started by broadly exploring the concept of transfer, both negative and positive, and in forward and reverse directions. In doing so, we identified various classifications of CLI across the ten dimensions put forth in Table 5.2 by Jarvis and Pavlenko (2008). Following this, we reviewed key studies on phonological (Section 5.3), lexical (Section 5.4), morphological (Section 5.5), and syntactic (Section 5.6) transfer along with other types such as discursive, pragmatic, and sociolinguistic (Section 5.7). While it appears that identifying types of CLI is fairly easy, there are a number of factors that can determine the degree to which transfer emerged or whether it happens at all. In Section 5.8, we noted that several of modulating factors have been identified, with language dominance, input frequency, and cross-linguistic similarity being the most studied.

Following our discussion on transfer, in Section 5.9 we transitioned to review other phenomena that arise when two languages exist in one mind, namely the ability to switch between the two language systems. In doing so, we looked at theoretical models that explain what facilitates language switching and what empirical studies tell us about the neural and electrophysiological activity that arises in language switching. Finally, in Section 5.10 we addressed dreaming and bilingualism. Although there is relatively little research in this area, we know that there are a number of factors that determine in what language bilinguals dream and that dreaming in an L2, contrary to popular belief, does not necessarily require or imply fluency in that language.

Review Questions

1. Discuss what is meant by "a bilingual is not two monolinguals in one person" (Grosjean, 1989, p. 3).
2. Describe some of the positive and negative effects arising from CLIs.
3. Discuss factors that affect the extent to which transfer occurs across languages.
4. Describe the different types of code-switching that have been identified by researchers in bilingualism.
5. Identify the factors that can determine the language in which bilinguals dream.

Further Reading

Elgort, I., Siyanova-Chanturia, A., & Brysbaert, M. (Eds.). (2023). *Cross-language influences in bilingual processing and second language acquisition*. Benjamins.

Jarvis, S., & Pavlenko, A. (2008). *Crosslinguistic influence in language and cognition*. Routledge.

Schwieter, J. W. (Ed.). (2015). *The Cambridge handbook of bilingual processing*. Cambridge University Press.

Tokowicz, A. (2015). *Lexical processing and second language acquisition*. Cambridge University Press.

CHAPTER SIX

Bilingual Lexical and Conceptual Memory

Learning Objectives

- Explore the notion that a bilingual brain may be a default, rather than an exception.
- Learn how concepts and words are mentally represented among bilinguals.
- Examine prominent models explaining how words are mapped onto concepts.
- Discover the degree of conceptual overlap between languages.

6.1 Introduction

Bilingualism, as we have defined it in Chapter 1, represents 60 percent of the world's population. Thus, it may be more appropriate to approach the multilingual mind as the default rather than an anomaly (Libben & Schwieter, 2019; Vaid & Meuter, 2017). In coming to this potential realization, researchers have kept sharp focus on two enduring questions: Is the mental lexicon of bilinguals integrated or separate? And are words accessed from the lexicon in a selective or nonselective manner? (See Kroll, 2017, for a review.) In light of the ample evidence that bilinguals can never completely "turn off" a language (see Chapter 2; but see Schmid, 2010, for a discussion on extreme cases of language attrition) and that a bilingual's two languages are constantly active to some degree, nonselective, dynamic explanations seem to be favored. In this chapter we will review these accounts by starting with a discussion on how our exploration of the bilingual mental lexicon allows for the opportunity to understand more deeply how lexical and conceptual knowledge interact and coexist in the mind (Section 6.2). Following this, in Section 6.3, we will look at how concepts are represented and distributed in the bilingual mind as evidenced by both behavioral and neuroscientific findings. We then synthesize important theoretical models explaining word-to-concept mapping in the bilingual memory (Section 6.4) and discuss important issues such as how the mind accommodates overlapping concepts in the context of bilingual/multilingual development (Section 6.5). In Section 6.6 we review connectionist models, and we conclude the chapter in Section 6.7.

6.2 The Bilingual Mental Lexicon as the Default

Libben and Schwieter (2019) discuss how an integrated lexical system can acquire, maintain, couple, and decouple the lexical elements of two or more languages. The authors build on claims by Libben, Goral, and Libben (2017a), which argue that modeling the bilingual mental lexicon requires an understanding of dynamicity and integration both as individual constructs and in their interactions with one another and key phenomena in bilingual lexical processing. New developments in mental lexicon research, which we will discuss throughout this chapter, have offered further implications for multilingual development and maintenance. Since the multilingual lexicon requires different languages to be separated yet interactive, Libben, Goral, and Libben argue that it must be a cognitive system that is organized in a way that it can act in a connected or isolated manner under dynamic conditions.

As noted by Libben and Schwieter (2019), the term *mental lexicon* is primarily rooted in psycholinguistics and, with regard to bilingual lexical access, our understanding has been widely informed by a single experimental paradigm: the lexical decision task. In this task, participants are presented with a string of letters on the screen and are asked to press a "yes" or "no" button as quickly and accurately as possible to indicate whether or not the string of letters is a real word. In the many lexical decision studies, the findings are sensitive to differences associated with lexical characteristics such as frequency, length, correctness, and part of speech. Libben, Goral, and Baayen (2017b) argue that the role of structurally complex words (e.g., compounds, multimorphemic, etc.) has consequences for the architecture of the multilingual lexicon and, thus, morphological complexity should be accounted for in psycholinguistic models of the mental lexicon. Structurally complex words (e.g., handy), for instance, are linked to simple words (e.g., hand) yet remain idiosyncratic in character. Accordingly, a core feature of the bilingual mental lexicon is the ability to manage lexical and morphological interference. According to Zhang, Van Heuven, and Conklin (2011) and Libben, Goral, and Baayen (2017b), connections within the multilingual lexicon do not involve whole words, and subword primes in an L2 facilitate compound recognition in an L1. In the upcoming sections we will unpack these claims by discussing how concepts are represented in the bilingual memory, along with prominent theoretical models that depict the architecture and functionality of the bilingual mental lexicon.

6.3 Conceptual and Lexical Representation in Bilinguals

Research in cognitive neuroscience demonstrates that for monolinguals and bilinguals, lexical and grammatical subsystems are connected to one another and to other cognitive (nonverbal) systems (Pulvermüller, 2003). Under this assumption, concepts "are organized in terms of distributed representations [in which] **conceptual representation in memory entails linked sensory, action, and linguistic-semantic knowledge**" (Athanasopoulos, 2015, p. 275; see also Section 3.3.1). The existence of language- or culture-specific conceptual units can be seen in concepts such as colors. For instance, Thierry et al. (2009) examined brain activation when processing colors such as blue and green among Greek and English monolinguals. Because Greek has two basic terms for blue, according to the degree of lightness, there was more brain activity when Greek speakers conceptualized *blue* compared to the English speakers. These contrasts were not apparent for *green* as this color only has one label in each language. Studies such as Thierry et al. demonstrate that for the most part, concepts across languages and cultures are not totally equivalent but rather share various degrees of overlap (Jarvis & Pavlenko, 2008). Other evidence of the nonequivalent nature of conceptual representations for bilinguals comes from processing emotion words in translation and lexical priming experiments. For example, Pavlenko (2009) notes that the Greek noun *stenahoria* is conceptually distributed to several notions in English ranging from discomfort to sadness or suffocation.

Important to our conversation about the overlapping nature of concepts and the words that represent them in the two languages is the role of **cognates**, or words that have phonological and/or orthographic meaning across languages. Studies show that processing cognates is modulated by the degree to which they phonologically and orthographically overlap (Comesaña et al., 2015; Dijkstra et al., 2010). In a recent study by Carrasco-Ortiz, Amengual, and Gries (2021), a group of L1 English learners of Spanish and a group of Spanish–English heritage bilinguals participated in lexical decision tasks in English and Spanish containing noncognates and cognates. The researchers were interested in seeing whether cognates with different degrees of phonological and orthographical overlap are equally represented in the bilingual lexicon and whether there are differences in cross-language competition when processing cognates in the L1 versus in the L2. The results demonstrated that cross-language orthographic and phonological similarity affected visual word recognition for both groups. Larger facilitation effects were observed when the orthographic overlap was greater. Phonological similarity, however, appeared to be dependent on the participants' language environment (i.e., English) rather than language dominance (i.e., English or Spanish), as evidenced by the stronger effect of English phonological representations on Spanish word recognition than the opposite direction. Overall, the findings support connectionist models such as the BIA Model that we discussed in Chapter 2, which we will also look at in more detail later in this chapter.

Finally, there are several phenomena associated with conceptual representation – including conceptual coexistence, transfer, shift, convergence, restructuring, and attrition – that appear not to be mutually exclusive. Complicating these issues, bilinguals may experience a combination of these phenomena at different developmental stages, which are modulated by various individual differences and external factors. In a review of conceptual representation in bilinguals, Athanasopoulos (2015) notes three fundamental assumptions, namely that it is: (a) distributed and multimodal; (b) shaped by cross-linguistic and cross-cultural variation of concepts; and (c) is developmental in nature such that the emergent links between concepts and their lexical representations can strengthen and weaken.

These three points have been further elaborated in several prevalent models, laying the groundwork for our understanding of the bilingual memory store and the process of lexical access during word recognition and production. We will look at these models next and organize them according to their emphasis on word-to-concept mapping, the distributed and overlapping nature of conceptual representation, or whether they take a connectionist approach.

6.4 Modeling Word-to-Concept Mapping and Mediation

Significant strides have been made with respect to modeling the bilingual memory and understanding how words are activated and accessed during speech production and perception. An appropriate starting point is to first discuss some hypotheses regarding the relationship between concepts and the lexical items that are mapped onto them, along with how activation flows through the conceptual and lexical systems. While some models, as we will see, hold that as concepts and words are activated and retrieved from the bilingual memory, the flow of activation is

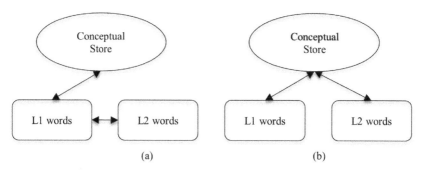

Figure 6.1 The Word Association Model (a) and the Concept Mediation Model (b)

lexically mediated for both languages, other models favor a conceptually mediated procedure.

6.4.1 Word Association and Concept Mediation Models

Perhaps the earliest hypotheses explaining the architecture of the bilingual memory came from Potter et al. (1984). In their study, the researchers put forth and tested two opposing accounts: The Word Association and Concept Mediation Models. The **Word Association Model** holds that for bilinguals, L2 words are connected to their conceptual representation only by association with their equivalent L1 words (see Figure 6.1a). The **Concept Association Mediation Model**, on the other hand, argues that L2 and L1 words are both directly connected to their conceptual representation (Figure 6.1b). The two models are examples of lexically and conceptually mediated processes, respectively.

Potter et al. conducted a set of experiments among highly proficient Chinese–English bilinguals and nonfluent English–French learners. Both groups were asked to complete word naming, picture naming, and word translation tasks, and an additional subgroup of Chinese–English bilinguals also semantically categorized words and pictures. The researchers hypothesized that if the Word Association Model could accurately predict the performance in these tasks, the participants should have quicker responses to L1 words than picture naming. Particularly, naming pictures in the L2 should be slower because participants must first identify the L1 name of the picture. On the other hand, if the Concept Mediation Model is accurate, pictures and words should elicit the same relative level of difficulty. The results showed that both highly proficient and less proficient participants had similar processing patterns: When the task was to produce an L2 word, participants were slower to do so from a picture cue

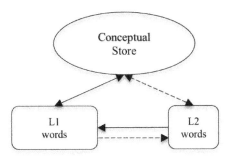

Figure 6.2 The Revised Hierarchical Model
Source: Kroll and Stewart (1994).

versus a to-be-translated L1 word. Given the assumption that concepts common to both words and pictures are activated and retrieved through task-specific processing that appears to be similar for both word and picture input, Potter et al.'s results align with the Concept Mediation Model but cannot be explained by the Word Association Model, suggesting that there is a direct association between L1 and L2 words.

6.4.2 Revised Hierarchical Model

One of the most influential models of bilingual memory is the RHM (Kroll & Stewart, 1994), shown in Figure 6.2, although we will also review later in this section some enduring criticism that it has faced over the years. In many ways, the RHM brings together and refines predictions from the Concept Mediation and Word Association Models with the developmental caveat that conceptual and lexical links (and, thus, the mediation and path of activation) have differential strengths. The model holds that **L2 proficiency is a modulating factor of these links**, such that at the beginning stages of L2 acquisition learners are heavily reliant on existing links between their L1 words and their conceptual representations before developing the ability to mediate directly between L2 words and concepts. As L2 proficiency increases, and consequently L2 lexical-conceptual links strengthen, there is less need to associate L2 words with their L1 equivalents to access meaning.

As seen in Figure 6.2, the RHM demonstrates a bilingual memory in which the size of the L1 and L2 lexicon is notably different, demonstrating distinct proficiency levels in the two languages. The model assumes weak and strong conceptual and lexical links, as depicted by the dotted and solid lines, respectively. The strongest path for L2 to L1 translation, for instance, is through association with the L1 word. Nevertheless, with increases in L2 proficiency, the L2 to L1 translation path may be conceptually mediated due to the fact that L2 words increasingly become more strongly mapped onto concepts. It appears as though the opposite may be true for the reverse direction: **Conceptual mediation is the preferred and more efficient path of lexicalization for L1 to L2 translation** (Kroll et al., 2010).

In Kroll and Stewarts' (1994) well-cited study, Dutch–English bilinguals completed picture and word naming tasks presented in either semantically categorized or randomized lists. The results showed that picture naming and word translation were both slower when lists included items belonging to the same semantic category. However, this category interference effect was no longer observed when the experiment alternated between picture naming and word naming. Furthermore, and most important from the study, in a third experiment comparing word translation in both directions, again in categorized or randomized lists, the results showed that category interference occurred when translating words from L1 to L2 but not in the reverse direction. Kroll and Stewart interpreted these findings as evidence for three key implications: (a) That the two translation directions engage different interlanguage connections; (b) that there is differential reliance on lexical and conceptual links; and (c) that the role of language proficiency is a determining factor of bilingual memory representations. In a later paper, Kroll et al. (2010) note that in the RHM's original form, it was incorrectly assumed that the weak link between L2 words and the conceptual store was bidirectional but that the asymmetry is more critical for production versus recognition (see Kroll et al., 2002; Schwieter & Sunderman, 2009).

There are a **few shortcomings of the RHM** which have drawn criticism from some researchers. First, the model has difficulties accounting for translation equivalence and a shift in language dominance that is often observed in bilingualism, particularly in cases where individuals move to environments where their L2 is the majority language and thus must rely mostly on it for communication. Studies on code-switching behavior (Heredia, 1997) and lexical access among bilinguals who have experienced a shift in language dominance (Basnight-Brown & Altarriba, 2007) have reported faster access to words in the L2, which was more dominant at the time of the studies (see Basnight-Brown, 2014, for a review).

Furthermore, it has been argued that the storage of L2 words may not necessarily be confined to the lexicon but may be represented as both lexical and conceptual entries if the words are acquired in an environment in which form and meaning are emphasized (Ferré, Sánchez-Casas,

& García, 2000; La Heij et al., 1996). For example, Duyck and Brysbaert (2004) reported that both balanced and less proficient Dutch–French bilinguals showed evidence of forward (L1-L2) and backward (L2-L1) translation priming effects, suggesting that even at a low L2 proficiency level, conceptual mediation is possible. The researchers argued, contrary to the RHM, that it is possible for less-proficient L2 leaners to access the visual, auditory, and semantic representations of L2 words directly, without the need to rely on their lexical equivalents in the L1. Similar effects of semantic influence on L2 lexical processing were observed in another study by Duyck and Brysbaert (2008) among Dutch–English–German trilinguals, but this time only in backward translation. The authors explained the findings as evidence that lexical form overlap between translation equivalents affects the degree of semantic activation, a notion which dual route models of word translation do not address. Additional findings suggesting concept mediation in backward translation were reported in a priming experiment by Schoonbaert et al. (2009), in which the authors argued that L1 words have richer semantic representations than L2 words. Consequently, L1 primes activate large parts of semantic nodes connected to L2 words whereas L2 primes activate a smaller percentage of the semantic node mapped onto L1 words.

Brysbaert and Duyck (2010) further elaborate these hypotheses in a systematic review of empirical research on the RHM. In their paper entitled "Is it time to leave behind the Revised Hierarchical Model of bilingual language processing after fifteen years of service?," the researchers highlighted some limitations of the model including that:

- there is little evidence for separate lexicons and language-selective access;
- the inclusion of excitatory connections between translation equivalents at the lexical level is likely to impede word recognition;
- the conceptual connections between words in the L2 are stronger than is suggested; and
- there is evidence of distinctions between language-dependent and language-independent semantic features.

Brysbaert and Duyck's (2010) view of the bilingual memory and word processing aligns with connectionist approaches, which we will discuss in Section 6.6. The authors state that although both lexical and semantic routes exist, what is critical is the extent to which each path contributes to overall activation. The authors argue that while one path is not necessarily faster than the other, there may be stronger connection weights (e.g., from L2 to L1 lexical nodes and from L1 to L2 semantic nodes) that consequently influence the degree of activation.

A final criticism of the RHM is that to consider word translation equivalents that share semantic qualities is problematic (Duyck & Brysbaert, 2004) and, similarly, to assume that during word retrieval, the same conceptual representations are accessed from both languages is potentially erroneous (Jared, Pei Yun Poh, & Paivio, 2013). Indeed, **some concepts only exist in one language and, therefore, cannot be linked to a lexical item in another language** (Pavlenko, 2009). We will now discuss some of the models that have addressed the degree of overlap in the bilingual conceptual system.

6.5 Modeling the Degree of Overlap of Conceptual Representations

During the 1990s and beyond, other models of bilingual conceptual representation and word processing entertained the notion that concepts in both languages do not fully overlap. The degree of such overlap is accounted for in these models. As a rudimentary example, consider the concept CAT. While a cat, as a living mammal, is the same regardless of the language one speaks, is CAT really the same for an English speaker as for a Spanish speaker? In other words, when asked to visualize a cat, is this mental picture and the associated attributes the same? Because of diverse language backgrounds and experiences, the answer is likely to be *no*. In this section, we will look at models that have addressed the potential distributed and overlapping nature of conceptual representation in bilinguals.

6.5.1 Distributed Feature Model

A more elaborate illustration of the CAT example just described can be explained through a model which depicts the distributed features that are shared between languages. It has been found that **there are processing differences between concrete words** (e.g., *pencil*, a word whose concept is highly concrete, making it easily visualized) **compared to abstract words** (e.g., *sadness*, a word whose concept is much less concrete, making it difficult to form an image representing it), such that translating concrete words is faster than abstract words (De Groot, 1992; Paivio, 1986; van Hell & de Groot, 1998). In the study by Paivio, it was also reported that concrete translation equivalents show greater semantic similarity in free association compared to abstract translation equivalents (see Paivio, 2010, for a further discussion).

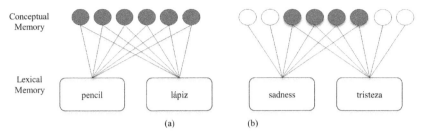

Figure 6.3 The Distributed Feature Model, showing different spreading activation for concrete translations (a) and abstract translations (b)
Note: Grey circles refer to overlapping representations; white circles refer to nonoverlapping representations.
Source: De Groot (1992).
Note: A black and white version of this figure will appear in some formats. For the color version, please refer to the plate section.

The first bilingual model to capture these hypotheses was de Groot's (1992) **Distributed Feature Model (DFM)**. In the model, concrete word translations are hypothesized to share more "conceptual nodes" than abstract words. As such, during lexical access, increased semantic overlap between concrete translations causes increased spreading activation, which, in turn, facilitates translation speed. Returning to our *pencil* and *sadness* examples of concrete and abstract words, respectively, the DFM would account for the degree of overlap in conceptual nodes differentially between these two types of words, as shown in the English–Spanish examples in Figure 6.3.

In a subsequent study supporting the DFM, van Hell and de Groot (1998) asked Dutch–English bilinguals to verbally produce the first word that came to mind when seeing target words in four different task conditions. The conditions included two within- and two between-language associations: Dutch stimulus/Dutch response; Dutch stimulus/English response; English stimulus/English response; and English stimulus/ Dutch response. The target words included nouns and verbs that varied in terms of their concreteness and cognate status. The results showed that for both within- and between-language contexts, retrieving an associated word was easier for concrete compared to abstract words, for cognates compared to noncognates, and for nouns compared to verbs. The authors argued that the findings support the DFM and extend its predictions such that certain translation and word types (e.g., concrete nouns and cognates) share larger parts of their conceptual representations than others (e.g., abstracts nouns, noncognates, and verbs). Van Hell and de Groot's study offers evidence that word-type processing effects in bilinguals may

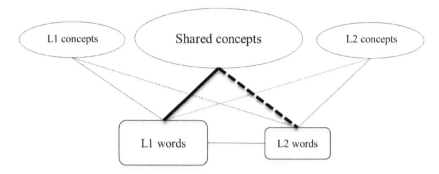

Figure 6.4 The Shared Distributed Asymmetrical Model
Source: Dong, Cui, and MacWhinney (2005).

be attributed to the extent to which their conceptual (and potentially orthographic and/or phonological) features are shared.

6.5.2 Shared Distributed Asymmetrical Model

Another model that emphasizes the complex overlapping nature of conceptual representations in bilingualism is the **Shared Distributed Asymmetrical Model** (**SDAM**; Dong, Cui, & MacWhinney, 2005). As in the RHM and DFM, it is assumed that there are two separate lexical stores for each language, with the L1 lexicon being larger than the developing L2 lexicon. Similarly, the differential strengths of associations between words and concepts are shown by the darkness of the lines, with dotted lines being weaker than solid ones. As shown in Figure 6.4, the SDAM is distinct in that it posits a common (shared) conceptual store for both languages but also two additional, smaller conceptual stores that are specific to each language.

In the study by Dong, Cui, and MacWhinney (2005), Chinese university students majoring in English participated in a classic priming experiment and a semantic-closeness ranking task. In the first experiment, participants saw a string of letters in English or Chinese immediately followed by either a real word in English or Chinese or a nonword. They were asked to determine whether the second string of letters was a real word or not by button press. In line with previous work (Kroll & Stewart, 1994), the results showed evidence for a shared conceptual storage, with asymmetrical links between L1 and L2 words and their conceptual representations. In the second experiment, participants were given target words that were accompanied by eight critical words, seven of which were related to the target and one which was completely unrelated. The participants were asked to rank the eight words in terms of how closely they were semantically related to the target as shown in (1). Interestingly, some of the critical words to be ranked were more associated with one language or the other. For example, among the critical words from the study shown in (1), *jealousy* may be more strongly associated with the English target word *green* than in its Chinese translation equivalent, given that in English, there exists a saying "green with envy" but not in Chinese.

(1)   Target word: *green*
       Critical words: yellow, light, speak, silly, young, tree, color, jealousy

The results from Experiment 2 indicated that bilinguals integrated conceptual differences across translation equivalents but also "demonstrated a 'separatist' tendency to maintain the L1 conceptual system in the representation of L1 words and to adopt the L2 conceptual system in the representation of L2 words" (Dong, Gui, & MacWhinney, 2005, p. 221). Other research has also used semantic rating tasks to examine the semantic overlap between translations and has found that words that share a translation meaning have stronger associations and are perceived as more semantically similar (Degani, Prior, & Tokowicz, 2011; Jiang, 2002). In a study by Degani and Tokowicz (2010), English speakers were taught Dutch words that either shared or did not share an English translation. The results showed that ambiguous words were more difficult to learn compared to words with translation equivalents. Upon eventually learning the words, the ambiguous Dutch words were consistently translated more slowly into English compared to those with translation equivalents. Furthermore, and more importantly, was the observation that lexical access and future retrieval were affected by whether there was a one-to-one mapping or one-to-many mapping of concepts in Dutch. The results of Degani and Tokowicz's study support the SDAM's hypothesis that when there are multiple translations between L1 and L2 words, many more concepts become activated compared to when there is a single translation between the two languages. Consequently, more time is required to retrieve the appropriate response. In addition to our understanding of the bilingual memory store, the SDAM has some pedagogical implications which can inform educational models of L2 learning (see Tytus, 2014, for a review).

6.5.3 Bilingual and Trilingual Modified Hierarchical Models

Many of the models we have discussed thus far focus on the relationship between word forms and meanings and examine factors such as

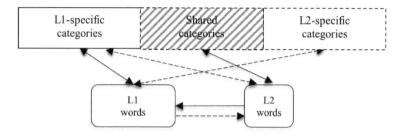

Figure 6.5 The Modified Hierarchical Model
Source: Pavlenko (2009).
Note: A black and white version of this figure will appear in some formats. For the color version, please refer to the plate section.

the strength of conceptual and lexical links and retrieval speeds. However, few studies address **the nature of the representation itself**, particularly from a developmental perspective. It has also been shown that conceptual restructuring occurs when new words accommodate word-to-concept mapping (Athanasopoulos, 2009, 2011; Athanasopoulos & Kasai, 2008; Cook et al., 2006). For instance, in the well-studied area of color concepts, it has been reported that, for bilinguals, color categories of an L1 can influence those of the L2, and vice versa (Pavlenko et al., 2017), and that conceptual category adjustment of colors in general occurs during L2 acquisition (Matusevych, Beekhuizen, & Stevenson, 2018).

Pavlenko (2009) proposed the **Modified Hierarchical Model (MHM)**, a multimodal representation of the bilingual conceptual system consisting of categories that are fully shared, partially overlapping, or entirely language-specific. The MHM presents a dynamic account of lexical and conceptual processing which addresses conceptual restructuring and transfer. According to the model, lexical concepts are multimodal mental representations that are inclusive of auditory, visual, kinesthetic, and perceptual information, and are stored in the implicit memory. These representations are not static and, therefore, dynamically change with language development and experiences. Furthermore, they are sensitive to other individual differences.

As shown in Figure 6.5, L1 and L2 words have asymmetric links connecting them to a conceptual store (as in the RHM), that is, not a single, shared entity, but rather a complex system of representations that range from fully shared, partially shared, or not shared between the two languages. Critically, and unique to the model, is that unlike approaching L2 development as being built around the strengthening of direct links between L2 words and concepts, the MHM views L2 learning as "conceptual restructuring and development of target-like linguistic categories" (Pavlenko, 2009, p. 150).

The MHM can be easily adapted to make predictions about the bilingual memory system when more than two languages are involved. These attempts were made by Benati and Schwieter (2017) and further discussed in Libben and Schwieter (2019). In the multilingual version of the MHM, the **Trilingual Modified Hierarchical Model (TMHM)** similarly argues that concepts can be fully shared, partially shared, or language-specific, but that both L2 and L3 word learning can trigger conceptual reorganizing. The model is shown in Figure 6.6.

The predictions of the TMHM address the complex issue of transfer and the effects of parallel language activation on how bilinguals process languages. The model posits that with proficiency development in the L2 and L3, stronger conceptual links are developed between the conceptual store and words in both languages; however, whether L3 words are associated with L1 or L2 words is unclear, as noted by Benati and Schwieter (2017):

The addition of an L3 implies that lexical mediation from the L3 to the L2 can occur, although empirical support would be needed to tease apart whether the preferred path of lexical mediation for the L3 would be via L1 or L2 words and whether these things are modulated by other factors. For instance, when an English (L1), Spanish (L2), Italian (L3) language learner is asked to name an L3 word (e.g., gatto), he/she may have to access its meaning by first associating it with the L2 word (e.g., gato) rather than with the L1 word cat. L3-to-L2 word association may be sensitive to factors such as cognate status, language typologies, lexical robustness (i.e., an element of proficiency in which automaticity of word retrieval is due to the familiarity with and frequency of its access; Schwieter & Sunderman, 2008, 2009), and overall proficiency level (p. 267).

The TMHM demonstrates that the cognitive dynamics of bilingual processing can be generalized to trilingual (and, in principle, n-lingual) cognitive architectures (Libben & Schwieter, 2019). Although cases of simultaneous bilingualism from early childhood are common, language learning among adolescents and adults typically develops across the lifespan. The consequence of this, as hypothesized in the TMHM, is that **the multilingual lexical-conceptual system is always in a dynamic state of readjustment**, where words can be recoupled and decoupled and the degree of conceptual overlap across the three languages changes as a result of an individual's unique language experiences. The specific nature of these experiences and individual differences, along with their effects on language processing and cognition in general continues to be a fruitful area for future research.

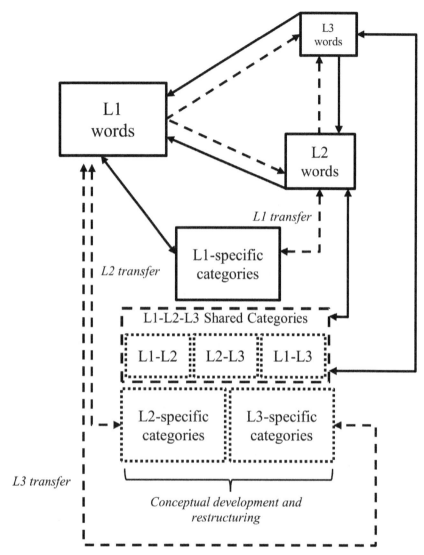

Figure 6.6 The Trilingual Modified Hierarchical Model
Source: Benati and Schwieter (2017).

6.5.4 The Sense Model

Asymmetrical effects in cross-language priming have been consistently reported in the literature such that primes in an L1 speed up the recognition of their L2 translation equivalents but not vice versa (Gollan,

Forster, & Frost, 1997; Jiang & Forster, 2001; Xia & Andrews, 2015; see Basnight-Brown & Altarriba, 2007, for a review). The RHM accounts for this finding, as noted in Section 6.4.2, by suggesting that because there is a weak link between the L2 lexicon and the conceptual store, primes in the L2 are unable to automatically activate their meaning, and thus do not produce significant L2–L1 effects. The opposite holds for priming in the L1–L2 direction: Because there is a strong link between the L1 lexicon and conceptual store, L1 primes quickly activate their corresponding concepts, and thus facilitate the retrieval of the L2 words also mapped onto them.

What is difficult for the RHM to account for, however, is that within-language masked repetition effects have also been found in the L2: Bilinguals are faster to respond to L2 words (e.g., cat) when preceded by a masked presentation of the same word but in a different case (e.g., "CAT") compared to a control prime (e.g., "TRUCK") (Finkbeiner, 2005; Gollan, Forster, & Frost, 1997; Jiang, 1999; Jiang & Forster, 2001). A further complication is that these priming effects may be task sensitive, such that translation priming for the L2–L1 direction only emerges in semantic categorization but not lexical decision tasks (Finkbeiner et al., 2004; Grainger & Frenck-Mestre, 1998).

Finkbeiner et al. (2004) hypothesized that the ratio of primed to unprimed senses associated with the target will affect translation priming. In the first three of six experiments, the researchers replicated previous findings (Grainger & Frenck-Mestre, 1998) that in a lexical decision task, L1 masked primes facilitate L2 lexical decisions but not vice versa and that these effects are symmetrical in a semantic categorization task. They argued that in addition to the asymmetrical nature between the conceptual store and L1 versus L2 words, semantic categorization tasks, as opposed to lexical decision tasks, elicit a filtering out process of category-irrelevant senses (i.e., to eliminate representational asymmetry) from the decision-making process.

Further to the findings from the first three experiments, Finkbeiner et al. (2004) argued that the role of polysemy across words in both languages can illuminate the differential range of the number of "senses" (i.e., the number of different ways that a word is used in the language) that translation pairs have. One of their examples of a pair of translation equivalents with a significantly different number of nonoverlapping senses compared to overlapping senses is the Japanese word *kuroi* and its English translation *black*. In Japanese and English, each of these words have many senses but perhaps only one of them, COLOR, is in common between the two. For example, the senses associated with *black* can range from drinking one's coffee *black* and going shopping on *Black* Friday to having a *black*

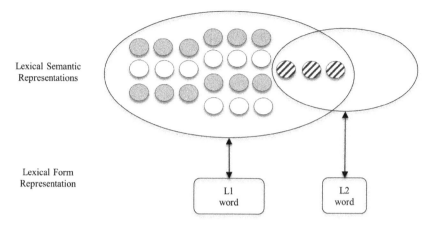

Lexical Semantic
Representations

Lexical Form
Representation

Figure 6.7 The Sense Model
Source: Finkbeiner et al. (2004).
Note: A black and white version of this figure will appear in some formats. For the color version, please refer to the plate section.

sense of humor. But among the senses associated with *kuroi* are guilty and well tanned, neither of which overlap with their English counterpart. In the case of an L2 learner, while each of the senses associated with the L2 word can be acquired, it is likely that even the most proficient L2 learners will have more robust senses in their dominant L1 compared to their L2.

In additional categorization and lexical decision tasks, these hypotheses were tested by Finkbeiner et al. (2004), but this time in within-language (L1–L1) contexts. In this experimental design, words in the participants' L1 (English) with many senses (e.g., "fly") were coupled with words with few senses (e.g., "mosquito"). According to the researchers, when words with many senses are used as primes for target words with few senses, a similar scenario to the L1–L2 priming direction is created. Likewise, the few-to-many priming direction should represent a situation similar to L2–L1 priming. The results from these within-language priming experiments mirrored findings from the first three experiments: During the lexical decision task, significant priming effects were observed in the many-to-few direction (e.g., FLY–mosquito) but no priming was obtained in the few-to-many direction (e.g., MOSQUITO–fly). For semantic categorization, however, priming was reported in both directions.

Based on these findings, Finkbeiner et al. put forth the **Sense Model** (see Figure 6.7). According to the Sense Model, the degree of overlap of the semantic senses between two translations is represented by the stripped circles while language-specific senses are shown in grey and white. Referencing the *black–kuroi* example, these stripped circles, therefore, refer to COLOR, since that is the only sense hypothesized to be shared between the two languages.

Although additional support for the Sense Model has been reported (e.g., Luo et al., 2013; Wang & Forster, 2010), several more recent studies have challenged some of its predictions. These criticisms have been specifically directed at the model's claim that the lack of L2–L1 (noncognate) priming stems from: (a) the inability of L2 primes to activate a sufficient proportion of the L1 targets' senses (Nakayama, Ida, & Lupker, 2016; Xia & Andrews, 2015); (b) whether representations of senses belong to both languages (core representations) or to a single language (language-specific representations) (Evans, 2020); and (c) what the role of word frequency is (Brysbaert, Mandera, & Keuleers, 2018; Chaouch-Orozco, Alonso, & Rothman, 2019, 2021; Nakayama, Lupker & Itaguchi, 2018). Other studies have shown that increasing the presentation time of an L2 prime (e.g., by as little as 150 ms) can lead to L2–L1 priming effects (Chen et al., 2014; Lee, Jang, & Choi, 2018), thus bringing into question whether only small portions of senses at the lexical-semantic level are activated by L2 words. Many of these criticisms seem to favor connectionist approaches, which we will discuss next.

6.6 Connectionist Models of Bilingual Memory

During the development of many of the aforementioned models, interest in connectionist accounts of bilingual memory grew among many researchers (see Dijkstra & Rekké, 2010; Zhao & Li, 2010). Connectionist views of word recognition and production argue that "processing speeds depend on the strength of connection weights between semantic, orthographic, and phonological components of the words being processed" (Basnight-Brown, 2014, p. 11). A key distinction between connectionist models and the models discussed in Sections 6.4 and 6.5 is that **connectionist models are computer- and mathematical-based models** which, their proponents argue, provide a better examination of the quantitative components of language processing and a more precise manipulation of variables (Dijkstra et al., 2011). Two important localist-connectionist views we will discuss here are the BIA Model, along with its updated versions, and the Multilink Model.

6.6.1 BIA Models

As discussed briefly in Chapter 2, the **BIA Model** (Dijkstra & Van Heuven, 1998) assumes that bilingual word recognition is a nonselective

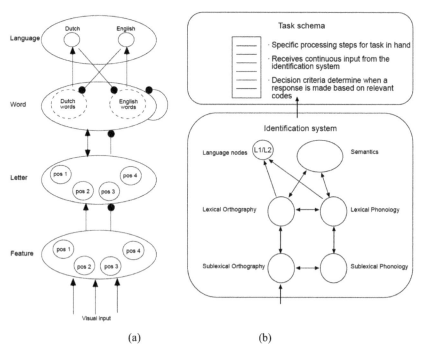

Figure 6.8 The Bilingual Interactive Activation Model (a) and the Bilingual Interactive Activation + Model (b)
Source: Dijkstra and Van Heuven (1998, 2002, respectively).

process (i.e., both language nodes are active and competing during processing) that consists of four layers of interactive levels. As portrayed in Figure 6.8a, when a bilingual sees a word, individual letter features are activated, which, in turn, activate the letters matching them. Words in both the L1 and L2 that share/include these letters are then activated. Finally, a language node acts as a filter, taking into account the degree of activation at the word level in order to facilitate the selection of the right word in the intended language.

Four years later, Dijkstra and Van Heuven (2002) updated the BIA to account for the role of phonology, semantics, and task demands during lexical access. In this revision, called the **BIA+ Model** (see Figure 6.8b), the word identification system feeds information about the activated representations from both languages to "a decision and response selection mechanism operating as part of a task schema" (p. 195). This extension underscores the complementary relationship between Green's Inhibitory Control Model (1998) (see Dijkstra, 1998, for a discussion). In the BIA+, language nodes are no longer hypothesized to serve as language filters; rather, their functions are

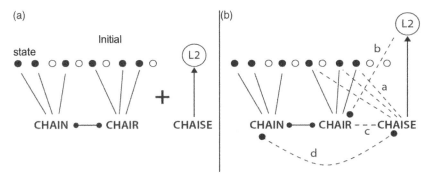

Figure 6.9 The Developmental Bilingual Interactive Activation Model
Note: Example refers to an L1 English speaker learning the French word *chaise* ("chair"). (a) refers to the initial stage of word learning in an L2; (b) represents the developmental changes in connectivity between word forms and semantics as a consequence of gains in and exposure to the L2.
Source: Grainger, Midgley, and Holcomb (2010).

restricted to "language membership representations within the identification system of which the activation level also reflects global lexical activity (because all activated words of one language feed activation forward to a language node)" (Dijkstra & Van Heuven, 2002, p. 186).

The BIA+ Model is more explicit than its BIA predecessor with regard to the time course of bilingual word recognition, the interactions between orthographic, phonological, and semantic representations, and language membership tags. Furthermore, the BIA+ distinguishes between linguistic and nonlinguistic influences on word recognition performance, such that linguistic context affects activation in the word identification system but nonlinguistic effects are restricted to the task/decision system. However, it does not reveal much about what may be occurring during L2 development (Basnight-Brown, 2014; Grainger, Midgley, & Holcomb, 2010). In a theoretical account by Grainger, Midgley, and Holcomb (2010), the authors bring together "the sequence of changes in L1–L2 connectivity that would allow an initial RHM model to develop into a BIA model" (p. 275). Their developmental version of the BIA, called the **BIA-d Model**, can be seen in Figure 6.9.

The BIA-d Model explains how individuals who already have an established L1 (i.e., late L2 learners) acquire and process L2 words across two largely overlapping phases of development. Figure 6.9 shows an example of an L1 English speaker learning or using an L2 French word. As shown in Figure 6.9a, prior to learning an L2 word the initial state is a set of L1 word forms (e.g., chair, chain, etc.) that are connected to a distributed network of semantic representations as posited by the DFM (de Groot, 1992; see also Kroll & de Groot, 1997). When being presented with a new L2 word such as *chaise*, and either being told (i.e., in classroom settings) or finding out (independently) that it means *chair* in English, there is coactivation of L1 and L2 word forms in addition to information that specifies to which language the word belongs (i.e., through an L2 language node). With practice and development, connections between the L2 word form, the equivalent word form in the L1, the corresponding semantic features, and the L2 language node strengthen (as shown by the dotted, open-ended lines in Figure 6.9b). As noted by Grainger, Midgley, and Holcomb, these strengthened connections, in turn, increase the degree of cross-language interference which is mitigated by developing inhibitory control (as shown by the dotted lines ending in circles) with both L2 and L1 words that are both formally similar and semantically incompatible. The developmental changes posited by the BIA-d are labeled (a)–(d) in Figure 6.9b and correspond to the following points:

(a) Excitatory connection strengths from L2 word forms to semantics gradually increase;
(b) Inhibitory connections from the L2 language node to L1 word forms gradually increase;
(c) Excitatory connections between L2 word forms and the word forms of their L1 translates gradually increase, and then decrease as the inhibitory input from the L2 language node increases and the L1 clamping process is dropped;
(d) Inhibitory connections develop from the L2 word form to other orthographically similar words in L2 and L1.
(Grainger, Midgley, & Holcomb, 2010, p. 278)

6.6.2 The Multilink Model

A final connectionist approach that we will discuss, the **Multilink Model**, is one of the newest models of the bilingual memory and has gained traction over the last decade or so. It was first developed by Rekké (2010) and Dijkstra and Rekké (2010) in response to a **need for a unified account of lexical-semantic processing** (Brysbaert & Duyck, 2010). While the BIA+ and RHM were originally conceptualized to explain bilingual word recognition and production/translation, respectively, the Multilink Model offers a **localist-connectionist view that accounts for word recognition, retrieval, and production processes**.

In a recent discussion on the Multilink Model, Dijkstra et al. (2019) describe how the model addresses several of the shortcomings found in

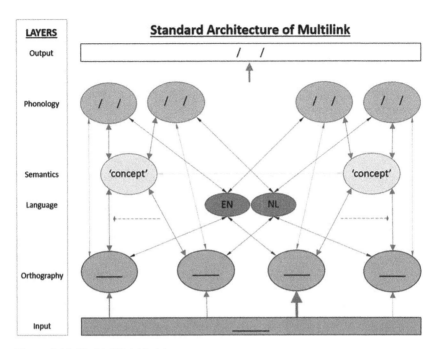

Figure 6.10 The Multilink Model
Source: Dijkstra et al. (2019).

previous models such as the BIA and BIA+. The authors state that some of the Multilink Model's unique characteristics are that it:

- allows the simulation of monolingual and bilingual processing of words that vary in frequency of usage, length, and cross-linguistic similarity;
- includes a task/decision system, it allows simulating word processing in psycholinguistic tasks such as lexical decision, orthographic and semantic priming, word naming, and word translation production; and
- can simulate performance of both high and low L2-proficiency bilinguals in these tasks [because] lexicon and parameter settings can be fine-tuned to L2-proficiency (Dijkstra et al., 2019, pp. 661–662).

As shown in Figure 6.10, a visually presented word first activates several lexical-orthographic representations which consequently activate their semantic and phonological representations in a language-nonselective manner. Language nodes determine language membership and activation flow is bidirectional.

A recent study by Vanlangendonck et al. (2020) tested the hypotheses of BIA+ and Multilink Models with a specific focus on how stimulus list composition and response competition affected the processing of cognates and interlingual homographs. The results demonstrated that changing a pure stimulus list to a mixed context turned faciliatory effects for cognates into inhibitory effects. Increased inhibition for interlingual homographs was also reported. The authors interpreted these results as evidence that "identical cognates benefit from their shared semantics relative to interlingual homographs without meaning overlap, reducing response competition effects in both pure and mixed stimulus lists" (p. 843). These contrastive effects of overlap of cross-linguistic form and response competition can be accounted for in both the BIA+ and Multilink frameworks.

As noted by Dijkstra et al. (2019), in its present state, the Multilink Model takes a simple, holistic view of semantic representations; but it does not consider the semantic spreading of activation between associated representations nor phonological differences in the onset of words. Furthermore, it does not directly represent the task/decision system (see Green, 1998) that is needed to select representations for output. Elaborating a task/decision system may help to offer an account of interlingual homograph processing. Ongoing empirical studies currently are testing and refining the model (Goertz, Wahl, & Dijkstra, in preparation; Pruijn, Peacock, & Dijkstra, in preparation).

Finally, perhaps the most apparent limitation of the Multilink Model, as with other statistical models of this nature, is that (human) computer programmers often implement the assumptions of the model, thus bringing into question the **ecological validity** of the design (Basnight-Brown, 2014). Although proponents of computational models are aware of this limitation, as suggested by Dijkstra et al.'s (2019) statement that "computational modelling of word retrieval requires making hard choices: about the general theoretical framework, lexical representations, and underlying processing mechanisms" (p. 676), these programming decisions actually present an opportunity: "Making these choices to specify a model clarifies one's thinking about general and specific theoretical issues" (p. 676).

6.7 Summary

In this chapter, we began by arguing that it is beneficial to view the mental lexicon as a system that is inherently set up for bi/multilingualism (Section 6.2). Because the majority of the world's population speaks more than one language, considering a "bilingual" mental lexicon as the default may be a more accurate way of exploring lexical and conceptual memory. Following this discussion, we examined how concepts and words are represented in the mind (Section 6.3), with particular emphasis on the dynamic, developmental nature of word-to-concept mapping and the distributed, overlapping characteristics of semantic representations. With this background, in Section 6.4 we reviewed several theoretical models of word processing – including word recognition, production, and translation. The first set of models included the Word Association Model, which assumed that L2 words are first processed through their L1 translation equivalent to access their shared meaning, and the Concept Mediation Model, which argued that both L1 and L2 words have direct access to their meaning. Drawing on these assumptions, the RHM essentially brought the two models together by suggesting that L2 learners move from word association to concept mediation as they become more proficient in their L2.

In Section 6.5 we then discussed another set of models that offer a more detailed account of the conceptual system by emphasizing the degree of overlap that exists between conceptual representations in the two languages. While the DFM differentiated concrete and abstract word translations as having more or fewer overlapping conceptual nodes, respectively, the SDAM depicted multiple conceptual stores: A shared one for both languages and two smaller, language-specific ones. The MHM and TMHM, which are largely informed by the RHM and DFM, view the conceptual store(s) as a complex set of representations that range from fully overlapping, partially overlapping, or not overlapping between the languages. According to these two models, not only do links between concepts and their lexical representations strengthen and weaken (as in the RHM), but conceptual restructuring and development of target-like linguistic categories occur as a natural part of L2/L3 acquisition. Following our treatment of the MHM and TMHM, we reviewed the Sense Model, which considers the role of polysemy in language. Although the Sense Model has only been partially supported or refuted in subsequent studies, it offers interesting insights on how the number of different ways that a word is used in a language (i.e., its "senses") implies different degrees of overlap of lexical-semantic representations.

In Section 6.6, we turned to two localist-connectionist models: The BIA/BIA+/BIA-d and the Multilink Models. In the updated version of the BIA, the well-cited BIA+, there are two interactive subsystems of bilingual word recognition: A word identification subsystem and a task/decision subsystem. The BIA-d offered a development view of these interactive subsystems. Finally, the most recent model rooted in connectionist traditions is the Multilink Model. Although developments to this model are still ongoing (Dijkstra et al., submitted), it offers promising new directions that can account for the processing of words that vary in frequency, length, and cross-linguistic similarity across several tasks, examining production, comprehension, and translation.

Review Questions

1. Discuss support for the notion that, for the brain, bilingualism, as opposed to monolingualism, may be a default.
2. Discuss the developmental nature of word-to-concept mapping and mediation. How and to what extent do concepts overlap between languages?
3. How does the Sense Model explain word processing?
4. How do connectionist models differ from models that incorporate distributed features into their predictions?
5. Explain the architecture of the bilingual mental lexicon as posited by the Multilink Model.

Further Reading

Altarriba, J., & Isurin, L. (Eds.). (2014). *Memory, language, and bilingualism: Theoretical and applied approaches*. Cambridge University Press.
Heredia, R., & Altarriba, J. (Eds.). (2014). *Foundations of bilingual memory*. Springer.
Heredia, R., & Cieślicka, A. (Eds.). (2020). *Bilingual lexical ambiguity resolution*. Cambridge University Press.

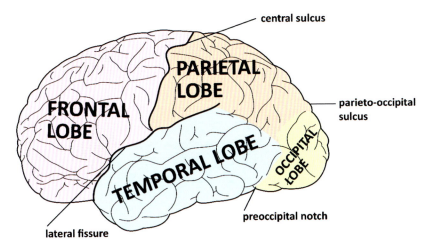

Figure 2.1 Lobes and fissures in the cortex

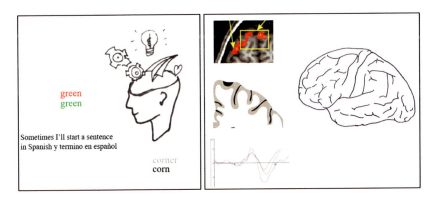

Figure 3.1 Difference between mind and brain

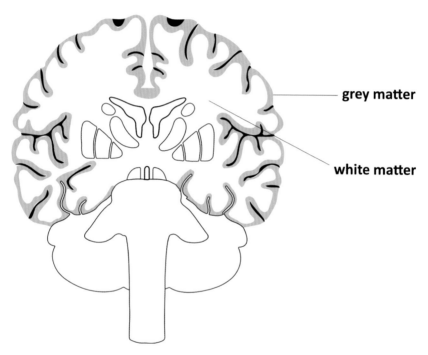

Figure 3.4 Grey and white matter in the brain

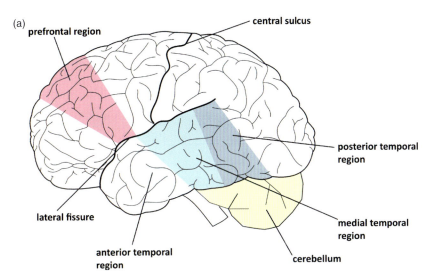

Figure 3.5 Localizing multiple memory and learning systems in the brain: View from the surface (a) and inside (b)

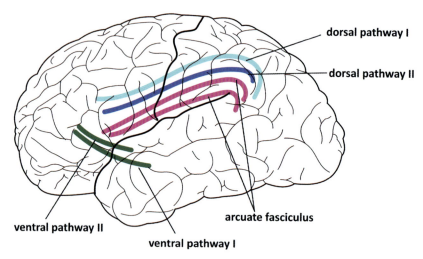

Figure 3.6 Arcuate fasciculus and ventral and dorsal pathways

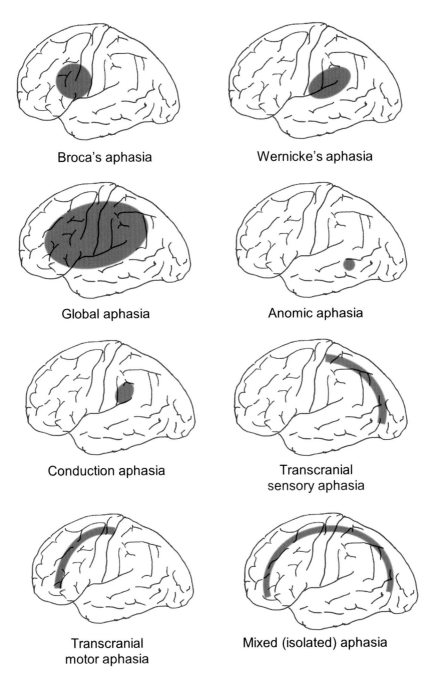

Broca's aphasia

Wernicke's aphasia

Global aphasia

Anomic aphasia

Conduction aphasia

Transcranial
sensory aphasia

Transcranial
motor aphasia

Mixed (isolated) aphasia

Figure 4.1 Example approximations of lesion sites that correlate to various types of aphasia

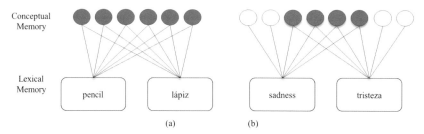

Figure 6.3 The Distributed Feature Model, showing different spreading activation for concrete translations (a) and abstract translations (b)

Note: Grey circles refer to overlapping representations; white circles refer to nonoverlapping representations.

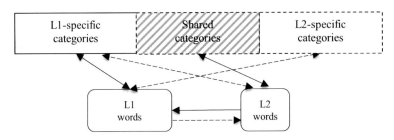

Figure 6.5 The Modified Hierarchical Model

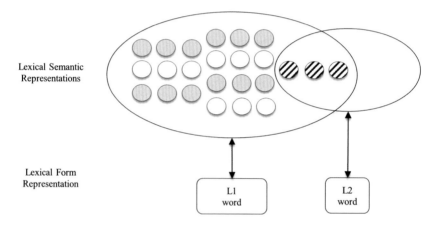

Lexical Semantic Representations

Lexical Form Representation

L1 word

L2 word

Figure 6.7 The Sense Model

CHAPTER SEVEN

Cognitive and Neurocognitive Effects of Bilingualism

Learning Objectives

- Gain insight into the cognitive effects related to bilingualism.
- Review effects of bilingualism in the neuroscientific domain.
- Learn about the mechanisms of cognitive functioning outside the language domain.
- Understand the complexity of bilingual effects on cognition and neurocognition.
- Gain an understanding of why findings in studies on bilingual effects are so inconclusive.

7.1 Introduction

In previous chapters, we have come across many details on linguistic effects of bilingualism. In this chapter, we will deal with the following questions:

- What are the consequences of learning and using two languages?
- What is the impact on cognition and on brain structure and function when learning and "juggling two languages in one mind"? (Kroll, 2008; Kroll et al., 2012).

These rather wide-ranging questions led us to opt for a broad approach to this topic. At the same time, we would like to note that **this chapter is not focused on the bilingual advantage debate**, that is, the assumption that bilinguals may benefit from bilingualism to such an extent that they perform better than monolinguals on a number of cognitive tasks, such as the Simon task, and so on. The main problem with current research on the bilingual advantage is that there is always at least one study showing no effect, sometimes even a disadvantage for the bilingual group. Until now, findings from studies conducted on this topic have been seriously doubted as some of them have clearly lacked robustness and reliability (see criticisms concerning methodological approaches and publication biases by de Bruin, Treccani, & Della Sala, 2015; Leivada et al., 2021; Paap, 2023; Paap & Greenberg, 2013; Paap et al., 2018; Paap, Johnson, &

Sawi, 2015b). Consequently, a bilingual advantage for the overall bilingual population has been neither proven nor disproven. Some researchers have suggested ending the quest for the bilingual advantage (e.g., Paap, Johnson, & Sawi, 2016) while others aim to reach a deeper understanding (e.g., Dick et al., 2019; Grundy, 2020; Poarch & Krott, 2019; Woumans & Duyck, 2015) or to enlarge the scope of the abilities possibly involved in the advantage (e.g., Festman & Schwieter, 2019; Greve et al., 2021).

Additionally, there is the famous **chicken-and-egg-dilemma**: *Which came first: the chicken or the egg?* Since even extremely young infants can show differences in their behavior after being exposed to two languages for a very short time, it is questionable whether all effects can be related exclusively to bilingualism. "Does an individual turn out to be multilingual because s/he has a higher level of cognitive control? Or does being bi- or multilingual train the person's cognitive control abilities with continuous use of two or more languages?" (Festman, 2021, p. 25). A two-sided approach is more likely:

- Either one could start off genetically well-equipped in terms of cognitive control abilities, memory capacity, auditory cortex, and eagerness to learn and thus develop great bi- or multilingual skills,
- or one could be born into a bi- or multilingual family and acquire two or more languages from early on, what might lead to enhanced cognitive skills due to additional training of bi/multilingualism) (Festman, 2021, p. 25).

Both approaches might ultimately lead to greater language proficiency in two or more languages and to excellent cognitive control abilities. Nonetheless, there might be subtle differences when looking at the details. Developmental studies (as suggested by Filippi, De Souza, & Bright, 2019) with longitudinal designs can help reveal the impact of multilingualism on language and cognition more clearly. The dynamic changes are due to the interplay among cognitive control, language proficiency, and a multifaceted experience which, in turn, may lead to processing efficiency and functional neural changes (see Li & Grant, 2016, for a review). Individual differences in genetics and environmental factors are paired with the diverse experiences of multilingual language users and lead to heterogeneous speaker profiles (see e.g., Festman, Poarch, & Dewaele, 2017, for individual learning trajectories of multilingual children). Based on the state-of-art concerning this highly complex issue, the "interplay between genetics, language use and communicative demands as well as general environmental factors yet awaits our understanding in general – and of its development in particular" (Festman, 2021, p. 25).

Therefore, in this chapter, we collected and summarized relevant information related to bilingualism and corresponding consequences and effects across different domains (mainly distinguished by their methodological approach). These effects include language processing/performance (see Table 7.1) and cognitive processing/performance on cognitive tasks (Table 7.2), and on the brain, based on neuroscientific studies (Table 7.3). In this way, we have tried to tease apart effects on the mind and consequences directly observed on the brain. Note that this artificial distinction is mainly motivated by diverging foci and methods of different scientific disciplines as related to the questions listed at the beginning of this section (see Chapter 1 on disciplines involved). In the upcoming sections, we will explore the various cognitive and neurocognitive effects of bilingualism.

7.2 Effects of Bilingualism and Necessary Adaptations

Results from infant studies, in particular, have repeatedly demonstrated the impact of a bilingual environment on infants' very early abilities. The perceived input from different languages is often characterized as **unpredictable**, since the languages that are heard might change every now and then, they might be mixed, and so on. The input is per se **variable**, because it offers a rich perceptual stimulation due to two languages being involved, with their different sounds, intonations, stress patterns, cultures, gestures, etc. What is more, the idiosyncratic way individual speakers use their languages multiplies if multilinguals use one or the other, a code-switched version, or even standard or dialectal variations of the languages. Bilingualism necessitates adaptations, and we will take a close look at them in the following sections.

7.3 Effects of Bilingualism on Attentional Abilities and Perceptual Learning

For infants, this variability already presumably triggers distinct processes in order to **fine-tune attentional abilities and perceptual learning**. Table 7.1 describes these sources as related to bilingualism and illustrates possible effects that have been reported in research on bilingual populations. Example studies are mentioned for further reading.

Furthermore, the same table provides an overview of different effects linked to being raised or confronted with two languages in relation to the type of input (e.g., sound and structure), the amount of input, along with speakers and their characteristics. These circumstances may lead to increased sensitivity, a more analytical approach to languages, enhanced discriminatory skills and opportunities for transfer,

Table 7.1 Parameters of bilingualism: Influence of language stimulation and input as training and transfer effects

Effects of bilingualism (assumptions, explanations, theories) …	… on language processing/cognition (behavioral evidence)	Example studies and reviews
Bilingualism offers variable, unpredictable input and rich stimulation		
The **attentional** system needs to be tuned to perceive and track information per language and to switch between two languages; **perceptual** learning needs to be refined to discriminate between the properties of the languages	**Specific adaptations are induced:** existence of two different languages (e.g., based on sounds, possible word endings, articulatory gestures) has to be noticed the perceptual system has to be tuned to discriminate between them. **Early bilinguals:** • show great sensitivity to novelty • seek new information • show great exploratory behavior (D'Souza et al., 2020) • disengage attention fast from an already familiar visual stimulus in order to shift attention to new stimulus • switch attention frequently between, e.g., two visual stimuli	Antón et al. (2014), Arredondo et al. (2017, 2022), Bak, Vega-Mendoza and Sorace (2014), Bosch and Sebastián-Gallés (1997), Cheour et al. (1998), Costa, Hernández and Sebastián-Gallés (2008), D'Souza et al. (2020), D'Souza and D'Souza (2021), Filippi, D'Souza and Bright (2019), Filippi et al. (2020), Kovács and Mehler (2009), Näätänen et al. (1997), Sebastián-Gallés et al. (2012) Review: Bialystok (2017), Costa and Sebastián-Galles (2014), Dal Ben et al. (2022), Festman (2021), Filippi and Bright (2023), Ouzia and Filippi (2016), Soveri et al. (2011)
Bilingualism involves input from and use of two languages including:		
Exposure to **speakers** from different languages	Enhanced extraction of talker-specific information encoded in the speech signal (Fecher and Johnson, 2019) **Sensitivity is increased:** • to interlocutor's linguistic knowledge • to reaction to language choice • to other people's knowledge (theory of mind) Adjustments of language choice according to communicative partner and situation	Fennell and Byers-Heinlein (2014), Fecher and Johnson (2019, 2022), Werker (2012) Review: Nicoladis and Smithson (2022), Yu, Kovelman and Wellman (2021)

	Bilinguals:	Antovich and Graf Estes (2018), Byers-Heinlein and Werker (2013), Hoff et al. (2012)
Two **language systems** need to be represented	learn to discriminate between, sort, and parse two language systems (e.g., phoneme repertoire and grammatical information of each language) establish links between concepts and word forms (often one concept but two word forms) gain "a sense of order during the acquisition processing" (Witney & Dewaele, 2018, p. 49)	Review: Costa and Sebastián-Gallés (2014), Hirosh and Degani (2018),
Input from and use of two languages along with exposure to **two cultures** and different **scripts**	Enhances metalinguistic awareness More abstract thinking about languages Improves awareness of differences and variability "a more analytic orientation to linguistic operations" (Chin & Wigglesworth, 2007, p. 62) "the child learns to see his language as one particular system among many, to view its phenomena under more general categories, and this leads to awareness of his l linguistic operations" (Vygotsky, 1962, p. 110)	Barac and Bialystok (2012), Chin and Wigglesworth (2007), Edwards and Christophersen (1988), Folke et al. (2016), Tran, Arredondo and Yoshida (2019), Yelland, Pollard and Mercuri (1993) Review: Bright, Ouzia and Filippi (2019), Hoff (2018), Lado et al. (2017), Paap et al. (2015a)
Role of languages relevant for the individual learner in school/ work context, society; **prestige of languages**	Immersion at school with regular language input and use, best if biliteracy is achieved and interaction with peers using the same languages Language of instruction (L1, L2, Lx) leads to higher competence, because it is more than a colloquial, day-by-day language Development of metalinguistic awareness Development of language skills in both languages	Bialystok, Luk and Kwan (2005), Trebits et al. (2022), Salomé, Casalis and Commissaire (2022), Witney and Dewaele (2018) Review: Kroll and Mendoza (2022), Rumlich (2020) For overview: Kersten and Winsler (2022) See Festman (2021) for review of international studies with different language combinations on the biliteracy effect, in particular for L3 learning

continued

Table 7.1 (cont.)

Effects of bilingualism (assumptions, explanations, theories) …	… on language processing/cognition (behavioral evidence)	Example studies and reviews
Less time per language – in terms of exposure/input and use and continuous interaction between two language systems	Smaller vocabulary per language Greater/possible difficulties with lexical access and during lexical competition Reduced semantic fluency, lexical retrieval failure Production of semantically or phonologically related words Cross-language interference Increased tip-of-the-tongue states, but comparable amount of immediate retrieval (Gollan & Silverberg, 2001) → Compensatory strategies, experimenting with existing skills, more gestures and code-switching	Gollan and Acenas (2004), Gollan and Brown (2006), Gollan et al. (2007), Ivanova and Costa (2008), Kreiner and Degani (2015), Legacy et al. (2018), Michel and Gollan (2005), Poulisse, Bongaerts and Kellerman (1984), Yan and Nicoladis (2009) Review: Hoff (2015), Ben-Zeev (1977), Hörder (2018), Pika, Nicoladis and Marentette (2006), Wermelinger et al. (2020). Gullberg (2012), Nicoladis (2008), Nicoladis and Smithson (2022)
One language (in case of dominant L1) available as basis for **intercomprehension and transfer, translanguaging,** and experiences with language learning → transfer opportunities – can use knowledge and experience from L1/L2 acquisition/learning	Linguistic structures, sound patterns, and grammatical systems can be transferred into the newly learned language Intercomprehension ability Jarvis and Pavlenko's (2008) claim: Multilinguals were "open to make more interlingual identifications between the target language and previously learned languages" (p. 205)	Hicks (2021), Jarvis and Pavlenko (2008), Kirsch and Duarte (2020), Melo-Pfeifer (2020), Pavlenko and Malt (2011), Peyer et al. (2010), Treffers-Daller and Sakel (2012), see Chapter 5 in this volume Review: Festman (2021), Montanari (2019)

as well as stronger compensatory strategies and increased language proficiency.

7.4 Effects of Bilingualism on Processing and Domain-General Control

The fact that bilinguals must handle two languages poses specific challenges for the processing system. While acquiring and using two languages, the system supposedly must cope with higher processing demands in order to keep up with production speed and the functionality of managing two languages, see Table 7.2 for an overview and summary.

7.5 Effects of Bilingualism on Brain Structure and Functioning

What is more, **L2 learning seemingly influences structure and functioning brain** (see Li, Legault, & Litcofsky, 2014, for a review). When a complex skill is acquired and then used, the brain reacts by restructuring the respective area to accommodate increased demands. Internal restructuring can be seen, for example, via initial structural changes of grey matter (see Pliatsikas, 2020, for a respective theory). There is a wealth of studies investigating changes on the brain level related to the requirements of bilingual processing based on a number of different points of structural or functional interest (see Table 7.3 for an overview and summary). One recent theory put forward by DeLuca et al. (2020) draws a conclusive picture of the relationship between bilingual experience and related neurocognitive adaptations.

7.6 Summary

Summing up, this chapter has presented a wealth of criteria characterizing the "bilingual experience," that is, the exposure to, acquiring, and using two languages. The impact of these criteria has been examined on three different levels: In terms of language processing, cognitive processing, and structural and functional changes in the brain. On all three levels, numerous studies have been conducted and many different methods have been employed, but no highly conclusive results have ensued. However, what can be said is that the bilingual experience is a change-inducing event leading to speedy adaptations on different levels of processing, with brain changes at its base to accommodate for additional demands and specific requirements.

Table 7.2 Parameters of bilingualism: Influence on (language) processing system and domain-general executive control processes

Source in bilingualism (assumptions, explanations, theories)	Effect on domain-general executive control processes (behavioral evidence)	Example studies and reviews
Two language systems → in general: **greater effort**/ higher processing demands because of greater demands on a control system and/or less frequent use of each language (Costa & Sebastián-Gallés, 2014) → need for adaptation	"More languages" also means "more demands" for the processing system compared to monolingualism (Festman, 2013; cf. Costa & Sebastián-Gallés, 2014); requires more efficient processing of these language demands (Calabria et al., 2018; Claussenius-Kalman & Hernandez, 2019)	Abutalebi (2008), Luk et al. (2012), Festman and Mosca (2016), Sá-Leite, Fraga, and Comesaña (2019), Schmidtke (2018) Review: Valian (2016)
Parallel/joint activation and **constant competition** between two languages for **selection** (e.g., from among potential lexical candidates within and across languages), conflict between two language systems, possible interference → **avoidance of cross-language interference**	Domain-general control processes are needed: EF are drawn upon inhibition **control attention** to language representations and language processing in a way not required for monolinguals; **attention to relevant linguistic features**, efficiency in **filtering out irrelevant information**: less interference in conflict resolution	Green (1998), Kroll et al. (2008), Rodríguez-Fornells et al. (2005), Thierry and Wu (2007), Wu and Thierry (2013) Review: Filippi and Bright (2023), Kroll et al. (2015), Marian and Spivey (2003), Bialystok (2018a), Bialystok and Martin (2004), Martin-Rhee and Bialystok (2008), Costa et al. (2008, 2009)
Need for **mental flexibility**	Increases cognitive flexibility (Abutalebi and Green, 2007) Flexible **switching** between tasks	Barbu, Gillet, and Poncelet (2020), Poulin-Dubois et al. (2022), Nicoladis, Hui, and Wiebe (2018) Review: Grote et al. (2021)

Abutalebi and Green (2013): • "single-language context" = restriction on using only one language in certain situations (e.g., in school). • The "dual-language context" = the use of two languages in a certain context (only one is used with an interlocutor at a given time), no code-switching between the two languages, however, the speaker intentionally keeps both languages ready for use • "Dense code-switching" = the use of both languages and "copious" switching between them (Green, 2018) Mechanisms in current situation, e.g., inhibition → need to act according to context/ different control processes	Monitoring (the process of evaluation whether there is a need to apply cognitive control) → Great need for controlling and monitoring the two languages (only in single- and dual-language contexts) Eight control processes that are differentially recruited as a function of the type of interactional context for language use (goal maintenance, conflict monitoring, interference suppression, salient cue detection, selective response inhibition, task disengagement, task engagement, and opportunistic planning)	Costa et al. (2009), Czapka and Festman (2021), Dong and Li (2015), Kałamała et al. (2020), Kheder and Kaan (2021), Lai and O'Brien (2020), Liu et al. (2019), Markiewicz, Mazaheri, and Krott (2023), Poarch and van Hell (2012b), Singh and Mishra (2013), Teubner-Rhodes et al. (2016)
Regular experience of managing two languages	→ Improves WM capacity and its efficiency: Temporary maintenance and constant updating of information relative to the content of language production	Antón, Carreiras, and Duñabeitia (2019) Review: Monnier et al. (2022), Grundy and Timmer (2016)

continued

Table 7.2 (cont.)

Source in bilingualism (assumptions, explanations, theories)	Effect on domain-general executive control processes (behavioral evidence)	Example studies and reviews
BILINGUAL BY PROFESSION Translators/interpreters; specific dual-language condition which is present right from the start of interpretation training	Effects on EF revealed in performance shortly after the onset of formal intense training are dependent on time on task, i.e., the hours of practice and with years of professional experience	Elmer et al. (2010), Köpke and Nespoulous (2006), Elmer, Hänggi, and Jäncke (2014), Santilli et al. (2019) Review: Ferreira, Schwieter, and Festman (2020)
Simultaneous interpreters (SI): Need for perception of key information in the incoming sound stream and comprehension of the constantly unfolding speech	Enhanced auditory perception (verbal and nonverbal sounds) for expert SIs → improves: abilities to extract and recognize relevant information from complex auditory input, sensitivity to semantic rather than syntactic features, and capacity to understand unfolding text	Elmer, Hänggi, and Jäncke et al. (2014); sentence comprehension (Bajo, Padilla, & Padilla, 2000); detecting semantic errors (Fabbro, Gran, & Gran, 1991; Yudes et al., 2013)
Professionally required: Storing new information and processing it in parallel **Strong impact on memory capacities**	Expert SIs show a more general memory advantage compared to trainees Great at manipulating information in WM and processing sublexical phonological representations; large memory spans	Babcock and Vallesi (2017), Christoffels, de Groot, and Kroll (2006), Signorelli, Haarmann, and Obler (2012), Yudes, Macizo, and Bajo (2011), Yudes et al. (2013) Review: Ferreira, Schwieter, and Festman (2020)

Enhanced training of retrieval of highly specific lexical items under time pressure	Good at efficient within- and cross-language processing and managing of unfamiliar information	Word knowledge/wider vocabulary (Christoffels, de Groot, & Kroll, 2006), phonological and semantic verbal fluency (Santilli et al., 2019)
Processing of multiple tasks	Need for monitoring and updating WM Superior performance in monitoring and updating for SI (n-back task in an easy and a dual-task condition)	Morales et al. (2015)

LIFELONG BILINGUALISM

Lifelong use of two languages, switching, trained ability to adapt to language contexts → greater cognitive reserve (= resistance of certain aspects of cognition to brain damage, i.e., reducing detrimental effects of aging on cognition, e.g., neurodegenerative diseases)	Delays behavioral symptoms of neurodegenerative disorders (e.g., Alzheimer's disease), delay of onset of dementia and of mild cognitive impairment	Alladi et al. (2013, 2017), Bak and Alladi (2014), Bialystok, Craik, and Freedman (2007), Papageorgiou et al. (2019), Woumans et al. (2015) Review: Antoniou (2019), Bialystok (2017, 2021), Degirmenci et al. (2022), Del Maschio et al. (2018)

Table 7.3 Parameters of bilingualism: Effects on brain structure and functioning

Source in bilingualism (assumptions, explanations, theories)	Effect on brain (neuroscientific evidence)	Example studies and reviews
Experience modifies aspects of brain function and structure (Herholz & Zatorre, 2012) **Experience-dependent neuroplasticity** of the brain → specific **adaptations of neural networks:** • **Changes in anatomical features in specific brain areas,** • **changes of cortical organization to enhance local processing,** • **changes in connectivity** between specific regions to enhance processing	Evidence for structural brain changes associated with learning a foreign language → differences in brain structure for both grey matter density and white matter integrity following even brief periods of L2 learning (cf. Bialystok, 2017)	Review: Berken et al. (2016), Li, Legault, and Litcofsky (2014), DeLuca et al. (2020), Pfenninger, Festman, and Singleton (2023), Pliatsikas (2020), Tao et al. (2021)
Networks for acquisition and processing of L1/L2 are **similar** (e.g., overlap in brain networks involved in language selection and nonverbal task switching (Abutalebi & Green, 2007; De Baene et al., 2015; Luk et al., 2012)), and more → control is needed	A domain-general system is recruited for language control: **Language control relies on lateral PFCs and the basal ganglia** This particular network in the bilingual brain is stronger than in monolinguals	Ansaldo, Ghazi-Saidi, and Adrover-Roig (2015), Luk et al. (2010) Review: Buchweitz and Prat (2013), Stocco et al. (2012)

Need **to keep languages separate yet switch** between them Adaptive control hypothesis (Green & Abutalebi, 2013)	**Control mechanisms are recruited for preventing interference** from nontarget-languages **and for switching**	Abutalebi and Green (2008), Garbin et al. (2010) Review: Banich & Compton (2018), Liu and Cao (2016), Vinerte and Sabourin (2019), Ye and Zhou (2009)
Constant use of two or more languages and switching between languages might **strengthen general nonlinguistic abilities**, observed in better task performance on cognitive tasks known as **bilingual cognitive advantage** (Bialystok, 1999)	**Strengthening of a "domain-general processing resource"** in the dorso-lateral PFC ACC – particularly involved in conflict resolution with regard to language processing (Abutalebi et al., 2012) ACC **might be the area which has undergone "special tuning"** in order to manage multiple languages simultaneously (Del Maschio & Abutalebi, 2019)	Filippi, D'Souza, and Bright (2019), Hernandez et al. (2001) Review: Del Maschio and Abutalebi (2019)
Need for flexible selection and application of rules when using multiple languages (Grundy, Pavlenko, & Bialystok, 2020)	**"Train" the processing system** (i.e., the fronto-striatal loops which send signals to the PFC) (cf. Wattendorf et al., 2014)	Bilinguals showed increased activation in the basal ganglia compared to monolinguals when learning and applying novel mathematical rules faster than their monolingual peers (Stocco & Prat, 2014) Review: Vinerte and Sabourin (2019)

continued

Table 7.3 (cont.)

Source in bilingualism (assumptions, explanations, theories)	Effect on brain (neuroscientific evidence)	Example studies and reviews
Even relatively short exposure to another language impacts on the neural architecture	Exposure to another language initially **affects in particular the local cortical grey matter** volume and subsequently subcortical and white matter restructuring when proficiency improves (Pliatsikas, 2020)	Grey matter density increased with the time spent in a five-month foreign language class in a longitudinal study (Stein et al., 2012) Review: Pliatsikas (2020)
Dynamic Restructuring Model (DRM) (Pliatsikas, 2020): Stages of structural adaptation according to increasing language experience, interrelation with speaker's experiences of language learning and switching • **Initially cortical** including the IFG, ACC, inferior parietal lobule/superior parietal lobule, and hippocampus; • **Then subcortical and white matter tracts:** Increased structural connectivity between regions, impacting on several white matter tracts, increases in subcortical grey matter (e.g., caudate, putamen, and thalamus), dynamic nature of these adaptations • **Finally** efficient processing and control: Increases in cerebellar grey matter and decreases in frontal connectivity	Structural changes reflected in changed **grey matter density** (e.g., in the **left inferior frontal cortex and left inferior parietal cortex**) Changes in cortical thickness	Mechelli et al. (2004), Liu et al. (2021c), Pliatsikas, DeLuca, and Voits (2020) Increased grey matter density in the left inferior parietal region, a primary center for language processing, was positively correlated to the participant's degree of bilingualism (Mechelli et al., 2004) Review: Hayakawa and Marian (2019), Pliatsikas (2020), Archila-Suerte et al. (2018), Claussenius-Kalman et al. (2020), Pliatsikas, DeLuca, and Voits (2020), Vaughn et al. (2021)

Higher processing demands for bilinguals Stronger involvement of language production and cognitive control areas:	**Increased activation in some language-related regions,** e.g., in five areas of the left hemisphere involved in speech production: the dorsal precentral gyrus, pars triangularis, and opercularis (of the IFC), superior temporal gyrus, and planum temporale (Parker Jones et al., 2012)	Abutalebi (2008), Abutalebi et al. (2012), Costumero et al. (2015), Cargnelutti, Tomasino, and Fabbro (2019b), Hernandez and Li (2007), Liu and Cao (2016), Nichols and Joanisse (2016), Palomar-García et al. (2015) Review: Luk et al. (2012)
Increased language **processing demands** as a function of L2 learning Processing of several languages requires **efficient communication between language and language control** areas, which are spread across the brain.	Changes in **white matter** between language-related brain areas (e.g., changes in white matter integrity reflecting increased myelination of the connecting tracts in left hemisphere language areas and their right hemisphere analogs as well as in the frontal lobe) Differential diffusivity patterns in white matter tracts in bilinguals	Schlegel, Rudelson, and Tse (2012) **Increased integrity of white matter** for early, lifelong bilinguals (Luk et al., 2011) and sequential, highly immersed bilinguals (Pliatsikas et al., 2017) Review: Berken et al. (2016), Anderson et al. (2018), Hämäläinen et al. (2017), Luk et al. (2011), Pliatsikas, Moschopoulou, and Saddy (2015), Rossi et al. (2017)
Language proficiency, amount of exposure to the languages as well as amount/type of language use and speaker environment **Neural convergence hypothesis** (Green, 2003), which suggests that qualitative differences between L1 and L2 speakers disappear with increasing L2 proficiency	**Degree of proficiency** seems to be more important than age of L2 acquisition **Language proficiency can overrule the initial modulations of AoA on the differences of brain activation** Based on **continued neuroplasticity, later language learners could be provided with compensatory mechanisms**	Abutalebi, Cappa, and Perani (2001), Consonni et al. (2013), Nichols and Joanisse (2016), Perani et al. (1998) Review: Hernandez (2013), Hernandez and Li (2007), Pfenninger, Festman, and Singleton (2023)

continued

Table 7.3 (cont.)

Source in bilingualism (assumptions, explanations, theories)	Effect on brain (neuroscientific evidence)	Example studies and reviews
	to achieve L2 proficiency (cf. Berken et al., 2016, for an example of L2 articulatory proficiency). Or in Li, Legault, and Litcofsky's (2014) words, "in contrast to predictions of the critical period hypothesis, L2 learning, even if it occurs late in adulthood, leads to both behavioral and neural changes that may approximate" (p. 302)	
Difference in AoA of multiple languages	Impact on the degree of **homogeneity of brain activation** of later learned languages: early multilinguals seem to have a more homogeneous brain activation for each of their languages, but more individual variability was observed for later learned languages	Fernández-Coello et al. (2016), Wattendorf et al. (2014) Review: Claussenius-Kalman and Hernandez (2019)
AoA and extensiveness of exposure	Less extensive brain activation for the earlier language to which they were exposed to a greater extent	Perani et al. (2003)
Inflicted language loss: Koreans at ages 3–8 adopted into French families	Reversibility of plastic changes associated with language acquisition in the first few years of life L2 may become represented in the very areas that normally represent the L1	Pallier et al. (2003)

	Enhanced state of alertness: ERP components enhanced (N1, P3, LRP)	Timmer, Costa, and Wodniecka (2021), Timmer, Wodniecka, and Costa (2021)
Surrounded by words from two languages		
Specific language use habits Single language context Both languages ready for use in a dual language context Dense code-switching	Neural adaptations: Implement sustained inhibition of the nontarget language by changes in the dorsal left frontal cortex and the parietal cortex are executed	Green and Abutalebi (2013) Review: Grundy, Anderson, and Bialystok (2017)
	Additional involvement of the thalamus and basal ganglia: allows for attention to cues indicating which language is more appropriate and for choice of that language as target language Particular involvement of left inferior frontal and right cerebellar circuits to allow for language switching and morphosyntactic integration of both languages	
BILINGUAL BY PROFESSION Intensive training programs in interpreting = **parallel processing of input and output**	Increase in the volume of grey matter in regions that are involved in semantic processing, learning, motor control, and domain-general EFs	Hervais-Adelman, Moser-Mercer, and Golestani (2015)

continued

Table 7.3 (cont.)

Source in bilingualism (assumptions, explanations, theories)	Effect on brain (neuroscientific evidence)	Example studies and reviews
SI trainees	**Increased cortical thickness** in temporal, parietal, and dorsal premotor regions that are important to phonetic, lexico-semantic, and executive functions **Increased activity** in frontobasal and perisylvian regions, with maximal recruitment of linguistic and cognitive control hubs (e.g., superior temporal and PFCs)	Hervais-Adelman et al. (2017) Hervais-Adelman et al. (2014) Review: García (2019)
Interpreter trainees and translator trainees after training	**Increase of structural connectivity** in the frontal-basal ganglia subnetwork typically associated with domain-general and language-specific cognitive control and in the cerebellum and the supplementary motor area, an important proposed language control network	Van de Putte et al. (2018)
Professional interpreters with sustained interpreting practice after years of experience	Reductions in volume of the bilateral middle anterior cingulate gyrus, the middle anterior insula, the superior middle gyrus, the pars triangularis	Elmer, Hänggi, and Jäncke (2014) Similarly, changes in grey matter density have been observed as reflections of lifelong bilingualism (Abutalebi et al., 2014, 2015)

Professional interpreters	Changes in grey matter density of these areas as well as of the caudate nucleus (areas are key to verbal and nonverbal functions such as WM and phonetic processing, as well as sensory-to-motor coupling)	Becker et al. (2016)
	Greater grey matter density in left frontal lobes and volumetric increase in this cognitive control area	
	Higher global functional efficiency in the left frontal pole and more functional connectivity to the left inferior and middle temporal gyri (during switching and dual tasks)	
LIFELONG BILINGUALISM Sustained, lifelong use of two languages	Promotes cognitive reserve in the elderly	Bak and Alladi (2014), Alladi et al. (2013), Alladi et al. (2017), Guzmán-Vélez and Tranel (2015), Kim et al. (2019), Heredia, Blackburn, and Vega (2020), Perani and Abutalebi (2015), Voits et al. (2020) Review: Lee (2022), Vega-Mendoza, Alladi, and Bak (2019)

continued

Table 7.3 (cont.)

Source in bilingualism (assumptions, explanations, theories)	Effect on brain (neuroscientific evidence)	Example studies and reviews
Lifelong use and prolonged duration of bilingual experience Degree of bilingual engagement	Increased efficiency in language control (shift from reliance on task-relevant cortical regions toward subcortical structures or posterior regions such as the cerebellum, as well as decreased white matter structure in frontal regions) White matter integrity in corpus callosum maintained	DeLuca, Rothman, and Pliatsikas (2019), Nichols and Joanisse (2016), Gold, Johnson, and Powell (2013), Grundy, Pavlenko, and Bialystok (2020), DeLuca and Voits (2022), Pliatsikas et al. (2021)
Continuous brain plasticity	"the brain remains much more malleable throughout the lifespan than previously claimed, meaning there is **no sharp decline in neurological plasticity culminating around puberty in general** (see Fuchs & Flügge, 2014) and certainly not as related to language" (DeLuca et al., 2019a, p. 175)	Review: DeLuca et al. (2019a), Pfenninger, Festman, and Singleton (2023)

The brain seems to adapt "on demand" – depending on length and intensity of bilingual experiences (cf. section "Bilingual by profession" in Table 7.3); therefore, the new surge of proposals for including measures that examine in depth the bilingual experience, for example, the adaptive control hypothesis (Green & Abutalebi, 2013) or language entropy (Gullifer & Titone, 2020) comes as no surprise. What is more, the brain adapts from early on, even in infants, allowing for early indications of the effects of bilingual experience with respect, in particular, to perception and attentional aspects (see Table 7.1). Finally, a lifelong bilingual experience results in a significant increase of efficiency of processes related to bilingualism and relevant domain-general processes. The experience-dependent alterations in the brain at various locations, with varying intensities, and on different timelines seem to fit our current understanding of the cognitive neuroscientific effects of bilingualism much better than earlier notions positing separate brain areas for processing and representing each language. This earlier, radical differential localization account seems outdated given the main conclusion that **brain activation overlaps to a large degree** for mono- and bilinguals as well as for early and late bilinguals (Banich & Compton, 2018; Paradis, 2004).

Review Questions

1. Which specific characteristics of bilingual experiences induce changes at the language level?
2. Which specific characteristics of bilingual experiences induce changes at the cognitive level?
3. Which specific characteristics of bilingual experiences induce changes at the brain level?
4. Why is it possible for bilingual experiences to result in changes in infants?
5. Why do language proficiency and related variables in bilingual experiences overrule the initial effects of early bilingualism?

Further Reading

Mishra, M., & Abutalebi, J. (Eds.). (2020). Cognitive consequences of bilingualism [Special issue]. *Journal of Cultural Cognitive Science*, *4*(2).

Pliatsikas, C. (2020). Understanding structural plasticity in the bilingual brain: The Dynamic Restructuring Model. *Bilingualism: Language and Cognition*, *23*(2), 459–471.

Schwieter, J. W. (Ed.). (2016). *Cognitive control and consequences of multilingualism*. Benjamins.

Small, S., & Watkins, K. (Eds.). (2021). Bilingualism and executive function [Special issue]. *Neurobiology of Language, 2*(4).

Van den Noort, M., Bosch, P., & Struys, E. (Eds.). (2020). Individual variation and the bilingual advantage: Factors that modulate the effect of bilingualism on cognitive control and cognitive reserve [Special issue]. *Behavioral Sciences, 9*(12).

CHAPTER EIGHT

Conclusion

Learning Objectives

- Understand how linguistic, cognitive, and neuroscientific research approaches complement one another in the quest toward understanding bilingualism on a cognitive neuroscientific level.
- Learn about why there cannot be an "easy story" to tell regarding the effects of bilingualism on language, the mind, and the brain.
- Reflect on the differences between treating bilingualism as a dichotomous or a continuous variable in research.
- Gain an overview of new ways of understanding the bilingual experience.
- Understand the necessity of including relevant factors (social, cultural, educational, input-specific, etc.) in study designs involving bilinguals.
- Identify current research gaps in the literature on the cognitive neuroscience of bilingualism.

8.1 Introduction

A great deal of research over the twentieth century has informed our understanding of language, cognition, and the brain. Bilingualism, as we mentioned in Chapter 1, is a reality for the majority of people today, and thus is an excellent way to research these areas from different angles. In this book, we brought together these different perspectives, scientific disciplines, and their methods. Although plentiful, the existing research we have included is by no means complete. Therefore, in addition to many research articles, we have referenced reviews, empirical studies, and further readings for additional overviews. Of course, it is impossible to cover all areas in great depth, so we hope that readers will be inspired to deepen their knowledge by being guided by the references and further reading suggestions throughout the book. As bilingualism research is a very productive field of science stretching over several scientific disciplines, new articles are continuously being published, so it is worthwhile for the interested reader to keep abreast of the most recent literature.

Our understanding of two languages in one brain is continuously developing, becoming more detailed and precise – but it is still only a fragment of what needs to be understood to fully grasp the workings of the brain and the impact of a great number of influential factors (see Bialystok, Craik, & Luk, 2012).

8.2 Complexity as the Main Issue

One of the main conclusions to be drawn from our discussions is that bilingualism, language, the brain, and behavior all are complex; consequently, there cannot be an "easy story" to tell regarding the effects of bilingualism on language, the mind, and the brain. Given this complexity, one might ask: Is it possible that all bilinguals can be "the same" in one respect – reflecting the reasoning behind group-wise comparisons to monolinguals? Or is it more likely that individual differences, including various language histories, together with social environments and different trajectories, complicate things further?

Currently, as we have outlined, there are many foundations of bilingualism research, and we will close this book by drawing attention to them to inspire more research. First, earlier (and rather dichotomous) ideas of early versus late bilinguals, monolinguals versus bilinguals, the critical period, and the bilingual advantage – to name but a few – have been intensely researched, have produced conflicting results, have undergone immense discussion, and have been rebutted to some extent. Today, there is a call to treat bilingualism as a **continuous variable** (Luk & Bialystok, 2013; but see e.g., Champoux-Larsson & Dylman, 2021, for an operationalization of bilingualism as dichotomous and continuous variable and a comparison of task results, or Kremin & Byers-Heinlein, 2021, for newer statistical models that combine both). In a study by Sulpizio et al. (2020), the authors showed the unique contributions and modulation of distinct factors (e.g., language proficiency, AoA of L2, and language use) on resting-state functional connectivity and suggested that bilingualism be investigated as a "gradient measure."

Second, there is still **no clear definition of bilingualism** (cf. Chapter 1, de Bot, 2019, and Surrain & Luk, 2019, for new efforts of systematizing labels and descriptions). There are specific questionnaires which collect language history, and there is the possibility of these providing **aggregated scores** for language proficiency, language dominance, and language immersion levels (see Li et al., 2020). To advance these dialogues and to offer solutions, Marian and Hakayawa (2021; see also for a discussion of earlier options to assess and quantify bilingualism) recently put forward the idea of a "**bilingual quotient**" or degree of bilingualism (Anderson et al., 2018), while other researchers are on a quest to determine a "**bilingual signature**" (e.g., Jasińska & Petitto, 2014; Kovelman et al., 2008) or, more recently, "**bilingual phenotype(s)**" (Beatty-Martínez & Titone, 2021; de Leon et al., 2020; Green, Crinion, & Price, 2006; Navarro-Torres et al., 2021).

Third, the **frequency and recency** of language use (per item or language) have long been suggested as critical criteria determining language availability or loss (Paradis, 2004). Today, these aspects have come back into focus (e.g., Korenar, Treffers-Daller, & Pliatsikas, 2022) when putting forward **usage-based approaches** to bilingualism.

In this book, we have described at great length that language acquisition is largely **experience-dependent and how experiences impact language development, cognition, and the brain at different levels**. Thus, it is fundamental to portray bilinguals' experiences in acquiring, learning, and using their languages, and to include these in an informative, thorough, and concise way in studies. A bilingual's language use, or "**bilingual experience**" as it is often called today, has been categorized in many different ways (e.g., DeLuca, Rothman, & Pliatsikas, 2019b, 2020). Grosjean (2001, 2013) has put forward the **language mode** hypothesis, while Green and Abutalebi (2013) have suggested three different language use contexts in their **adaptive control hypothesis**. More recently, Gullifer and Titone (2020) proposed "**language entropy**" as a way to include social diversity in a bilingual's language use.

Fourth, although research today includes **many more variables** compared to past studies, there is still a need for the inclusion of more influential factors and a rich characterization and description of the participants involved in studies (e.g., Green & Abutalebi, 2016). Moreover, there is a continuous call for attention to be paid to "**understudied factors** contributing to variability in cognitive performance related to language learning" (cf. Long et al., 2020, for their paper with this title).

Of course, a while ago, in a book on research methods, Marian (2008) rightly pointed out: "it is not possible to control for every single **potentially confounding variable**" (p. 18), and therefore suggests: "When designing a study, consider the factors that are most likely to pose a problem for that particular research question and focus on those" (p. 18). To make a decision about what most likely poses a problem, we probably have to gain a more complete picture of possible confounding variables and their impact on the topic under investigation. What is more, many of the variables are interrelated and interact with one another (Del Maschio & Abutalebi, 2019), making it even more difficult to disentangle them when designing studies and analyzing data. Until we see the full picture, we need to be careful when investigating single pieces of the bilingual mosaic. One attempt to grasp the impact of **moderator variables** in research along the lines of the bilingual advantage has been undertaken by Festman, Czapka, and Winsler (2023) (see Dash, Joanette, & Ansaldo, 2022) for concrete suggestions, in particular regarding statistical approaches).

Fifth, as language use often involves **interaction**, researchers called for the inclusion of **language processing contexts** (e.g., Wu & Thierry, 2010) and **social contexts** (Luk & Grundy, 2023). For instance, language use is embedded in cultural context; therefore cultural background does play a role (see e.g., Barac & Bialystok, 2012; Tran, Arredondo, & Yoshida, 2019), as does **SES** (e.g., Grote, Scott, & Gilger, 2021; Naeem et al., 2018), because an impoverished environment has a negative impact on cognitive development and brain volume and structure (Kishiyama et al., 2009; Noble et al., 2012; see e.g., Ursache & Noble, 2016, for a review). Some researchers have succeeded in shifting our predominantly **Western-oriented view of bilingualism** to other multilingual countries, for example, Africa and India (Alladi et al., 2013; Iyer et al., 2014; Mishra, 2015).

Crucially, it is important to consider Ortega's (2020) plea that "unique and language-shaping experience of minoritization" should no longer be overlooked and "heritage speakers and their languages must be understood as connected to **minoritized communities** and to the experience of inequitable multilingualism" (p. 15; see also Ortega, 2019). Because the discourse of brain science affirms middle-class values/lifestyles by invoking cultural practices and preferences specific to this group in the discourse's explication of the "ideal" environment for "stimulating" neurological development (Nadesan, 2002, p. 429), there is also a **strong need for more cross-cultural comparisons** (cf. Kidd, Donnelly, & Christiansen, 2018; Nielsen & Haun, 2016) and respective differences across cultures (Pfenninger, Festman, & Singleton, 2023).

Sixth, language learning is an intriguing topic when taking the **social environment of schools** and all that comes with this into consideration. Social psychology is one main approach, but research into the realm of education should also be undertaken. Many of these factors, including **learning, motivation, self-concept development, emotional effects of classroom experience,** and **foreign language anxiety** (see e.g., Blakemore & Frith, 2005; Bruhn et al., 2023; Dewaele & Li, 2020; Gregersen & Mercer, 2022; Lambert, 1980; Renninger & Hidi, 2019; Wright, Boun, & García, 2017) have been largely overlooked in cognitive neuroscience studies on those participants who experienced languages in the school context.

Research on **immersion** effects have been popular, but a distinction should be made between immersion in the school context with language lessons and opportunities to use both languages versus being immersed only in the L2, the language of education in that school (e.g., Bialystok, 2018b; Gillet, Barbu, & Poncelet, 2020; Trebits et al., 2022; see Kersten & Winsler, 2022, for an overview). Additionally, there is an interesting line of research on adults' immersion (Bice, Yamasaki, & Prat, 2020; DeLuca, Rothman, & Pliatsikas, 2019; Försterling et al., 2023; Linck, Kroll, & Sunderman, 2009; Osterhout et al., 2006; Pliatsikas et al., 2017, 2020; Soares et al., 2021; Zhang et al., 2021). Note that immersion in this latter context can differ substantially from immersive school programs and thus must be clearly defined and described in all studies involving it.

Seventh, some researchers are in favor of a **lifespan perspective** or developmental approaches in portraying how experiences with learning and using languages interact with development and aging (Claussenius-Kalman, Hernandez, & Li, 2021; Filippi & Bright, 2023; Filippi, D'Souza, & Bright, 2019; Luk & Rothman, 2022; Pfenninger, Festman, & Singleton, 2023). The first studies on the lifespan aspect of neuroplasticity are also worth exploring (e.g., Del Maschio et al., 2018; for theory, see Pliatsikas, 2020). Considering the lifelong use of languages, it is obviously not easy to grasp and quantify the **dynamic nature of language.**

Language proficiency is usually categorized via subjective measures such as self-reports and self-ratings. Objective measures (including standardized tests, assessments, etc.) are preferable; however, they also only give a momentary indication of language performance, not necessarily of competence, and certainly do not represent language abilities across the lifespan. Differences in language proficiency, learning context, and a person's individual differences pose significant challenges for research on bilingualism, with respect to methodological aspects in particular, but also concerning the generalizability of findings as applied to the entire bilingual population. As has been shown throughout the book, language use – as the use of any skill – increases proficiency, reduces processing demands, and increases efficiency. This can be captured in different ways, be it a reduction of errors, an increase in processing speed (e.g., response times), modulations in ERP components, or amount of regional activation, to give just a few examples. In terms of bilingualism research, it is consequently important that the use of both languages, separately and in combination, be portrayed in research studies. Therefore, switching behavior is one additional aspect to be taken into consideration. Rodriguez-Fornells et al. (2012) were the first to come up with a **bilingual switching questionnaire**; more recently, Olson (2022) presented a "Bilingual Code-Switching Profile" questionnaire, whereas Jylkkä et al. (2020) focused on the assessment of **momentary switching** behavior rather than the retrospective self-reports used in most other questionnaires.

Similarly, as Pfenninger, Festman, and Singleton (2023) have pointed out, some language acquisition processes are, from early on, highly sensitive to environmental input and thus to the encounter of specific and unique environments. The dynamic nature even of **language quality characteristics** should not be overlooked as it commonly changes over time, even in young children. Although initial input for newborns and infants may be strongly dominated by their mothers, as children grow older, they are commonly exposed to different speakers and caregivers and *their* respective language input (e.g., Golinkoff et al., 2019). Even more so, as families differ in size (depending on the cultural community) siblings can play a role in modifying language input at home (cf. Bridges & Hoff, 2014; Brody, 2004; Duncan & Paradis, 2020; Tsinivits & Unsworth, 2021).

Furthermore, **high instructional quality and emotional support** in daycare have been found to play crucial roles in the development of languages. After attending kindergarten, children showed better language, preacademic, and social skills if they received sensitive and stimulating interactions with the teacher, compared to those institutions which only provided moderate responsiveness and sensitivity (Burchinal et al., 2008, 2010). Unfortunately, "the most **disadvantaged children** are least likely to attend center-based childcare or organized preschools early in their lives, and the programs they do attend are likely to be of lower quality than the programs used by higher-income families" (Huston & Bentley, 2010, p. 426). This contrast again not only highlights the need to carefully portray the circumstances of participants' living and learning, but also shows the aspects that need to be improved in order to reduce educational inequity and inequality. This being said, it should not be automatically assumed that children from lower SES families receive less verbal input (see e.g., Sperry, Sperry, & Miller, 2019, who carefully studied the amount of language exposure in young children's environments and came to this conclusion). Importantly, if there is only acoustic input, a child does not necessarily have or use the opportunity for language interaction and communicative improvement of language skills, as such language might not be directed to the child. Relatedly, it was found that variability of language outcomes across children with cochlear implants was dependent on whether language was only overheard or actually child-directed (Arjmandi, Houston, & Dilley, 2022). Critically, Golinkoff et al. (2019) highlight the "importance of retaining focus on the vital ingredient to language learning – quality speech directed to children rather than overheard speech" (p. 985).

Eighth, the field is still struggling with the problems of the **reliability, validity, task impurity, and ecological validity** of executive function tests (see e.g., Antoniou, 2019; Blanco-Elorrieta & Pylkkänen, 2018; Burgess, 2004; Burgess et al., 1998; Czapka & Festman, 2021; Friedman, 2016; Miyake et al., 2000; Paap & Sawi, 2016; Soveri et al., 2018; Wallisch et al., 2018). On top of that, there is a clear need for a **conclusive theory** – on which the bilingual advantage could be based and which could guide research in the future (Blanco-Elorrieta & Caramazza, 2021; de Bruin, Dick, & Carreiras, 2021; Paap & Sawi, 2014). Due to the complexity of language, cognition, and the brain that we have outlined throughout this book, it is not surprising that no coherent theory has been put forth.

Ninth, group comparisons between mono- and bilinguals seem less informative today than in earlier times. This change of interest and research design might be explained by the differences in questions asked related to bilingualism. For one, it no longer seems necessary to disprove the notion that learning another language might be detrimental to a person's development or cognitive health, as was suggested in earlier times. The bilingual advantage debate has clearly shown that possible cognitive effects do not play out for every bilingual individual in the same way. The shift for designing research in the field of bilingualism seems to be necessarily more **interdisciplinary in nature, given the scope of the topic, favoring more longitudinal designs to reveal developmental aspects of bilingualism and how relevant factors modulate language-, cognitive-, and brain-related outcomes**. Such *within-group comparisons* across time allow for some reduction of confounding variables which might distort the results, since the same participants are tested; only the time changes and, along with this, maturational effects, learning, and experience. Unfortunately, four major issues darken the otherwise bright attraction for longitudinal designs: (a) there is a high financial burden in times when research funding has been severely cut, making such studies in less wealthy countries even more unlikely; (b) there is a high likelihood of participants dropping out over the course of time (by moving away, withdrawing their willingness to participate, etc.); (c) there is a need for large participant samples to be representative of the multifaceted bilingual population; and (d) the time aspect itself (language development investigations looking, e.g., at lexical development of children over the first six years of life take up six years of data collection). Ideally, such longitudinal studies would also investigate bilingual development in different areas, including language, cognitive, or neuroscientific in nature. Only collaborations across different labs with **multicenter studies** (a term borrowed from health research) could possibly realize such an endeavor. In embracing such a research design, studies could be conducted in multiple, independent research centers following the same procedure, leading to a large sample size from different speech communities and allowing for generalizability of the findings.

Recent very interesting longitudinal or large-scale studies in the field of bilingualism, for example investigating brain adaptations in reference to learning an L2 or the bilingual advantage, are signaling current possibilities and the way to pursue these (e.g., DeLuca, Rothman, & Pliatsikas, 2019; Dick et al., 2019; Filippi & Bright, 2023; Hartanto, Toh, & Yang, 2019; Legault et al., 2019; Liu et al., 2021a, 2021b; Mukadam et al., 2018).

8.3 Summary

This book has shed light on changes inflicted on language, cognition, and the brain itself by learning an L2, rather than focusing on the advantages and disadvantages of being bilingual. To obtain a more realistic picture of bilingualism including its assets (i.e., what is easier, what are the gains) and its difficulties (what struggles do speakers experience, what is exhausting and leads to high consumption of mental resources), we have drawn on research from different disciplines that were introduced in Chapter 1. Fernández-López and Perea (2019) have spelled out suggestions on how to end the "bilingual war(s)." We conclude this chapter and book with a noteworthy citation: "As a field, we are in the early stages of understanding the precise aspects of bilingual experience that give rise to different trajectories and outcomes [...]. By providing a rich characterization of bilingual speakers in terms of their habits of language use and in relation to their interactional context, we can more effectively extract signals from noise" (Beatty-Martínez & Titone, 2021, p. 6).

Review Questions

1. Which factors make language, its acquisition, and processing so complex?
2. Which aspects of bilingualism can explain why cognition, its development, and processing are so complex?
3. Why is the brain, its malleability, and processing so difficult to research?

4. Discuss why more studies on bilingualism are necessary for our understanding of language, mind, and brain.
5. What must be considered and integrated in research designs in future studies?

Further Reading

Andrews, E. (2014). *Neuroscience and multilingualism*. Cambridge University Press.

Fabbro, F. (1999). *The neurolinguistics of bilingualism: An introduction*. Taylor & Francis.

Garraffa, M., Sorace, A., & Vender, M., with Schwieter, J. W. (2023). *Bilingualism matters: Language learning across the lifespan*. Cambridge University Press.

Grosjean, F., & Li, P. (2013). *The psycholinguistics of bilingualism*. Wiley-Blackwell.

Kersten, K., & Winsler, A. (Eds.). (2023). *Understanding variability in second language acquisition, bilingualism, and cognition: A multi-layered perspective*. Taylor & Francis.

Willem, R. (Ed.). (2015). *Cognitive neuroscience of natural language use*. Cambridge University Press.

References

Abo, M., Senoo, A., Watanabe, S., Miyano, S., Doseki, K., Sasaki, N., ... & Yonemoto, K. (2004). Language-related brain function during word repetition in post-stroke aphasics. *NeuroReport*, *15*, 1891–1894.

Abutalebi, J. (2008). Neural aspects of second language representation and language control. *Acta Psychologica*, *128*(3), 466–478.

Abutalebi, J., & Green, D. (2007). Bilingual language production: The neurocognition of language representation and control. *Journal of Neurolinguistics*, *20*, 242–275.

Abutalebi, J., & Green, D. (2008). Control mechanisms in bilingual language production: Neural evidence from language switching studies. *Language and Cognitive Processes*, *23*, 557–582.

Abutalebi, J., & Green, D. (2016). Neuroimaging of language control in bilinguals: Neural adaptation and reserve. *Bilingualism: Language and Cognition*, *19*(4), 689–698.

Abutalebi, J., Canini, M., Della Rosa, P. A., Sheung, L. P., Green, D. W., & Weekes, B. S. (2014). Bilingualism protects anterior temporal lobe integrity in aging. *Neurobiology of Aging*, *35*(9), 2126–2133.

Abutalebi, J., Cappa, S., & Perani, D. (2001). The bilingual brain as revealed by functional neuroimaging. *Bilingualism: Language and Cognition*, *4*(2), 179–290.

Abutalebi, J., Cappa, S., & Perani, D. (2005). What can functional neuroimaging tell us about the bilingual brain? In J. Kroll & A. de Groot (Eds.), *Handbook of bilingualism: Psycholinguistic approaches* (pp. 497–515). Oxford University Press.

Abutalebi, J., Della Rosa, P., Ding, G., Weekes, B., Costa, A., & Green, D. (2013). Language proficiency modulates the engagement of cognitive control areas in multilinguals. *Cortex*, *49*(3), 905–911.

Abutalebi, J., Della Rosa, P., Green, D. W., Hernandez, M., Scifo, P., Keim, R., ... & Costa, A. (2012). Bilingualism tunes the anterior cingulate cortex for conflict monitoring. *Cerebral Cortex*, *22*(9), 2076–2086.

Abutalebi, J., Guidi, L., Borsa, V., Canini, M., Della Rosa, P. A., Parris, B. A., & Weekes, B. S. (2015). Bilingualism provides a neural reserve for aging populations. *Neuropsychologia*, *69*, 201–210.

Abutalebi, J., Miozzo, A., & Cappa, S. F. (2000). Do subcortical structures control 'language selection' in polyglots? Evidence from pathological language mixing. *Neurocase*, *6*, 51–56.

Abutalebi, J., Rosa, P., Tettamanti, M., Green, D., & Cappa, S. (2009). Bilingual aphasia and language control: A follow-up fMRI and intrinsic connectivity study. *Brain and Language, 109*, 141–156.

Agustín-Llach, M. (2019). The impact of bilingualism on the acquisition of an additional language: Evidence from lexical knowledge, lexical fluency, and (lexical) cross-linguistic influence. *International Journal of Bilingualism, 23*(5), 888–900.

Albert, M., & Obler, L. (1978). *The bilingual brain: Neuropsychological and neurolinguistic aspects of bilingualism.* Academic Press.

Al-Hoorie, A. H., & MacIntyre, P. D. (Eds.). (2019). *Contemporary language motivation theory: 60 years since Gardner and Lambert (1959).* Multilingual Matters.

Alladi, S., Bak, T. H., Duggirala, V., Surampudi, B., Shailaja, M., Shukla, A. K., et al. (2013). Bilingualism delays age at onset of dementia, independent of education and immigration status. *Neurology, 81*, 22.

Alladi, S., Bak, T., Mekala, S., Rajan, A., Chaudhuri, J., Mioshi, E., ... & Duggirala, V. (2015). Impact of bilingualism on cognitive outcome after stroke. *Stroke, 47*(1), 258–261.

Alladi, S., Bak, T. H., Shailaja, M., Gollahallo, D., Rajan, A., Surampudi, B., et al. (2017). Bilingualism delays the onset of behavioral but not aphasic forms of frontotemporal dementia. *Neuropsychologia, 99*, 207–212.

Amengual, M. (2016). Cross-linguistic influence in the bilingual mental lexicon: Evidence of cognate effects in the phonetic production and processing of a vowel contrast. *Frontiers in Psychology, 7*(617), 1–17.

Amengual, M., & Chamorro, P. (2015). The effects of language dominance in the perception and production of the Galician mid vowel contrasts. *Phonetica, 72*, 207–236.

Amengual, M., & Simonet, M. (2020). Language dominance does not always predict cross-linguistic interactions in bilingual speech production. *Linguistic Approaches to Bilingualism, 10*(6), 847–872.

Anderson, J. A., Grundy, J. G., De Frutos, J., Barker, R. M., Grady, C., & Bialystok, E. (2018). Effects of bilingualism on white matter integrity in older adults. *Neuroimage, 167*, 143–150.

Anderson, J. A., Mak, L., Keyvani Chahi, A., & Bialystok, E. (2018). The language and social background questionnaire: Assessing degree of bilingualism in a diverse population. *Behavior Research Methods, 50*(1), 250–263.

Anderson, N. J., Graham, S. A., Prime, H., Jenkins, J. M., & Madigan, S. (2021). Linking quality and quantity of parental linguistic input to child language skills: A meta-analysis. *Child Development, 92*(2), 484–501.

Andrews, E. (2019). Cognitive neuroscience and multilingualism. In J. W. Schwieter (Ed.), *The handbook of the neuroscience of multilingualism* (pp. 19–47). Wiley.

Andric, M., & Small, S. L. (2015). fMRI methods for studying the neurobiology of language under naturalistic conditions. In R. M. Willems (Ed.), *Cognitive neuroscience of natural language use* (pp. 8–28). Cambridge University Press.

Angelovska, T., & Hahn, A. (Eds.). (2017). *L3 syntactic transfer: Models, new developments, and implications.* Benjamins.

Ansaldo, A., & Saidi, L. (2014). Aphasia therapy in the age of globalization: Crosslinguistic therapy effects in bilingual aphasia. *Behavioral Neurology, 2014*(603085), 1–10.

Ansaldo, A. I., Ghazi-Saidi, L., & Adrover-Roig, D. (2015). Interference control in elderly bilinguals: Appearances can be misleading. *Journal of Clinical and Experimental Neuropsychology, 37*(5), 455–470.

Ansaldo, A., Ghazi Saidi, L., & Ruiz, A. (2009). Model-driven intervention in bilingual aphasia: Evidence from a case of pathological switching. *Aphasiology, 9*, 1–16.

Ansaldo, A., Marcotte, K., Scherer, L., & Raboyeau, G. (2008). Language therapy and bilingual aphasia: Clinical implications of psycholinguistic and neuroimaging research. *Journal of Neurolinguistics, 21*(6), 539–557.

Antón, E., Carreiras, M., & Duñabeitia, J. A. (2019). The impact of bilingualism on executive functions and working memory in young adults. *PloS One, 14*(2), e0206770.

Antón, E., Duñabeitia, J. A., Estévez, A., Hernández, J. A., Castillo, A., Fuentes, L. J., ... & Carreiras, M. (2014). Is there a bilingual advantage in the ANT task? Evidence from children. *Frontiers in Psychology, 5*, 398.

Antoniou, M. (2019). The advantages of bilingualism debate. *Annual Review of Linguistics, 5*, 395–415.

Antovich, D. M., & Graf Estes, K. (2018). Learning across languages: Bilingual experience supports dual language statistical word segmentation. *Developmental Science, 21*(2), e12548.

Aoyama, K. (2003). Perception of syllable-initial and syllable-final nasals in English by Korean and Japanese speakers. *Second Language Research, 19*, 251–265.

Archila-Suerte, P., Woods, E. A., Chiarello, C., & Hernandez, A. E. (2018). Neuroanatomical profiles of bilingual children. *Developmental Science, 21*(5), e12654

Argyri, E., & Sorace, A. (2007). Crosslinguistic influence and language dominance in older bilingual children. *Bilingualism: Language and Cognition, 10*(1), 79–99.

Arjmandi, M. K., Houston, D., & Dilley, L. C. (2022). Variability in quantity and quality of early linguistic experience in children with cochlear implants: Evidence from analysis of natural auditory environments. *Ear and Hearing, 43*(2), 685–698.

Arredondo, M. M., Aslin, R. N., & Werker, J. F. (2022). Bilingualism alters infants' cortical organization for attentional orienting mechanisms. *Developmental Science*, *25*(2), e13172.

Arredondo, M. M., Hu, X. S., Satterfield, T., & Kovelman, I. (2017). Bilingualism alters children's frontal lobe functioning for attentional control. *Developmental Science*, *20*(3), e12377.

Athanasopoulos, P. (2009). Cognitive representation of color in bilinguals: The case of Greek blues. *Bilingualism: Language and Cognition*, *12*(1), 83–95.

Athanasopoulos, P. (2011). Cognitive restructuring in bilingualism. In A. Pavlenko (Ed.), *Thinking and speaking in two languages* (pp. 29–65). Multilingual Matters.

Athanasopoulos, P. (2015). Conceptual representation in bilinguals. In J. W. Schwieter (Ed.), *The Cambridge handbook of bilingual processing* (pp. 275–292). Cambridge University Press.

Athanasopoulos, P., & Kasai, C. (2008). Language and thought in bilinguals: The case of grammatical number and nonverbal classification preferences. *Applied Psycholinguistics*, *29*(1), 105–121.

Babcock, L., & Vallesi, A. (2017). Are simultaneous interpreters expert bilinguals, unique bilinguals, or both? *Bilingualism: Language and Cognition, 20*(2), 403–417.

Baddeley, A. D. (1986). *Working memory*. Oxford University Press.

Baillet, S. (2017). Magnetoencephalography for brain electrophysiology and imaging. *Nature Neuroscience*, *20*(3), 327–339.

Bajo, M. T., Padilla, F., & Padilla, P. (2000). Comprehension processes in simultaneous interpreting. In A. Chesterman, N. Gallardo San Salvador, & Y. Gambier (Eds.), *Translation in context* (pp. 127–142). Benjamins.

Bak T. H., & Alladi S. (2014). Can being bilingual affect the onset of dementia? *Future Neurology, 9*, 101–103.

Bak, T. H., Vega-Mendoza, M., & Sorace, A. (2014). Never too late? An advantage on tests of auditory attention extends to late bilinguals. *Frontiers in Psychology*, *5*, 485.

Bakker, I., Takashima, A., van Hell, J. G., Janzen, G., & McQueen, J. M. (2015). Tracking lexical consolidation with ERPs: Lexical and semantic-priming effects on N400 and LPC responses to newly-learned words. *Neuropsychologia*, *79*, 33–41.

Banich, M. T., & Compton, R. J. (2018). *Cognitive neuroscience* (4th ed.). Cambridge University Press.

Barac, R., & Bialystok, E. (2012). Bilingual effects on cognitive and linguistic development: Role of language, cultural background, and education. *Child Development*, *83*(2), 413–422.

Barbu, C. A., Gillet, S., & Poncelet, M. (2020). Investigating the effects of language-switching frequency on attentional and executive functioning in proficient bilinguals. *Frontiers in Psychology*, *11*, 1078.

Bardel, C., & Falk, Y. (2007). The role of the second language in third language acquisition: The case of Germanic syntax. *Second Language Research*, 23(4), 459–484.

Basnight-Brown, D. (2014). Models of lexical access and bilingualism. In R. Heredia & J. Altarriba (Eds.), *Foundations of bilingual memory* (pp. 85–107). Springer.

Basnight-Brown, D., & Altarriba, J. (2007). Differences in semantic and translation priming across languages: The role of language direction and language dominance. *Memory & Cognition, 35*, 953–965.

Basser, P. J. (1995). Inferring microstructural features and the physiological state of tissues from diffusion-weighted images. *NMR in Biomedicine*, 8(7), 333–344.

Basso, A., Capitani, E., & Moraschini, S. (1982). Sex differences in recovery from aphasia. *Cortex*, *18*(3), 469–475.

Bates, E., & MacWhinney, B. (1989). Functionalism and the Competition Model. In B. MacWhinney & E. Bates (Eds.), *The crosslinguistic study of sentence processing* (pp. 3–73). Cambridge University Press.

Beatens Beardsmore, H. (1986). *Bilingualism: Basic principles* (Vol. 1). Multilingual Matters.

Beatty-Martínez, A., & Dussias, P. (2017). Bilingual experience shapes language processing: Evidence from codeswitching. *Journal of Memory and Language*, *95*, 173–189.

Beatty-Martínez, A. L., & Titone, D. A. (2021). The quest for signals in noise: Leveraging experiential variation to identify bilingual phenotypes. *Languages*, *6*(4), 168.

Becker, M., Schubert, T., Strobach, T., Gallinat, J., & Kühn, S. (2016). Simultaneous interpreters vs. professional multilingual controls: Group differences in cognitive control as well as brain structure and function. *Neuroimage*, *134*, 250–260.

Benati, A., & Schwieter, J. W. (2017). Input processing and processing instruction: Pedagogical and cognitive considerations for L3 acquisition. In T. Angelovska & A. Hahn (Eds.), *L3 syntactic transfer: Models, new developments, and implications* (pp. 253–275). Benjamins.

Ben-Zeev, S. (1977). The influence of bilingualism on cognitive strategy and cognitive development. *Child Development*, *48*(3), 1009–1018.

Bergelson, E., Soderstrom, M., Schwarz, I. C., Rowland, C. F., Ramirez-Esparza, N., ... & Cristia, A. (2022). Everyday language input and production in 1001 children from 6 continents. *PNAS*. https://doi.org/10.31234/osf.io/fjr5q.

Berk, L. (2015). *Child development*. Pearson Higher Education AU.

Berken, J. A., Gracco, V. L., Chen, J. K., & Klein, D. (2016). The timing of language learning shapes brain structure associated with articulation. *Brain Structure and Function, 221*(7), 3591–3600.

Best, C. C., & McRoberts, G. W. (2003). Infant perception of non-native consonant contrasts that adults assimilate in different ways. *Language and Speech, 46*(2–3), 183–216.

Bialystok, E. (1999). Cognitive complexity and attentional control in the bilingual mind. *Child Development, 70*(3), 636–644.

Bialystok, E. (2017). The bilingual adaptation: How minds accommodate experience. *Psychological Bulletin, 143*(3), 233–262.

Bialystok, E. (2018a). Bilingualism and executive function: What's the connection? In D. Miller, F. Bayram, J. Rothman, & L. Serratrice (Eds.), *Bilingual cognition and language: The state of the science across its subfields* (pp. 283–305). Benjamins.

Bialystok, E. (2018b). Bilingual education for young children: Review of the effects and consequences. *International Journal of Bilingual Education and Bilingualism, 21*(6), 666–679.

Bialystok, E. (2021). Bilingualism: Pathway to cognitive reserve. *Trends in Cognitive Sciences, 25*(5), 355–364.

Bialystok, E., & Craik, F. (2015). Cognitive consequences of bilingualism: Executive control and cognitive reserve. In J. W. Schwieter (Ed.), *The Cambridge handbook of bilingual processing* (pp. 571–585). Cambridge University Press.

Bialystok, E., & Martin, M. M. (2004). Attention and inhibition in bilingual children: Evidence from the dimensional change card sort task. *Developmental Science, 7*(3), 325–339.

Bialystok, E., Craik, F. I., & Freedman, M. (2007). Bilingualism as a protection against the onset of symptoms of dementia. *Neuropsychologia, 45*(2), 459–464.

Bialystok, E., Craik, F. I., & Luk, G. (2012). Bilingualism: Consequences for mind and brain. *Trends in Cognitive Sciences, 16*(4), 240–250.

Bialystok, E., Luk, G., & Kwan, E. (2005). Bilingualism, biliteracy, and learning to read: Interactions among languages and writing systems. *Scientific Studies of Reading, 9*(1), 43–61.

Bialystok, E., Poarch, G., Luo, L., & Craik, F. (2014). Effects of bilingualism and aging on executive function and working memory. *Psychology and Aging, 29*, 696–705.

Bice, K., Yamasaki, B. L., & Prat, C. S. (2020). Bilingual language experience shapes resting-state brain rhythms. *Neurobiology of Language, 1*(3), 288–318.

Bijeljac-Babic, R., Nassurally, K., Havy, M., & Nazzi, T. (2009). Infants can rapidly learn words in a foreign language. *Infant Behavior and Development, 32*(4), 476–480.

Black, S., & Behrmann, M. (1994). Localization in alexia. In A. Kertesz (Ed.), *Localization and neuroimaging in neuropsychology* (pp. 331–376). Academic Press.

Blakemore, S. J., & Choudhury, S. (2006). Development of the adolescent brain: Implications for executive function and social cognition. *Journal of Child Psychology and Psychiatry, 47*(3–4), 296–312.

Blakemore, S. J., & Frith, U. (2005). *The learning brain: Lessons for education*. Blackwell.

Blanco-Elorrieta, E., & Caramazza, A. (2021). On the need for theoretically guided approaches to possible bilingual advantages: An evaluation of the potential loci in the language and executive control systems. *Neurobiology of Language, 2*(4), 452–463.

Blanco-Elorrieta, E., & Pylkkänen, L. (2017). Bilingual language switching in the lab vs. in the wild: The spatio-temporal dynamics of adaptive language control. *Journal of Neuroscience, 37*, 9022–9036.

Blanco-Elorrieta, E., & Pylkkänen, L. (2018). Ecological validity in bilingualism research and the bilingual advantage. *Trends in Cognitive Sciences, 22*(12), 1117–1126.

Blanco-Elorrieta, E., Emmorey, K., & Pylkkänen, L. (2018). Language switching decomposed through MEG and evidence from bimodal bilinguals. *Proceedings of the National Academy of Sciences, 115*(39), 201809779.

Bloomfield, L. (1933). *Language*. Holt, Rinehart, & Winston.

Bongartz, C. (2002). *Noun combination in interlanguage: Typology effects in complex determiner phrases*. Niemeyer.

Bornstein, M. H., Hahn, C. S., & Putnick, D. L. (2016). Long-term stability of core language skill in children with contrasting language skills. *Developmental Psychology, 52*(5), 704–716.

Bosch, L., & Sebastián-Gallés, N. (1997). Native-language recognition abilities in 4-month-old infants from monolingual and bilingual environments. *Cognition, 65*(1), 33–69.

Botes, E., Dewaele, J. M., & Greiff, S. (2020). The foreign language classroom anxiety scale and academic achievement: An overview of the prevailing literature and a meta-analysis. *Journal for the Psychology of Language Learning, 2*(1), 26–56.

Böttger, H. (2016). *Neurodidaktik des frühen Sprachenlernens: Wo die Sprache zuhause ist* (Vol. 4654). utb.

Böttger, H., & Sambanis, M. (2017). *Sprachen Lernen in der Pubertät*. Narr.

Brady, M., Kelly, H., Godwin, J., Enderby, P., & Campbell, P. (2016). Speech and language therapy for aphasia following stroke. *Cochrane Database of Systematic Reviews, 6*, CD000425.

Brauer, J., Anwander, A., Perani, D., & Friederici, A. D. (2013). Dorsal and ventral pathways in language development. *Brain and Language*, *127*(2), 289–295.

Breitenstein, C., Jansen, A., Deppe, M., Foerster, A. F., Sommer, J., Wolbers, T., & Knecht, S. (2005). Hippocampus activity differentiates good from poor learners of a novel lexicon. *Neuroimage*, *25*(3), 958–968.

Brewer, J. B., Zhao, Z., Desmond, J. E., Glover, G. H., & Gabrieli, J. D. (1998). Making memories: Brain activity that predicts how well visual experience will be remembered. *Science*, *281*(5380), 1185–1187.

Bridges, K., & Hoff, E. (2014). Older sibling influences on the language environment and language development of toddlers in bilingual homes. *Applied Psycholinguistics*, *35*(2), 225–241.

Bright, P., Ouzia, J., & Filippi, R. (2019). Multilingualism and metacognitive processing. In J. Schwieter (Ed.), *The handbook of the neuroscience of multilingualism* (pp. 355–371). Wiley-Blackwell.

Broca, P. (1861). Perte de la parole. Ramollissement chronique en destruction partielle de lobe antérieur gauche de cerveau. *Bulletin de la Société d' Anthropologie*, *2*, 235–238.

Brodmann, K. (1909). *Vergleichende Lokalisationslehre der Großhirnrinde in ihren Prinzipien dargestellt auf Grund des Zellenbaues*. Leipzig.

Brody, G. H. (2004). Siblings' direct and indirect contributions to child development. *Current Directions in Psychological Science*, *13*(3), 124–126.

Brooks, R., & Meltzoff, A. N. (2005). The development of gaze following and its relation to language. *Developmental Science*, *8*(6), 535–543.

Bruhn, A. C., Genzer, M., Thies, L., Koch, M. J., & Kersten, K. (2023). The interplay of young learners' verbal self-concept and linguistic competences over time in monolingual and bilingual institutions. In Böttger, H., & Schlüter, N. (Eds.), *Fortschritte im frühen Fremdsprachenlernen. Konferenzband zur 5. Tagung im Dezember 2021* (pp. 94–124). Schriftbild.

Bruhn, A. C., Miller, L., Mähler, C., Ponto, K., & Kersten, K. (2022). Can type of schooling compensate for low SES? Investigating effects of instruction and SES on cognitive skills. In Kersten, K., & Winsler, A. (Eds.), *Understanding variability in second language acquisition, bilingualism, and cognition: A multi-layered perspective* (pp. 292–320). Routledge.

Brysbaert, M., & Duyck, W. (2010). Is it time to leave behind the Revised Hierarchical Model of bilingual language processing after fifteen years of service? *Bilingualism: Language and Cognition*, *13*, 359–371.

Brysbaert, M., & Mitchell, D. (1996). Modifier attachment in sentence processing: Evidence from Dutch. *The Quarterly Journal of Experimental Psychology*, *49A*, 664–695.

Brysbaert, M., Mandera, P., & Keuleers, E. (2018). The word frequency effect in word processing: An updated review. *Current Directions in Psychological Science*, *27*, 45–50.

Buchweitz, A., & Prat, C. (2013). The bilingual brain: Flexibility and control in the human cortex. *Physics of Life Reviews*, *10*(4), 428–443.

Buchweitz, A., Shinkareva, S. V., Mason, R. A., Mitchell, T. M., & Just, M. A. (2012). Identifying bilingual semantic neural representations across languages. *Brain and Language*, *120*(3), 282–289.

Buonomano, D. V., & Merzenich, M. M. (1998). Cortical plasticity: From synapses to maps. *Annual Review of Neuroscience*, *21*(1), 149–186.

Burchinal, M., Howes, C., Pianta, R., Bryant, D., Early, D., Clifford, R., & Barbarin, O. (2008). Predicting child outcomes at the end of kindergarten from the quality of pre-kindergarten teacher–child interactions and instruction. *Applied Development Science*, *12*(3), 140–153.

Burchinal, M., Vandergrift, N., Pianta, R., & Mashburn, A. (2010). Threshold analysis of association between child care quality and child outcomes for low-income children in pre-kindergarten programs. *Early Childhood Research Quarterly*, *25*(2), 166–176.

Burgess, P. W. (2004). Theory and methodology in executive function research. In P. Rabbitt (Ed.), *Methodology of frontal and executive function* (pp. 87–121). Routledge.

Burgess, P. W., Alderman, N., Evans, J. O. N., Emslie, H., & Wilson, B. A. (1998). The ecological validity of tests of executive function. *Journal of the International Neuropsychological Society*, *4*(6), 547–558.

Byers-Heinlein, K. (2015). Methods for studying infant bilingualism. In J. W. Schwieter (Ed.), *The Cambridge handbook of bilingual processing* (pp. 133–154). Cambridge University Press.

Byers-Heinlein, K., & Lew-Williams, C. (2013). Bilingualism in the early years: What the science says. *LEARNing Landscapes*, *7*(1), 95–112.

Byers-Heinlein, K., & Werker, J. F. (2013). Lexicon structure and the disambiguation of novel words: Evidence from bilingual infants. *Cognition*, *128*(3), 407–416.

Calabria, M., Costa, A., Green, D. W., & Abutalebi, J. (2018). Neural basis of bilingual language control. *Annals of the New York Academy of Sciences*, *1426*(1), 221–235.

Caramazza, A., Miceli, G., Silveri, M. C., & Laudanna, A. (1985). Reading mechanisms and the organisation of the lexicon: Evidence from acquired dyslexia. *Cognitive Neuropsychology*, *2*(1), 81–114.

Cappa, S., Cavallotti, G., & Vignolo, L. (1981). Phonemic and lexical errors in fluent aphasia: Correlation with lesion site. *Neuropsychologia*, *19*(2), 171–177.

Cargnelutti, E., Tomasino, B., & Fabbro, F. (2019a). Language brain representation in bilinguals with different age of appropriation and proficiency of the second language: A meta-analysis of functional imaging studies. *Frontiers in Human Neuroscience*, *13*, 154.

Cargnelutti, E., Tomasino, B. & Fabbro, F. (2019b). Aphasia in the multilingual population. In J. W. Schwieter (Ed.), *The handbook of the neuroscience of multilingualism* (pp. 533–552). Wiley-Blackwell.

Carrasco-Ortiz, H., Amengual, M., & Gries, S. Th. (2021). Cross-language effects of phonological and orthographic similarity in cognate word recognition: The role of language dominance. *Linguistic Approaches to Bilingualism*, 11(3), 389–417.

Casey, B. J. (2013). The teenage brain: An overview. *Current Directions in Psychological Science*, *22*(2), 80–81.

Casey, B. J., & Caudle, K. (2013). The teenage brain: Self control. *Current Directions in Psychological Science*, *22*(2), 82–87.

Casey, B. J., Tottenham, N., Liston, C., & Durston, S. (2005). Imaging the developing brain: What have we learned about cognitive development? *Trends in Cognitive Sciences*, *9*(3), 104–110.

Cattan, S., Fitzsimons, E., Goodman, A., Phimister, A., Ploubidis, G., & Wertz, J. (2022). Early childhood inequalities. *Institute for Fiscal Studies*, 1–5.

Champoux-Larsson, M. F., & Dylman, A. S. (2021). Different measurements of bilingualism and their effect on performance on a Simon task. *Applied Psycholinguistics*, *42*(2), 505–526.

Chaouch-Orozco, A., Alonso, J., & Rothman, J. (2019). Word frequency and the elusiveness of the L2-L1 (masked) translation priming effect. Paper presented at *The 32nd CUNY Conference on Human Sentence Processing*, University of Colorado Boulder, United States.

Chaouch-Orozco, A., Alonso, J., & Rothman, J. (2021). Individual differences in bilingual word recognition: The role of experiential factors and word frequency in cross-language lexical priming. *Applied Psycholinguistics*, *42*(2), 447–474.

Chee, M., Caplan, D., Soon, C., Sriram, N., Tan, E., … & Weekes, B. (1999). Processing of visually presented sentences in Mandarin and English studied with fMRI. *Neuron*, *23*(1), 127–137.

Chee, M., Tan, E., & Thiel, T. (1999). Mandarin and English single word processing studied with functional magnetic resonance imaging. *The Journal of Neuroscience*, *19*, 3050–3056.

Chen, B., Zhou, H., Gao, Y., & Dunlap, S. (2014). Cross-language translation priming asymmetry with Chinese-English bilinguals: A test of the sense model. *Journal of Psycholinguist Research*, *43*, 225–240.

Chen, X., & Schwartz, M. (Eds.). (2018). Morphological awareness and literacy in second language learners: A cross-language perspective [Special issue]. *Reading and Writing*, *31*(8), 1685–1694.

Cheour, M., Ceponiene, R., Lehtokoski, A., Luuk, A., Allik, J., Alho, K., & Näätänen, R. (1998). Development of language-specific phoneme representations in the infant brain. *Nature Neuroscience, 1*, 351–353.

Chin, N. B., & Wigglesworth, G. (2007). *Bilingualism: An advanced resource book*. Routledge.

Christoffels, I., de Groot, A., & Kroll, J. (2006). Memory and language skills in simultaneous interpreters: The role of expertise and language proficiency. *Journal of Memory and Language, 54*(3), 324–345.

Chung, S., Chen, X., & Geva, E. (2019). Deconstructing and reconstructing cross-language transfer. *Journal of Neurolinguistics, 50*, 149–161.

Claussenius-Kalman, H. L., & Hernandez, A. E. (2019). Neurocognitive effects of multilingualism throughout the lifespan: A developmental perspective. In J. W. Schwieter (Ed.), *The handbook of the neuroscience of multilingualism* (pp. 655–684). Wiley-Blackwell.

Claussenius-Kalman, H., Hernandez, A. E., & Li, P. (2021). Expertise, ecosystem, and emergentism: Dynamic developmental bilingualism. *Brain and Language, 222*, 105013.

Claussenius-Kalman, H., Vaughn, K. A., Archila-Suerte, P., & Hernandez, A. E. (2020). Age of acquisition impacts the brain differently depending on neuroanatomical metric. *Human Brain Mapping, 41*(2), 484–502.

Coffey, J. R., Shafto, C. L., Geren, J. C., & Snedeker, J. (2022). The effects of maternal input on language in the absence of genetic confounds: Vocabulary development in internationally adopted children. *Child Development, 93*(1), 237–253.

Cohen, D., & Cuffin, B. N. (1983). Demonstration of useful differences between magnetoencephalogram and electroencephalogram. *Electroencephalography and Clinical Neurophysiology, 56*(1), 38–51.

Cohen, N. J., & Squire, L. R. (1980). Preserved learning and retention of pattern-analyzing skill in amnesia: Dissociation of knowing how and knowing that. *Science, 210*(4466), 207–210.

Colomé, A. (2001). Lexical activation in bilinguals' speech production: Language-specific or language-independent? *Journal of Memory and Language, 45*, 721–736.

Colver, A., & Longwell, S. (2013). New understanding of adolescent brain development: Relevance to transitional healthcare for young people with long term conditions. *Archives of Disease in Childhood, 98*(11), 902–907.

Comesaña, M., Ferré, P., Romero, J., Guasch, M., Soares, A., & García-Chico, T. (2015). Facilitative effect of cognate words vanishes when reducing the orthographic overlap: The role of stimuli list composition. *Journal of Experimental Psychology. Learning, Memory, and Cognition, 41*(3), 614–635.

Conner, P., Goral, M., Anema, I., Borodkin, K., Haendler, Y., Knoph, M., ... & Moeyaert, M. (2018). The role of language proficiency and linguistic similarity in crosslinguistic treatment effects in aphasia. *Clinical Linguistics & Phonetics*, *32*, 739–757.

Connor, L., Obler, L., Tocco, M., Fitzpatrick, P., & Albert, M. (2001). Effect of socioeconomic status on aphasia severity and recovery. *Brain and Language*, 78, 254–257.

Consonni, M., Cafiero, R., Marin, D., Tettamanti, M., Iadanza, A., Fabbro, F., & Perani, D. (2013). Neural convergence for language comprehension and grammatical class production in highly proficient bilinguals is independent of age of acquisition. *Cortex*, *49*(5), 1252–1258.

Cook, V. (Ed.) (2002). *Portraits of the L2 user*. Multilingual Matters.

Cook, V., Bassetti, B., Kasai, C., Sasaki, M., & Takahashi, J. (2006). Do bilinguals have different concepts? The case of shape and material in Japanese L2 users of English. *International Journal of Bilingualism*, *10*(2), 137–152.

Cook, V., Iarossi, E., Stellakis, N., & Tokumaru, Y. (2003). Effects of the L2 on the syntactic processing of the L1. In V. Cook (Ed.), *Effects of the second language on the first* (pp. 193–213). Multilingual Matters.

Costa, A., & Santesteban, M. (2004). Lexical access in bilingual speech production: Evidence from language switching in highly proficient bilinguals and L2 learners. *Journal of Memory and Language*, *50*(4), 491–511.

Costa, A., & Sebastián-Gallés, N. (2014). How does the bilingual experience sculpt the brain? *Nature Reviews Neuroscience*, *15*(5), 336.

Costa, A., Caramazza, A., & Sebastián-Gallés, N. (2000). The cognate facilitation effect: Implications for models of lexical access. *Journal of Experimental Psychology: Learning, Memory, and Cognition*, *26*, 1283–1296.

Costa, A., Colomé, À., & Caramazza, A. (2000). Lexical access in speech production: The bilingual case. *Psicologica*, *21*(2), 403–437.

Costa, A., Colomé, A., Gómez, O., & Sebastián-Gallés, N. (2003). Another look at cross-language competition in bilingual speech production: Lexical and phonological factors. *Bilingualism: Language and Cognition*, *6*, 167–179.

Costa, A., Hernández, M., Costa-Faidella, J., & Sebastián-Gallés, N. (2009). On the bilingual advantage in conflict processing: Now you see it, now you don't. *Cognition*, *113*(2), 135–149.

Costa, A., Hernández, M., & Sebastián-Gallés, N. (2008). Bilingualism aids conflict resolution: Evidence from the ANT task. *Cognition*, *106*(1), 59–86.

Costa, A., Santesteban, M., & Ivanova, I. (2006). How do highly proficient bilinguals control their lexicalization process?: Inhibitory and language-specific selection mechanisms are both functional. *Journal*

of Experimental Psychology Learning Memory and Cognition, 32(5),
1057–1074.

Costumero, V., Rodríguez-Pujadas, A., Fuentes-Claramonte, P., & Avila,
C. (2015). How bilingualism shapes the functional architecture of the
brain: A study on executive control in early bilinguals and monolinguals.
Human Brain Mapping, 36(12), 5101–5112.

Crews, F., He, J., & Hodge, C. (2007). Adolescent cortical development: A
critical period of vulnerability for addiction. *Pharmacology Biochemistry
and Behavior, 86*(2), 189–199.

Croft, S., Marshall, J., Pring, T., & Hardwick, M. (2010). Therapy for naming
difficulties in bilingual aphasia: Which language benefits? *International
Journal of Language and Communication Disorders, 46*(1), 48–62.

Csizér, K., & Magid, M. (Eds.). (2014). *The impact of self-concept on
language learning.* Multilingual Matters.

Curtiss, S. (1977). *Genie: A psycholinguistic study of a modern day "wild
child".* Academic Press.

Czapka, S., & Festman, J. (2021). Wisconsin Card Sorting Test reveals a
monitoring advantage but not a switching advantage in multilingual
children. *Journal of Experimental Child Psychology, 204*, 105038.

D'Souza, D., & D'Souza, H. (2021). Bilingual adaptations in early
development. *Trends in Cognitive Sciences, 25*(9), 727–729.

D'Souza, D., Brady, D., Haensel, J. X., & D'Souza, H. (2020). Is mere
exposure enough? The effects of bilingual environments on infant
cognitive development. *Royal Society Open Science, 7*(2), 180–191.

Dąbrowska, E. (2012). Different speakers, different grammars: Individual
differences in native language attainment. *Linguistic Approaches to
Bilingualism, 2*(3), 219–253.

Dailey, S., & Bergelson, E. (2022). Language input to infants of different
socioeconomic statuses: A quantitative meta-analysis. *Developmental
Science, 25*(3), e13192.

Dal Ben, R., Killam, H., Pour Iliaei, S., & Byers-Heinlein, K. (2022).
Bilingualism affects infant cognition: Insights from new and open data.
Open Mind, 6, 88–117.

Damasio, H., Tranel, A., Grabowski, T., Adolphs, R., & Damasio, A.
(2004). Neural systems behind word and concept retrieval. *Cognition, 92*,
179–229.

Dash, T., Joanette, Y., & Ansaldo, A. I. (2022). Multifactorial approaches
to study bilingualism in the aging population: Past, present, future.
Frontiers in Psychology, 13, 917959.

De Angelis, G., & Selinker, L. (2001). Interlanguage transfer and competing
linguistic systems in the multilingual mind. In J. Cenoz, B. Hufeisen, &
U. Jessner (Eds.), *Crosslinguistic influence in third language acquisition:
Psycholinguistic perspectives* (pp. 42–58). Multilingual Matters.

De Baene, W., Duyck, W., Brass, M., & Carreiras, M. (2015). Brain circuit for cognitive control is shared by task and language switching. *Journal of Cognitive Neuroscience, 27*(9), 1752–1765.

de Bot, K. (2004). The multilingual lexicon: Modelling selection and control. *International Journal of Multilingualism, 1*(1), 17–32.

de Bot, K. (2008). Review article: The imaging of what in the multilingual mind? *Second Language Research, 24*(1), 111–133.

de Bot, K. (2009). Multilingualism and aging. In T. Bhatia & W. Ritchie (Eds.), *The new handbook of second language acquisition* (pp. 425–442). Emerald Group.

de Bot, K. (2019). *Defining and assessing multilingualism.* In J. W. Schwieter (Ed.), *The handbook of the neuroscience of multilingualism* (pp. 3–18). Wiley-Blackwell.

de Bruin, A., Dick, A. S., & Carreiras, M. (2021). Clear theories are needed to interpret differences: Perspectives on the bilingual advantage debate. *Neurobiology of Language, 2*(4), 433–451.

de Bruin, A., Treccani, B., & Della Sala, S. (2015). Cognitive advantage in bilingualism: An example of publication bias? *Psychological Science, 26*(1), 99–107.

De Cat, C. (2021). Socioeconomic status as a proxy for input quality in bilingual children? *Applied Psycholinguistics, 42*(2), 301–324.

De Groot, A. (1992). Bilingual lexical representation: A closer look at conceptual representations. In R. Frost & L. Katz (Eds.), *Orthography, phonology, morphology, and meaning* (pp. 389–412). Elsevier.

De Groot, A. (1993). Word-type effects in bilingual processing tasks: Support for a mixed representational system. In R. Schreuder & B. Weltens (Eds.), *The bilingual lexicon* (pp. 27–51). Benjamins.

de Groot, A. (2011). *Language and cognition in bilinguals and multilinguals: An introduction.* Routledge.

de Groot, A., & Starreveld, P. (2015). Parallel language activation in bilingual's word production and its modulating factors: A review and computer simulations. In J. W. Schwieter (Ed.), *The Cambridge handbook of bilingual processing* (pp. 389–415). Cambridge University Press.

de Groot, A., Dannenburg, L., & Van Hell, J. (1994). Forward and backward word translation by bilinguals. *Journal of Memory and Language, 33*, 600–629.

De Houwer, A. (1990). *The acquisition of two languages from birth: A case study.* Cambridge University Press.

De Houwer, A. (1995). Bilingual language acquisition. In P. Fletcher & B. MacWhinney (Eds.), *The handbook of child language* (pp. 219–250). Blackwell.

De Houwer, A. (2009). *Bilingual first language acquisition.* Multilingual Matters.

De Houwer, A. (2011). Language input environments and language development in bilingual acquisition. *Applied Linguistics Review*, *2*, 221–240.

De Houwer, A. (2021). *Bilingual development in childhood*. Cambridge University Press.

de Leon, J., Grasso, S. M., Welch, A., Miller, Z., Shwe, W., Rabinovici, G. D., ... & Gorno-Tempini, M. L. (2020). Effects of bilingualism on age at onset in two clinical Alzheimer's disease variants. *Alzheimer's & Dementia*, *16*(12), 1704–1713.

Degani, T., & Tokowicz, N. (2010). Ambiguous words are harder to learn. *Bilingualism: Language and Cognition*, *13*, 299–314.

Degani, T., Prior, A., & Tokowicz, N. (2011). Bidirectional transfer: The effect of sharing a translation. *European Journal of Cognitive Psychology*, *23*, 18–28.

Degirmenci, M. G., Grossmann, J. A., Meyer, P., & Teichmann, B. (2022). The role of bilingualism in executive functions in healthy older adults: A systematic review. *International Journal of Bilingualism*, 13670069211051291.

Dehaene, S., Dupoux, E., Mehler, J., Cohen, L., Paulesu, E., Perani, D., ... & Le Bihan, D. (1997). Anatomical variability in the cortical representation of first and second language. *NeuroReport*, *8*(17), 3809–3815.

Del Maschio, N., & Abutalebi, J. (2019). Language organization in the bilingual and multilingual brain. In J. Schwieter, (Ed.), *The handbook of the neuroscience of multilingualism* (pp. 197–213). Wiley-Blackwell.

Del Maschio, N., Sulpizio, S., Gallo, F., Fedeli, D., Weekes, B. S., & Abutalebi, J. (2018). Neuroplasticity across the lifespan and aging effects in bilinguals and monolinguals. *Brain and Cognition*, *125*, 118–126.

DeLuca, V., & Voits, T. (2022). Bilingual experience affects white matter integrity across the lifespan. *Neuropsychologia*, *169*, 108191.

DeLuca, V., Rothman, J., & Pliatsikas, C. (2019). Linguistic immersion and structural effects on the bilingual brain: A longitudinal study. *Bilingualism: Language and Cognition*, *22*(5), 1160–1175.

DeLuca, V., Miller, D., Pliatsikas, C., & Rothman, J. (2019a). Brain adaptations and neurological indices of processing in adult second language acquisition: Challenges for the critical period hypothesis. In J. W. Schwieter (Ed.), *The handbook of the neuroscience of multilingualism* (pp. 170–196). Wiley-Blackwell.

DeLuca, V., Rothman, J., Bialystok, E., & Pliatsikas, C. (2019b). Redefining bilingualism as a spectrum of experiences that differentially affects brain structure and function. *Proceedings of the National Academy of Sciences*, *116*(15), 7565–7574.

DeLuca, V., Rothman, J., Bialystok, E., & Pliatsikas, C. (2020). Duration and extent of bilingual experience modulate neurocognitive outcomes. *NeuroImage*, *204*, 116222.

DeLuca, V., Segaert, K., Mazaheri, A., & Krott, A. (2020). Understanding bilingual brain function and structure changes? U bet! A unified bilingual experience trajectory model. *Journal of Neurolinguistics*, *56*, 100930.

Desmet, T., & Duyck, W. (2007). Bilingual language processing. *Language and Linguistics Compass*, *1*(3), 168–194.

Dewaele, J. M. (2010). *Emotions in multiple languages*. Palgrave Macmillan.

Dewaele, J. M. (2015). Bilingualism and multilingualism. In K. Tracy, C. Illie & T. Sandel (Eds.), *The International encyclopedia of language and social interaction* (pp. 1–11). Wiley.

Dewaele, J. M., & Li, C. (2020). Emotions in second language acquisition: A critical review and research agenda. *Foreign Language World*, *196*(1), 34–49.

Diamond, A. (2007). Interrelated and interdependent. *Developmental Science*, *10*(1), 152–158.

Diamond, B., & Shreve, G. (2019). Translation, interpreting, and the bilingual brain: Implications for executive control and neuroplasticity. In J. W. Schwieter (Ed.), *The handbook of the neuroscience of multilingualism* (pp. 485–507). Wiley-Blackwell.

Dick, A. S., Garcia, N. L., Pruden, S. M., Thompson, W. K., Hawes, S. W., Sutherland, M. T., … & Gonzalez, R. (2019). No evidence for a bilingual executive function advantage in the ABCD study. *Nature Human Behaviour*, *3*(7), 692–701.

Diebold, A. R. (1961). Incipient bilingualism. *Language*, *37*(1), 97–112.

Dijkstra, T. (1998). From tag to task: Coming to grips with bilingual control issues. *Bilingualism: Language and Cognition*, *1*, 51–66.

Dijkstra, T., van Geffen, A., Hieselaar, W., & Peeters, D. (submitted). *Multilink+: A computational model for printed word retrieval in different language, participant groups, and tasks.*

Dijkstra, A., & Van Heuven, W. (1998). The BIA model and bilingual word recognition. In J. Grainger & A. Jacobs (Eds.), *Localist connectionist approaches to human cognition* (pp. 189–225). Erlbaum.

Dijkstra, T., & Van Heuven, W. (2002). The architecture of the bilingual word recognition system: From identification to decision. *Bilingualism: Language and Cognition*, *5*, 175–197.

Dijkstra, T., & Rekké, S. (2010). Towards a localist-connectionist model of word translation. *The Mental Lexicon*, *5*, 403–422.

Dijkstra, T., Grainger, J., & Van Heuven, W. (1999). Recognition of cognates and interlingual homographs: The neglected role of phonology. *Journal of Memory and Language*, *41*, 496–518.

Dijkstra, T., Haga, F., Bijsterveld, A., & Sprinkhuizen-Kuyper, I. (2011). Lexical competition in localist and distributed connectionist models of L2 acquisition. In J. Altarriba & L. Isurin (Eds.), *Memory, language, and bilingualism: Theoretical and applied approaches* (pp. 48–73). Cambridge University Press.

Dijkstra, T., Miwa, K., Brummelhuis, B., Sappelli, M., & Baayen, H. (2010). How cross-language similarity and task demands affect cognate recognition. *Journal of Memory and Language, 62*(3), 284–301.

Dijkstra, T., Wahl, A., Buytenhuijs, F., Van Halem, N., Al-Jibouri, Z., De Korte, M., & Rekké, S. (2019). Multilink: A computational model for bilingual word recognition and word translation. *Bilingualism: Language and Cognition, 22*(4), 657–679.

Dong, Y., Gui, S., & MacWhinney, B. (2005). Shared and separate meanings in the bilingual lexical memory. *Bilingualism: Language and Cognition, 8*, 221–238.

Dong, Y., & Li, P. (2015). The cognitive science of bilingualism. *Language and Linguistics Compass, 9*(1), 1–13.

Dörnyei, Z. (2005). *The psychology of the language learner: Individual differences in second language acquisition*. Erlbaum.

Dörnyei, Z. (2009). *The psychology of second language acquisition*. Oxford University Press.

Dörnyei, Z. (2019). From integrative motivation to directed motivational currents: The evolution of the understanding of L2 motivation over three decades. In M. Lamb, K. Cizér, & S. Ryan (Eds.), *The Palgrave handbook of motivation for language learning* (pp. 39–69). Palgrave Macmillan.

Dörnyei, Z., & Ryan, S. (2015). *The psychology of the language learner revisited*. Routledge.

Dow-Edwards, D., MacMaster, F. P., Peterson, B. S., Niesink, R., Andersen, S., & Braams, B. R. (2019). Experience during adolescence shapes brain development: From synapses and networks to normal and pathological behavior. *Neurotoxicology and Teratology, 76*, 106834.

Driemeyer, J., Boyke, J., Gaser, C., Büchel, C., & May, A. (2008). Changes in gray matter induced by learning – Revisited. *PloS One, 3*(7), e2669.

Dudai, Y., Karni, A., & Born, J. (2015). The consolidation and transformation of memory. *Neuron, 88*(1), 20–32.

Duncan, T. S., & Paradis, J. (2020). Home language environment and children's second language acquisition: The special status of input from older siblings. *Journal of Child Language, 47*(5), 982–1005.

Dussias, P. (2004). Parsing a first language like a second: The erosion of L1 parsing strategies in Spanish-English bilinguals. *International Journal of Bilingualism, 8*, 355–371.

Duyck, W. (2005). Translation and associative priming with cross-lingual pseudohomophones: Evidence for nonselective phonological activation in bilinguals. *Journal of Experimental Psychology: Learning, Memory, and Cognition, 31*, 1340–1359.

Duyck, W., & Brysbaert, M. (2004). Forward and backward number translation requires conceptual mediation both in balanced and unbalanced bilinguals. *Journal of Experimental Psychology: Human Perception and Performance, 30*, 889–906.

Duyck, W., & Brysbaert, M. (2008). Semantic access in number word translation: The role of cross-lingual lexical similarity. *Experimental Psychology, 55*, 73–81.

Duyck, W., Van Assche, E., Drieghe, D., & Hartsuiker, R. (2007). Visual word recognition by bilinguals in a sentence context: evidence for nonselective lexical access. *Journal of Experimental Psychology: Learning, Memory, and Cognition, 33*, 663–679.

Edmonds, L., & Kiran, S. (2006). Effect of semantic naming treatment on crosslinguistic generalization in bilingual aphasia. *Journal of Speech, Language and Hearing Research, 49*, 729–748.

Edwards, D., & Christophersen, H. (1988). Bilingualism, literacy, and meta-linguistic awareness in preschool children. *British Journal of Developmental Psychology, 6*(3), 235–244.

Edwards, J. (2004). Foundations of bilingualism. In T. Bhatia & W. Ritchie (Eds.), *The handbook of bilingualism* (pp. 7–31). Blackwell.

El Hachioui, H., Visch-Brink, E., de Lau, L., van de Sandt-Koenderman, M., Nouwens, F., … & Dippel, W. (2017). Screening tests for aphasia in patients with stroke: A systematic review. *Journal of Neurology, 264*(2), 211–220.

Elmer, S., Hänggi, J., & Jäncke, L. (2014). Processing demands upon cognitive, linguistic, and articulatory functions promote grey matter plasticity in the adult multilingual brain: Insights from simultaneous interpreters. *Cortex, 54*, 179–189.

Elmer, S., Meyer, M., & Jäncke, L. (2010). Simultaneous interpreters as a model for neuronal adaptation in the domain of language processing. *Brain and Research, 1317*, 147–156.

Elston-Güttler, K., Gunter, T., & Kotz, S. (2005). Zooming into L2: Global language context and adjustment affect processing of interlingual homographs in sentences. *Cognitive Brain Research, 25*, 57–70.

Enderby, P., Wood, V., Wade, D., & Hewer, R. (1987). The Frenchay Aphasia Screening Test: A short, simple test for aphasia appropriate for non-specialists. *International Rehabilitation Medicine, 8*, 166–170.

Erdocia, K., & Laka, I. (2018). Negative transfer effects on L2 word order processing. *Frontiers in Psychology, 9*, 337.

Escudero, P., & Boersma, P. (2004). Bridging the gap between L2 speech perception research and phonological theory. *Studies in Second Language Acquisition, 26*, 551–585.

Eubank, L. (1993). On the transfer of parametric values in L2 development. *Language Acquisition, 3*(3), 183–208.

Eubank, L., Bischof, J., Huffstutler, A., Leek, P., & West, C. (1997). "Tom eats slowly cooked eggs": Thematic-verb raising in L2 knowledge. *Language Acquisition, 6*, 171–199.

Evans, G. (2020). *Bilingual semantics: Intra- and inter-sense mapping in the case of two languages.* Unpublished doctoral dissertation, Bangor University, Wales.

Fabbro, F. (1999). *The neurolinguistics of bilingualism: An introduction.* Psychology Press.

Fabbro, F. (2001). The bilingual brain: Cerebral representation of languages. *Brain and Language, 79*(2), 211–222.

Fabbro F., & Cargnelutti, E. (2018). *Neuroscienze del Bilinguismo (Neuroscience of Bilingualism).* Astrolabio.

Fabbro, F., Gran, B., & Gran, L. (1991). Hemispheric specialization for semantic and syntactic components of language in simultaneous interpreters. *Brain and Language, 41*, 1–42.

Fabbro, F., Moretti, R., & Bava, A. (2000). Language impairments in patients with cerebellar lesions. *Journal of Neurolinguistics, 13*, 173–188.

Fabbro, G., Skrap, M., & Aglioti, S. (2000). Pathological switching between languages after frontal lesions in a bilingual patient. *Journal of Neurology, Neurosurgery, & Psychiatry, 68*, 650–652.

Fabiano-Smith, L., & Goldstein, B. (2010). Phonological cross-linguistic effects in bilingual Spanish–English speaking children. *Journal of Multilingual Communication Disorders, 3*(1), 56–63.

Farah, M. J. (2018). Socioeconomic status and the brain: Prospects for neuroscience-informed policy. *Nature Reviews Neuroscience, 19*(7), 428–438.

Faroqi, Y., & Chengappa, S. (1996). Trace deletion hypothesis and its implications for intervention with a multilingual agrammatic aphasic patient. *Osmania Papers in Linguistics, 22–23*, 79–106.

Faroqi-Shah, Y., Frymark, T., Mullen, R., & Wang, B. (2010). Effect of treatment for bilingual individuals with aphasia: A systematic review of the evidence. *Journal of Neurolinguistics, 23*, 319–341

Fecher, N., & Johnson, E. K. (2019). Bilingual infants excel at foreign-language talker recognition. *Developmental Science, 22*(4), e12778

Fecher, N., & Johnson, E. K. (2022). Revisiting the talker recognition advantage in bilingual infants. *Journal of Experimental Child Psychology, 214*, 105276.

Fennell, C., & Byers-Heinlein, K. (2014). You sound like Mommy: Bilingual and monolingual infants learn words best from speakers typical of their language environments. *International Journal of Behavioral Development*, *38*(4), 309–316.

Fernald, A., & Simon, T. (1984). Expanded intonation contours in mothers' speech to newborns. *Developmental Psychology*, *20*(1), 104–113.

Fernald, A., & Weisleder, A. (2015). Twenty years after "meaningful differences," it's time to reframe the "deficit" debate about the importance of children's early language experience. *Human Development*, *58*(1), 1–4.

Fernald, A., Marchman, V. A., & Weisleder, A. (2013). SES differences in language processing skill and vocabulary are evident at 18 months. *Developmental Science*, *16*(2), 234–248.

Fernandez, B., Cardebat, D., Demonet, J., Joseph, P., Mazaux, J., … & Allard, M. (2004). Functional MRI follow-up study of language processes in healthy subjects and during recovery in a case of aphasia. *Stroke*, *35*, 2171–2176.

Fernández-Coello, A., Havas, V., Juncadella, M., Sierpowska, J., Rodríguez-Fornells, A., & Gabarrós, A. (2016). Age of language acquisition and cortical language organization in multilingual patients undergoing awake brain mapping. *Journal of Neurosurgery*, *126*(6), 1912–1923.

Fernández-López, M., & Perea, M. (2019). The bilingualism wars: Is the bilingual advantage out of (executive) control? *Psicológica*, *40*(1), 26–33.

Ferré, P., Sánchez-Casas, R., & García, J. (2000). Conexiones léxicas y conceptuales en la adquisición de una segunda lengua: Datos del castellano y del alemán. *Cognitiva*, *13*, 131–152.

Ferreira, A., Schwieter, J. W., & Festman, J. (2020). Cognitive and neurocognitive effects from the unique bilingual experiences of interpreters. *Frontiers in Psychology*, *11*, 548755.

Festman, J. (2012). Language control abilities of late bilinguals. *Bilingualism: Language and Cognition*, *15*(3), 580–593.

Festman, J. (2013). The complexity-cost factor in bilingualism. *Behavioral and Brain Sciences*, *36*(4), 355.

Festman, J. (2021). Learning and processing multiple languages: The more the easier? *Language Learning*, *71*(S1), 121–162.

Festman, J., & Clahsen, H. (2016). How Germans prepare for the English past tense: Silent production of inflected words during EEG. *Applied Psycholinguistics*, *37*(2), 487–506.

Festman, J., & Mosca, M. (2016). Influence of preparation time on language control. In J. W. Schwieter (Ed.), *Cognitive control and consequences in the multilingual mind* (pp. 145–171). Benjamins.

Festman, J., & Münte, T. F. (2012). Cognitive control in Russian–German bilinguals. *Frontiers in Psychology*, *3*, 115.

Festman, J., & Schwieter, J. W. (2019). Self-concepts in reading and spelling among mono-and multilingual children: Extending the bilingual advantage. *Behavioral Sciences*, *9*(4), 39.

Festman, J., Czapka, S., & Winsler, A. (2023). How many moderators does is take till we know… that too many bilingual advantage effects have died. In K. Kersten & A. Winsler (Eds.), *Understanding variability in second language acquisition, bilingualism, and cognition: A multi-layered perspective* (pp. 80–127). Routledge.

Festman, J., Poarch, G. J., & Dewaele, J. M. (2017). *Raising multilingual children*. Multilingual Matters.

Festman, J., Rodriguez-Fornells, A., & Münte, T. F. (2010). Individual differences in control of language interference in late bilinguals are mainly related to general executive abilities. *Behavioral and Brain Functions*, *6*(1), 1–12.

Filippa, M., Della Casa, E., D'amico, R., Picciolini, O., Lunardi, C., Sansavini, A., & Ferrari, F. (2021). Effects of early vocal contact in the neonatal intensive care unit: Study protocol for a multi-centre, randomised clinical trial. *International Journal of Environmental Research and Public Health*, *18*(8), 1–15.

Filippi, R., & Bright, P. (2023). A cross-sectional developmental approach to bilingualism: Exploring neurocognitive effects across the lifespan. *Ampersand, 10*, 100097.

Filippi, R., Ceccolini, A., Periche-Tomas, E., Papageorgiou, A., & Bright, P. (2020). Developmental trajectories of control of verbal and non-verbal interference in speech comprehension in monolingual and multilingual children. *Cognition, 200*, 104252.

Filippi, R., D'Souza, D., & Bright, P. (2019). A developmental approach to bilingual research: The effects of multi-language experience from early infancy to old age. *International Journal of Bilingualism*, *23*(5), 1195–1207.

Finkbeiner, M. (2005). Task-dependent L2-L1 translation priming: An investigation of the separate memory systems account. In J. Cohen, K. T. McAlister, K. Rolstad, & J. MacSwan (Eds.), *Proceedings of the 4th International symposium on bilingualism* (pp. 741–750). Cascadilla.

Finkbeiner, M., Forster, K., Nicol, J., & Nakamura, K. (2004). The role of polysemy in masked semantic and translation priming. *Journal of Memory and Language, 51*, 1–22.

Flamand-Roze, C., Falissard, B., Roze, E., Maintigneux, L., Beziz, J., Chacon A, … & Denier, C. (2011). Validation of a new language screening tool for patients with acute stroke: The Language Screening Test (LAST). *Stroke, 42*, 1224–1229.

Flege, J., Bohn, O.-S., & Jang, S. (1997). Effects of experience on non-native speakers' production and perception of English vowels. *Journal of Phonetics, 25*, 437–470.

Folke, T., Ouzia, J., Bright, P., De Martino, B., & Filippi, R. (2016). A bilingual disadvantage in metacognitive processing. *Cognition, 150*, 119–132.

Försterling, M., Hainke, L., Redkina, A., & Sauseng, P. (2023). Influence of bilingualism on behavioral and electrophysiological parameters of cognitive control: No clear effects of immersion, stimulus language, and word similarity. *Journal of Psychophysiology, 37*(2), 88–100.

Foulkes, D., Meier, B., Strauch, I., Ken, N., Bradley, L., & Hollifield, M. (1993). Linguistic phenomena and language selection in the REM dreams of German-English bilinguals. *International Journal of Psychology, 28*(6), 871.

Friedman, N. P. (2016). Research on individual differences in executive functions: Implications for the bilingual advantage hypothesis. *Linguistic Approaches to Bilingualism, 6*(5), 535–548.

Fuchs, E., & Flügge, G. (2014). Adult neuroplasticity: More than 40 years of research. *Neural Plasticity,* 541870.

Galvez, A. & Hinckley, J. (2003). Transfer patterns of naming treatment in a case of bilingual aphasia. *Brain and Language, 87*(1), 173–174.

Gapany, D., Murukun, M., Goveas, J., Dhurrkay, J., Burarrwanga, V., & Page, J. (2022). Empowering aboriginal families as their children's first teachers of cultural knowledge, languages, and identity at Galiwin'ku FaFT Playgroup. *Australasian Journal of Early Childhood, 47*(1), 20–31.

Garbin, G., Sanjuan, A., Forn, C., Bustamante, J. C., Rodríguez-Pujadas, A., Belloch, V., ... & Ávila, C. (2010). Bridging language and attention: Brain basis of the impact of bilingualism on cognitive control. *NeuroImage, 53*(4), 1272–1278.

García, A. (2019). *The neurocognition of translation and interpreting.* Benjamins.

Garcia-Alvarado, S., Arreguin, M. G., & Ruiz-Escalante, J. A. (2022). Mexican-American preschoolers as co-creators of zones of proximal development during retellings of culturally relevant stories: A participatory study. *Journal of Early Childhood Literacy, 22*(2), 232–253.

Gaser, C., & Schlaug, G. (2003). Brain structures differ between musicians and non-musicians. *Journal of Neuroscience, 23*(27), 9240–9245.

Gerard, L., & Scarborough, D. (1989). Language-specific lexical access of homographs by bilinguals. *Journal of Experimental Psychology: Learning, Memory, and Cognition, 15*(2), 305–315.

Gil, M., & Goral, M. (2004). Nonparallel recovery in bilingual aphasia: Effects of language choice, language proficiency, and treatment. *International Journal of Bilingualism, 8*, 191–219.

Gillet, S., Barbu, C. A., & Poncelet, M. (2020). Exploration of attentional and executive abilities in French-Speaking children immersed in Dutch since 1, 2, 3, and 6 years. *Frontiers in Psychology, 11*, 587574.

Goertz, R., Wahl, A., & Dijkstra, T. (in preparation). Translating interlingual homographs: Empirical and simulation data.

Golberg, H., Paradis, J., & Crago, M. (2008). Lexical acquisition over time in minority first language children learning English as a second language. *Applied Psycholinguistics, 29*(1), 41–65.

Gold, B. T., Johnson, N. F., & Powell, D. K. (2013). Lifelong bilingualism contributes to cognitive reserve against white matter integrity declines in aging. *Neuropsychologia, 51*(13), 2841–2846.

Goldrick, M., Putnam, M., & Schwartz, L. (2016). Coactivation in bilingual grammars: A computational account of code mixing. *Bilingualism: Language and Cognition, 19*(5), 857–876.

Golinkoff, R. M., Hoff, E., Rowe, M. L., Tamis-LeMonda, C. S., & Hirsh-Pasek, K. (2019). Language matters: Denying the existence of the 30-million-word gap has serious consequences. *Child Development, 90*(3), 985–992.

Gollan, T. H., & Acenas, L. A. R. (2004). What is a TOT? Cognate and translation effects on tip-of-the-tongue states in Spanish-English and Tagalog-English bilinguals. *Journal of Experimental Psychology: Learning, Memory, and Cognition, 30*(1), 246.

Gollan, T. H., & Brown, A. S. (2006). From tip-of-the-tongue (TOT) data to theoretical implications in two steps: When more TOTs means better retrieval. *Journal of Experimental Psychology: General, 135*(3), 462.

Gollan, T. H., & Silverberg, N. B. (2001). Tip-of-the-tongue states in Hebrew–English bilinguals. *Bilingualism: Language and Cognition, 4*(1), 63–83.

Gollan, T. H., Fennema-Notestine, C., Montoya, R. I., & Jernigan, T. L. (2007). The bilingual effect on Boston Naming Test performance. *Journal of the International Neuropsychological Society, 13*(2), 197–208.

Gollan, T., Forster, K., & Frost, R. (1997). Translation priming with different scripts: Masked priming with cognates and noncognates in Hebrew-English bilinguals. *Journal of Experimental Psychology: Learning, Memory, and Cognition, 23*, 1122–1139.

Gollan, T., Montoya, R., Fennema-Notestine, C., & Morris, S. (2005). Bilingualism affects picture naming but not picture classification. *Memory & Cognition, 33*, 1220–1234.

Gómez-Ruiz, I., & Aguilar-Alonso, Á. (2011). Capacity of the Catalan and Spanish versions of the bilingual aphasia test to distinguish between healthy aging, mild cognitive impairment and Alzheimer's disease. *Clinical Linguistics & Phonetics, 25*, 444–463.

Goral, G., Levy, E., & Kastl, R. (2009). Cross-language treatment generalization: A case of trilingual aphasia. *Brain and Language, 103*, 1–18.

Goral, M. (2019). Acquired reading disorders in bilingualism. In J. W. Schwieter (Ed.), *The handbook of the neuroscience of multilingualism* (pp. 592–607). Wiley-Blackwell.

Goral, M., Naghibolhosseini, M., & Conner, P. (2013). Asymmetric inhibitory treatment effects in multilingual aphasia. *Cognitive Neuropsychology*, *30*, 564–577.

Goral, M., Rosas, J., Conner, P., Maul, K., & Obler, L. (2012). Effects of language proficiency and language of the environment on aphasia therapy in a multilingual. *Journal of Neurolinguistics*, *25*, 538–551.

Gorno-Tempini, M., Dronkers, N., Rankin, K., Ogar, J., Phengrasamy, L., Rosen, H., ... & Miller, B. (2004). Cognition and anatomy in three variants of primary progressive aphasia. *Annals of Neurology*, *55*(3), 335–346.

Gorno-Tempini, M., Hillis, A., Weintraub, S., Kertesz, A., Mendez, M., Cappa, S., ... & Grossman, M. (2011). Classification of primary progressive aphasia and its variants. *Neurology*, *76*(11), 1006–1014.

Goswami, U. (2008). Principles of learning, implications for teaching: A cognitive neuroscience perspective. *Journal of Philosophy of Education*, *42*(3–4), 381–399.

Grainger, J., & Frenck-Mestre, C. (1998). Masked priming by translation equivalents in proficient bilinguals. *Language and Cognitive Processes*, *13*, 601–623.

Grainger, J., Midgley, K., & Holcomb, P. (2010). Re-thinking the bilingual interactive-activation model from a developmental perspective (BIA-d). In M. Kail & M. Hickmann (Eds.), *Language acquisition across linguistic and cognitive systems* (pp. 267–284). Benjamins.

Green, D. (1986). Control, activation, and resource: A framework and a model for the control of speech in bilinguals. *Brain and Language*, *27*, 210–223.

Green, D. (1998). Mental control of the bilingual lexico-semantic system. *Bilingualism: Language and Cognition*, *1*(2), 67–81.

Green, D. (2003). The neural basis of the lexicon and the grammar in L2 acquisition. In R. van Hout, A. Hulk, F. Kuiken & R. Towell. (Eds.), *The interface between syntax and the lexicon in second language acquisition* (pp. 197–208). Benjamins.

Green, D. (2018). Language control and code-switching. *Languages*, *3*(2), Article 8.

Green, D., & Abutalebi, J. (2008). Understanding the link between bilingual aphasia and language control. *Journal of Neurolinguistics*, *21*, 558–576.

Green, D., & Abutalebi, J. (2013). Language control in bilinguals: The adaptive control hypothesis. *Journal of Cognitive Psychology*, *25*(5), 515–530.

Green, D., & Abutalebi, J. (2016). Language control and the neuroanatomy of bilingualism: In praise of variety. *Language, Cognition and Neuroscience, 31*(3), 340–344.

Green, D., & Wei, L. (2014). A control process model of code-switching. *Language, Cognition and Neuroscience, 29,* 499–511.

Green, D., & Wei, L. (2016). Codeswitching and language control. *Bilingualism: Language and Cognition, 19*(5), 883–884.

Green, D., Crinion, J., & Price, C. J. (2006). Convergence, degeneracy, and control. *Language Learning, 56,* 99–125.

Gregersen, T., & Mercer, S. (Eds.). (2022). *The Routledge handbook of the psychology of language learning and teaching.* Routledge.

Greve, W., Koch, M., Rasche, V., & Kersten, K. (2021). Extending the scope of the "cognitive advantage" hypothesis: Multilingual individuals show higher flexibility of goal adjustment. *Journal of Multilingual and Multicultural Development,* 1–17.

Grosjean, F. (1989). Neurolinguists, beware! The bilingual is not two monolinguals in one person. *Brain and Language, 36*(1), 3–15.

Grosjean, F. (1998). Studying bilinguals: Methodological and conceptual issues. *Bilingualism: Language and Cognition, 1,* 131–149.

Grosjean, F. (2001). The bilingual's language modes. In J. Nicol (Ed.), *One mind, two languages: Bilingual language processing* (pp. 1–22). Wiley-Blackwell.

Grosjean, F. (2010). *Bilingual life and reality.* Harvard University Press.

Grosjean, F. (2013). Bilingual and monolingual language modes. In C. A. Chapelle (Ed.), *The Encyclopedia of Applied Linguistics,* (pp. 489–493). Blackwell.

Grossman, M. (2010). Primary progressive aphasia: Clinicopathological correlations. *Nature Reviews: Neurology, 6*(2), 88–97.

Grote, K. S., Russell, E. E., Bates, O., & Gonzalez, R. (2021). Bilingual cognition and growth mindset: A review of cognitive flexibility and its implications for dual-language education. *Current Issues in Education, 22*(2).

Grote, K. S., Scott, R. M., & Gilger, J. (2021). Bilingual advantages in executive functioning: Evidence from a low-income sample. *First Language, 41*(6), 677–700.

Grundy, J. G. (2020). The effects of bilingualism on executive functions: An updated quantitative analysis. *Journal of Cultural Cognitive Science, 4*(2), 177–199.

Grundy J. G., & Timmer K. (2016). Bilingualism and working memory capacity: A comprehensive meta-analysis. *Second Language Research, 3,* 325–340.

Grundy, J. G., Anderson, J. A., & Bialystok, E. (2017). Neural correlates of cognitive processing in monolinguals and bilinguals. *Annals of the New York Academy of Sciences, 1396*(1), 183–201.

Grundy, J. G., Pavlenko, E., & Bialystok, E. (2020). Bilingualism modifies disengagement of attention networks across the scalp: A multivariate ERP investigation of the IOR paradigm. *Journal of Neurolinguistics, 56*, 100933.

Guion, S., Flege, J., Liu, S., & Yeni-Komshian, G. (2000). Age of learning effects on the duration of sentences produced in a second language. *Applied Psycholinguistics, 21*, 205–228.

Gullberg, M. (2012). Bilingualism and gesture. In T. K. Bhatia & W. C. Ritchie (Eds.), *The handbook of bilingualism and multilingualism* (pp. 417–437). Wiley-Blackwell.

Gullifer, J. W., & Titone, D. (2020). Characterizing the social diversity of bilingualism using language entropy. *Bilingualism: Language and Cognition, 23*(2), 283–294.

Guzmán-Vélez E., & Tranel D. (2015). Does bilingualism contribute to cognitive reserve? Cognitive and neural perspectives. *Neuropsychology, 29*, 139–150.

Hackman, D. A., & Farah, M. J. (2009). Socioeconomic status and the developing brain. *Trends in Cognitive Sciences, 13*(2), 65–73.

Hämäläinen, M., Hari, R., Ilmoniemi, R. J., Knuutila, J., & Lounasmaa, O. V. (1993). Magnetoencephalography – Theory, instrumentation, and applications to noninvasive studies of the working human brain. *Reviews of Modern Physics, 65*(2), 413.

Hämäläinen, S., Sairanen, V., Leminen, A., & Lehtonen, M. (2017). Bilingualism modulates the white matter structure of language-related pathways. *NeuroImage, 152*, 249–257.

Hartanto, A., Toh, W. X., & Yang, H. (2019). Bilingualism narrows socioeconomic disparities in executive functions and self-regulatory behaviors during early childhood: Evidence from the early childhood longitudinal study. *Child Development, 90*(4), 1215–1235.

Hasselgren, A. (1994). Lexical teddy bears and advanced learners: A study into the ways Norwegian students cope with English vocabulary. *International Journal of Applied Linguistics, 4*, 237–260.

Hattie, J. (2008). *Visible learning: A synthesis of over 800 meta-analyses relating to achievement.* Routledge.

Haugen, E. (1953). *The Norwegian language in America, a study in bilingual behavior* (Vol. 1). University of Pennsylvania Press.

Haugen, E. (1973). Bilingualism, language contact and immigrant language in the United States: A research report 1956–1970. In T.

Sebeok (Ed.), *Current trends in linguistics* (Vol. 10, pp. 505–591). Mouton.

Hauser-Grüdl, N., Guerra, L., Witzmann, F., Leray, E., & Müller, N. (2010). Cross-linguistic influence in bilingual children: Can input frequency account for it? *Lingua, 120*(11), 2638–2650.

Haxby, J. V., Gobbini, M. I., Furey, M. L., Ishai, A., Schouten, J. L., & Pietrini, P. (2001). Distributed and overlapping representations of faces and objects in ventral temporal cortex. *Science, 293*(5539), 2425–2430.

Hayakawa, S., & Marian, V. (2019). Consequences of multilingualism for neural architecture. *Behavioral and Brain Functions, 15*(1), 1–24.

Hebb, D. O. (1949). *Organization of behavior*. Wiley.

Heller, A. S., & Casey, B. J. (2016). The neurodynamics of emotion: Delineating typical and atypical emotional processes during adolescence. *Developmental Science, 19*(1), 3–18.

Heredia, R. R. (1997). Bilingual memory and hierarchical models: A case for language dominance. *Current Directions in Psychological Science, 6*, 34–39.

Heredia R. R., Blackburn A. M., & Vega L. V. (2020). Moderation-mediation effects in bilingualism and cognitive reserve. *Frontiers in Psychology, 11*, 572555.

Herholz, S. C., & Zatorre, R. J. (2012). Musical training as a framework for brain plasticity: Behavior, function, and structure. *Neuron, 76*(3), 486–502.

Hermans, D., Bongaerts, T., de Bot, K., & Schreuder, R. (1998). Producing words in a foreign language: Can speakers prevent interference from their first language? *Bilingualism: Language and Cognition, 1*, 213–229.

Hernandez, A. E. (2013). *The bilingual brain*. Oxford University Press.

Hernandez, A. E., & Li, P. (2007). Age of acquisition: Its neural and computational mechanisms. *Psychological Bulletin, 133*(4), 638.

Hernandez, A. E., Dapretto, M., Mazziotta, J., & Bookheimer, S. (2001). Language switching and language representation in Spanish–English bilinguals: An fMRI study. *NeuroImage, 14*(2), 510–520.

Hernandez, A. E., Martinez, A., & Kohnert, K. (2000). In search of the language switch: An fMRI study of picture naming in Spanish–English bilinguals. *Brain and Language, 73*(3), 421–431.

Hervais-Adelman, A., Moser-Mercer, B., & Golestani, N. (2015). Brain functional plasticity associated with the emergence of expertise in extreme language control. *NeuroImage, 114*, 264–274.

Hervais-Adelman, A., Moser-Mercer, B., Michel, C., & Golestani, N. (2014). fMRI of simultaneous interpretation reveals the neural basis of extreme language control. *Cerebral Cortex, 25*, 4727–4739.

Hervais-Adelman, A., Moser-Mercer, B., Murray, M., & Golestani, N. (2017). Cortical thickness increases after simultaneous interpretation training. *Neuropsychologia*, 98, 212–219.

Heynick, F. (1983). *Theoretical and empirical investigation into verbal aspects of the Freudian model of dream generation.* Unpublished doctoral dissertation, University of Groningen, The Netherlands.

Hickok, G., & Poeppel, D. (2004). Dorsal and ventral streams: A framework for understanding aspects of the functional anatomy of language. *Cognition*, 92(1–2), 67–99.

Hicks, N. S. (2021). Exploring systematic orthographic crosslinguistic similarities to enhance foreign language vocabulary learning. *Language Teaching Research*, 13621688211047353.

Higby, E., Kim, J., & Obler, L. K. (2013). Multilingualism and the brain. *Annual Review of Applied Linguistics*, 33, 68–101.

Hillis, A., Wityk, R., & Tuffiash, E. (2001). Hypoperfusion of Wernicke's area predicts severity of semantic deficit in acute stroke. *Annals of Neurology*, 50, 561–566.

Hinckley, J. (2003). Picture naming treatment in aphasia yields greater improvement in L1. *Brain and Language*, 87(1), 171–172.

Hinton, C., Miyamoto, K., & Della-Chiesa, B. (2008). Brain research, learning, and emotions: Implications for education research, policy, and practice. *European Journal of Education*, 43(1), 87–103

Hirosh, Z., & Degani, T. (2018). Direct and indirect effects of multilingualism on novel language learning: An integrative review. *Psychonomic Bulletin & Review*, 25(3), 892–916.

Hirsh-Pasek, K., Adamson, L. B., Bakeman, R., Owen, M. T., Golinkoff, R. M., Pace, A., Yust P. K. S., & Suma, K. (2015). The contribution of early communication quality to low-income children's language success. *Psychological Science*, 26(7), 1071–1083.

Hoff, E. (2003). The specificity of environmental influence: Socioeconomic status affects early vocabulary development via maternal speech. *Child Development*, 74(5), 1368–1378.

Hoff, E. (2015). Language development in bilingual children. In E. L. Bavin & L. R. Naigles (Eds.), *The Cambridge handbook of child language* (pp. 483–503). Cambridge University Press.

Hoff, E. (2018). Bilingual development in children of immigrant families. *Child Development Perspectives*, 12(2), 80–86.

Hoff, E., & Core, C. (2013). Input and language development in bilingually developing children. *Seminars in Speech and Language*, 34(4), 215–226.

Hoff, E., Core, C., & Shanks, K. F. (2020). The quality of child-directed speech depends on the speaker's language proficiency. *Journal of Child Language*, 47(1), 132–145.

Hoff, E., Core, C., Place, S., Rumiche, R., Señor, M., & Parra, M. (2012). Dual language exposure and early bilingual development. *Journal of Child Language*, *39*(1), 1–27.

Hohenstein, J., Eisenberg, A., & Naigles, L. (2006). Is he floating across or crossing afloat? Cross-influence of L1 and L2 in Spanish-English bilingual adults. *Bilingualism: Language and Cognition*, *9*, 249–261.

Höhle, B., Bijeljac-Babic, R., & Nazzi, T. (2020). Variability and stability in early language acquisition: Comparing monolingual and bilingual infants' speech perception and word recognition. *Bilingualism: Language and Cognition*, *23*, 56–71.

Holland, A, Greenhouse, J., Fromm, D., & Swindell, C. (2014). Predictors of language restitution following stroke: A multivariate analysis. *Journal of Speech and Hearing Research*, *32*, 232–238.

Holleman, G. A., Hooge, I. T., Kemner, C., & Hessels, R. S. (2020). The 'real-world approach' and its problems: A critique of the term ecological validity. *Frontiers in Psychology*, *11*, 721.

Holtzheimer, P., Fawaz, W., Wilson, C., & Avery, D. (2005). Repetitive transcranial magnetic stimulation may induce language switching in bilingual patients. *Brain and Language*, *94*(3), 274–277.

Hörder, S. (2018), The correlation of early multilingualism and language aptitude. In S. M. Reiterer (Ed.). *Exploring language aptitude: Views from psychology, the language sciences, and cognitive neuroscience* (pp. 277–304). Springer.

Hoshino, N., & Kroll, J. (2008). Cognate effects in picture naming: Does cross-language activation survive a change of script? *Cognition*, *106*, 501–511.

Hu, R. (2016). The age factor in second language learning. *Theory and Practice in Language Studies*, *6*(11), 2164–2168.

Huettel, S. A., Song, A. W., & McCarthy, G. (2004). *Functional magnetic resonance imaging*. Sinauer Associates.

Hull, R., & Vaid, J. (2006). Laterality and language experience. *Laterality*, *11*, 436–464.

Huston, A. C., & Bentley, A. C. (2010). Human development in societal context. *Annual Review of Psychology*, *61*, 411–437.

Huttenlocher, P. R. (1979). Synaptic density in human frontal cortex-developmental changes and effects of aging. *Brain Research*, *163*(2), 195–205.

Huttenlocher, P. R. (2009). *Neural plasticity: The effects of environment on the development of the cerebral cortex*. Harvard University Press.

iLanguages.org (2023). *Multilingual people*. Retrieved on May 8, 2023 from https://ilanguages.org/bilingual.php.

Illes, J., Francis, W., Desmond, J., Gabrieli, J., Glover, G., Poldrack, R., Lee, C., & Wagner, A. (1999). Convergent cortical representation of semantic processing in bilinguals. *Brain and Language*, *70*(3), 347–363.

Indefrey, P. (2006). A meta-analysis of hemodynamic studies on first and second language processing: Which suggested differences can we trust and what do they mean? *Language Learning, 56*, 279–304.

Isel, F., Baumgaertner, A., Thrän, J., Meisel, J. M., & Büchel, C. (2010). Neural circuitry of the bilingual mental lexicon: Effect of age of second language acquisition. *Brain and Cognition, 72*(2), 169–180.

Itakura, H. (2002). Gender and pragmatic transfer in topic development. *Language, Culture, and Curriculum, 15*, 161–183.

Ivanova, I., & Costa, A. (2008). Does bilingualism hamper lexical access in speech production? *Acta Psychologica, 127*(2), 277–288.

Iyer, G. K., Alladi, S., Bak, T. H., Shailaja, M., Mamidipudi, A., Rajan, A., ... & Kaul, S. (2014). Dementia in developing countries: Does education play the same role in India as in the West? *Dementia & Neuropsychologia, 8*, 132–140.

Jacobs, B., Schall, M., & Scheibel, A. (1993). A quantitative dendritic analysis of Wernicke's area in humans. II. Gender, hemispheric, and environmental factors. *Journal of Comparative Neurology, 327*(1), 97–111.

Jared, D., Pei Yun Poh, R., & Paivio, A. (2013). L1 and L2 picture naming in Mandarin-English bilinguals: A test of bilingual dual coding theory. *Bilingualism: Language and Cognition, 16*, 383–396.

Jarvis, S. (2002). Topic continuity in L2 English article use. *Studies in Second Language Acquisition, 24*, 387–418.

Jarvis, S. (2003). Probing the effects of the L2 on the L1: A case study. In V. Cook (Ed.), *Effects of the second language on the first* (pp. 81–102). Multilingual Matters.

Jarvis, S., & Pavlenko, A. (2008). *Crosslinguistic influence in language and cognition.* Routledge.

Jasińska, K. K., & Petitto, L. A. (2014). Development of neural systems for reading in the monolingual and bilingual brain: New insights from functional near infrared spectroscopy neuroimaging. *Developmental Neuropsychology, 39*(6), 421–439.

Jiang, N. (1999). Testing processing explanations for the asymmetry in masked cross-language priming. *Bilingualism: Language and Cognition, 2*, 59–75.

Jiang, N. (2002). Form-meaning mapping in vocabulary acquisition in a second language. *Studies in Second Language Acquisition, 24*, 617–637.

Jiang, N., & Forster, K. (2001). Cross-language priming asymmetries in lexical decision and episodic recognition. *Journal of Memory and Language, 4*, 32–51.

Jiménez, T. C., Filippini, A. L., & Gerber, M. M. (2006). Shared reading within Latino families: An analysis of reading interactions and language use. *Bilingual Research Journal, 30*(2), 431–452.

Johnson, A., Valachovic, A., & George, K. (1998). Speech-language pathology practice in the acute care setting: A consultative approach. In F. Johnson & B. Jacobson (Eds.), *Medical speech-language pathology: A practitioner's guide* (pp. 96–130). Thieme.

Johnson, J., & Newport, E. (1989). Critical period effects in second language learning: The influence of maturational state on the acquisition of English as a second language. *Cognitive Psychology*, *21*(1), 60–99.

Jones, G., & Rowland, C. F. (2017). Diversity not quantity in caregiver speech: Using computational modeling to isolate the effects of the quantity and the diversity of the input on vocabulary growth. *Cognitive Psychology*, *98*, 1–21.

Jones, P. E. (1995). Contradictions and unanswered questions in the Genie case: A fresh look at the linguistic evidence. *Language & Communication*, *15*(3), 261–280.

Jung, J. (2005). Issues in acquisitional pragmatics. *Working Papers in TESOL and Applied Linguistics*, *2*(3), 1–34.

Junqué, C., Vendrell, P., & Vendrell-Brucet, J. (1989). Differential recovery in naming in bilingual aphasics. *Brain and Language*, *36*, 16–22.

Jylkkä, J., Soveri, A., Laine, M., & Lehtonen, M. (2020). Assessing bilingual language switching behavior with Ecological Momentary Assessment. *Bilingualism: Language and Cognition*, *23*(2), 309–322.

Kałamała, P., Szewczyk, J., Chuderski, A., Senderecka, M., & Wodniecka, Z. (2020). Patterns of bilingual language use and response inhibition: A test of the adaptive control hypothesis. *Cognition*, *204*, 104373.

Kaplan, R. (1966). Cultural thought patterns in inter-cultural education. *Language Learning*, *16*, 1–20.

Karbe, H., Thiel, A., Weber-Luxenburger, G., Herholz, K., Kessler, J., & Heiss W. (1998). Brain plasticity in poststroke aphasia: What is the contribution of the right hemisphere? *Brain and Language*, *64*, 215–230.

Karim, K., & Nassaji, H. (2013). First language transfer in second language writing: An examination of current research. *Iranian Journal of Language Teaching Research, 1*(1), 117–134.

Keels, M. (2009). Ethnic group differences in early head start parents' parenting beliefs and practices and links to children's early cognitive development. *Early Childhood Research Quarterly*, *24*(4), 381–397.

Kellerman, E. (1995). Crosslinguistic influence: Transfer to nowhere? *Annual Review of Applied Linguistics*, *15*, 125–150.

Kellerman, E., & Sharwood Smith, M. (Eds.). (1986). *Crosslinguistic influence in second language acquisition*. Pergamon.

Kelly, A. C., Di Martino, A., Uddin, L. Q., Shehzad, Z., Gee, D. G., Reiss, P. T., Marguliesm D. S., Castellanos, F. X., & Milham, M. P.

(2009). Development of anterior cingulate functional connectivity from late childhood to early adulthood. *Cerebral Cortex, 19*(3), 640–657.

Kersten, K., & Winsler, A. (Eds.). (2022). *Understanding variability in second language acquisition, bilingualism, and cognition: A multi-layered perspective.* Taylor & Francis.

Keys, K. (2002). First language influence on the spoken English of Brazilian students of EFL. *ELT Journal, 56,* 41–46.

Khachatryan, E., Vanhoof, G., Beyens, H., Goeleven, A., Thijs, V., & Van Hulle, M. (2016). Language processing in bilingual aphasia: A new insight into the problem. *Wiley Interdisciplinary Reviews: Cognitive Science, 7,* 180–196.

Khamis, R., Venkert-Olenik, D., & Gil, M. (1996). Bilingualism in aphasia: The effect of L2 treatment on language performance in L1. *Journal of Speech, Language and Hearing Research, 19,* 73–82.

Kheder, S., & Kaan, E. (2021). Cognitive control in bilinguals: Proficiency and code-switching both matter. *Cognition, 209,* 104575.

Kidd, E., Donnelly, S., & Christiansen, M. H. (2018). Individual differences in language acquisition and processing. *Trends in Cognitive Sciences, 22*(2), 154–169.

Kim K., Relkin, N., Lee, K., & Hirsch, J. (1997). Distinct cortical areas associated with native and second languages. *Nature, 388*(6638), 171–174.

Kim S., Jeon S. G., Nam Y., Kim H. S., Yoo D., Moon M. (2019). Bilingualism for dementia: Neurological mechanisms associated with functional and structural changes in the brain. *Frontiers in Neuroscience, 13,* 1224.

Kiran, S., & Iakupova, R. (2011). Understanding the relationship between language proficiency, language impairment and rehabilitation: Evidence from a case study. *Clinical Linguistics & Phonetics, 25*(6–7), 565–583.

Kiran, S., & Roberts, P. (2010). Semantic feature analysis treatment in Spanish-English and French-English bilingual aphasia. *Aphasiology, 24*(2), 231–261.

Kiran, S., & Thompson, C. (2019). Neuroplasticity of language networks in aphasia: Advances, updates, and future challenges. *Frontiers in Neurology, 10,* 295.

Kiran, S., Sandberg, C., Gray, T., Ascenso, E., & Kester, E. (2013). Rehabilitation in bilingual aphasia: Evidence for within- and between-language generalization. *American Journal of Speech-Language Pathology, 22*(2), 298–309.

Kirsch, C., & Duarte, J. (Eds.). (2020). *Multilingual approaches for teaching and learning: From acknowledging to capitalising on multilingualism in European mainstream education.* Routledge.

Kirsner, K., Brown, H., Abrol, S., Chadha, N., & Sharma, N. (1980). Bilingualism and lexical representation. *Quarterly Journal of Experimental Psychology*, *32*(4), 585–594.

Kishiyama, M. M., Boyce, W. T., Jimenez, A. M., Perry, L. M., & Knight, R. T. (2009). Socioeconomic disparities affect prefrontal function in children. *Journal of Cognitive Neuroscience*, *21*(6), 1106–1115.

Klein, D., Milner, B., Zatorre, R., Meyer, E., & Evans, A. (1995). The neural substrates underlying word generation: A bilingual functional-imaging study. *Proceedings of the National Academy of Sciences of the United States of America*, *92*(7), 2899–2903.

Klein, D., Milner, B., Zatorre, R., Zhao, V., & Nikelski, J. (1999). Cerebral organization in bilinguals: A PET study of Chinese–English verb generation. *NeuroReport*, *10*, 2841–2846.

Klein, D., Zatorre, R., Milner, B., Meyer, E., & Evans, A. (1994). Left putaminal activation when speaking a second language: Evidence from PET. *NeuroReport*, *5*(17), 2295–2297.

Knoph, M. (2013). Language intervention in Arabic-English bilingual aphasia: A case study. *Aphasiology*, *27*, 1440–1458.

Knoph, M., Simonsen, H., & Lind, M. (2017). Cross-linguistic transfer effects of verb-production therapy in two cases of multilingual aphasia. *Aphasiology, 31*(12), 1482–1509.

Koda, K. (2005). Learning to read across writing systems: Transfer, metalinguistic awareness, and second language reading development. In V. Cook (Ed.), *Second language writing systems* (pp. 311–334). Multilingual Matters.

Koda, K. (2008). Impacts of prior literacy experience on learning to read in a second language. In K. Koda & A. Zehler (Eds.), *Learning to read across languages: Cross-linguistic relationships in first- and second-language literacy development* (pp. 68–96). Routledge.

Kohnert, K. (2004). Cognitive and cognate-based treatments for bilingual aphasia: A case study. *Brain and Language, 91*(3), 294–302.

Kohnert, K. (2009). Cross-language generalization following treatment in bilingual speakers with aphasia: A review. *Seminars in Speech and Language, 30*(3), 174–186.

Köpke, B. (2002). Activation thresholds and non-pathological first language attrition. In F. Fabbro (Ed.), *Advances in the neurolinguistics of bilingualism* (pp. 119–142). Forum.

Köpke, B., & Nespoulous, J.-L. (2006). Working memory performance in expert and novice interpreters. *Interpreting*, *8*(1), 1–23.

Korenar, M., Treffers-Daller, J., & Pliatsikas, C. (2022). Two languages in one mind: Insights into cognitive effects of bilingualism from usage-based approaches. *Naše Řeč, 106*(1), 24–46.

Kovács, Á. M., & Mehler, J. (2009). Flexible learning of multiple speech structures in bilingual infants. *Science*, *325*(5940), 611–612.

Kovelman, I., Shalinsky, M. H., Berens, M. S., & Petitto, L. A. (2008). Shining new light on the brain's "bilingual signature": A functional near infrared spectroscopy investigation of semantic processing. *Neuroimage*, *39*(3), 1457–1471.

Krashen, S. D. (1976). Formal and informal linguistic environments in language acquisition and language learning. *Tesol Quarterly*, *10*(2), 157–168.

Kreiner, H., & Degani, T. (2015). Tip-of-the-tongue in a second language: The effects of brief first-language exposure and long-term use. *Cognition*, *137*, 106–114.

Kremin, L. V., & Byers-Heinlein, K. (2021). Why not both? Rethinking categorical and continuous approaches to bilingualism. *International Journal of Bilingualism*, *25*(6), 1560–1575.

Kroll, J. (2008). Juggling two languages in one mind. *Psychological Science Agenda, American Psychological Association*, *22*(1).

Kroll, J. (2017). The bilingual lexicon: A window into language dynamics and cognition. In M. Libben, M. Goral, & G. Libben (Eds.), *Bilingualism: A framework for understanding the mental lexicon* (pp. 27–48). Benjamins.

Kroll, J., & de Groot, A. (1997). Lexical and conceptual memory in the bilingual: Mapping form to meaning in two languages. In A. de Groot & J. Kroll (Eds.), *Tutorials in bilingualism: Psycholinguistic perspectives* (pp. 169–199). Erlbaum.

Kroll, J., & Mendoza, G. A. (2022). Bilingualism: A cognitive and neural view of dual language experience. In *Oxford research encyclopedias of psychology*, (pp. 1–21). Oxford University Press.

Kroll, J., & Stewart, E. (1994). Category interference in translation and picture naming: Evidence for asymmetric connections between bilingual memory representations. *Journal of Memory and Language*, *33*, 149–174.

Kroll, J., & Tokowicz, N. (2005). *Models of bilingual representation and processing: Looking back and to the future*. Oxford University Press.

Kroll, J. F., Bobb, S. C., Misra, M., & Guo, T. (2008). Language selection in bilingual speech: Evidence for inhibitory processes. *Acta Psychologica*, *128*(3), 416–430.

Kroll, J., Dussias, P. E., Bice, K., & Perrotti, L. (2015). Bilingualism, mind, and brain. *Annual Review of Linguistics*, *1*, 377.

Kroll, J., Dussias, P. E., Bogulski, C. A., & Kroff, J. R. V. (2012). Juggling two languages in one mind: What bilinguals tell us about language processing and its consequences for cognition. *Psychology of Learning and Motivation*, *56*, 229–262.

Kroll, J., Michael, E., Tokowicz, N., & Dufour, R. (2002). The development of lexical fluency in a second language. *Second Language Research*, *18*, 137–171.

Kroll, J., van Hell, J., Tokowicz, N., & Green, D. (2010). The Revised Hierarchical Model: A critical review and assessment. *Bilingualism: Language and Cognition*, *13*, 373–381.

Kuhl, P. K. (2010). Brain mechanisms in early language acquisition. *Neuron*, *67*(5), 713–727.

Kuhl, P. K., Tsao, F. M., & Liu, H. M. (2003). Foreign-language experience in infancy: Effects of short-term exposure and social interaction on phonetic learning. *Proceedings of the National Academy of Sciences*, *100*(15), 9096–9101.

Kuhlen, A. K., Allefeld, C., Anders, S., & Haynes, J.-D. (2015). Towards a multi-brain perspective on communication in dialogue. In R. M. Willems (Ed.), *Cognitive neuroscience of natural language use* (pp. 182–200). Cambridge University Press.

Kuo, L.-J., & Anderson, R. (2006). Morphological awareness and learning to read: A cross-language perspective. *Educational Psychologist*, *41*, 161–180.

Kutas, M., & Federmeier, K. D. (2011). Thirty years and counting: Finding meaning in the N400 component of the event related brain potential (ERP). *Annual Review of Psychology*, *62*, 621–647.

Kutas, M., Moreno, E., & Wicha, N. (2009). Code-switching and the brain. In B. Bullock & A. Toribio (Eds.), *The Cambridge handbook of linguistics code-switching* (pp. 289–306). Cambridge University Press.

Kuzmina, E., Goral, M., Norvik, M., & Weekes, B. (2019). What influences language impairment in bilingual aphasia? A meta-analytic review. *Frontiers in Psychology*, *10*, 445.

La Heij, W., Hooglander, A., Kerling, R., & van der Velden, E. (1996). Nonverbal context effects in forward and backward word translation: Evidence for concept mediation. *Journal of Memory and Language*, *35*, 648–665.

Lado, B., Bowden, H. W., Stafford, C., & Sanz, C. (2017). Two birds, one stone, or how learning a foreign language makes you a better language learner. *Hispania*, *100*(3), 361–378.

Lado, R. (1957). *Linguistics across cultures: Applied linguistics for language teachers*. University of Michigan Press.

Laganaro, M., Di Pietro, M., & Schnider, A. (2003). Computerised treatment of anomia in chronic and acute aphasia: An exploratory study. *Aphasiology*, *17*, 709–721.

Lai, G., & O'Brien, B. A. (2020). Examining language switching and cognitive control through the adaptive control hypothesis. *Frontiers in Psychology*, *11*, 1171.

Lambert, W. E. (1975). Culture and language as factors in learning and education. In A. Wolfgang (Ed.), *Education of immigrant students: Issues and answers* (pp. 55–83). Ontario Institute for Studies in Education.

Lambert, W. E. (1980). The social psychology of language: A perspective for the 1980s. In H. Giles, W. Robinson, & P. Smith (Eds.), *Language: Social psychological perspectives*(pp. 415–424). Pergamon.

Lambert, W. E. (1985). Some cognitive and sociocultural consequences of being bilingual. In J. E. Alatis & J. J. Staczek (Eds.), *Perspectives on bilingualism and bilingual education*. Georgetown University Press.

LaPointe, L. (Ed.). (2011). *Handbook of aphasia and brain-based cognitive-language disorders*. Thieme.

Laska, A., Hellblom, A., Murray, V., Kahan, T., & Von Arbin M. (2001). Aphasia in acute stroke and relation to outcome. *Journal of Internal Medicine, 249*(5), 413–422.

Laufer, B., & Eliasson, S. (1993). What causes avoidance in L2 learning: L1-L2 differences, L1-L2 similarity, or L2 complexity? *Studies in Second Language Acquisition, 15*, 35–48.

Lauro, J., Core, C., & Hoff, E. (2020). Explaining individual differences in trajectories of simultaneous bilingual development: Contributions of child and environmental factors. *Child Development, 91*(6), 2063–2082.

Lazar, R., Speizer, A., Festa, J., Krakauer, J., & Marshall, R. (2008). Variability in language recovery after first-time stroke. *Journal of Neurology, Neurosurgery, & Psychiatry, 79*, 530–534.

Lee, C. (2007). Does horse activate mother? Processing lexical tone in form priming. *Language and Speech, 50*(1), 101–123.

Lee, J. (2000). Analysis of pragmatic speech styles among Korean learners of English: A focus on complaint-apology speech act sequences. *Dissertation Abstracts International, 61*, 535A.

Lee, Y. Y. (2022). Bilingualism, dementia, and the neurological mechanisms in between: The need for a more critical look into dementia subtypes. *Frontiers in Aging Neuroscience, 14*, 872508.

Lee, Y. Y., Jang, E., & Choi, W. (2018). L2-L1 translation priming effects in a lexical decision task: Evidence from low proficient Korean-English bilinguals. *Frontiers in Psychology, 9*, 267.

Legacy, J., Zesiger, P., Friend, M., & Poulin-Dubois, D. (2018). Vocabulary size and speed of word recognition in very young French–English bilinguals: A longitudinal study. *Bilingualism: Language and Cognition, 21*(1), 137–149.

Legault, J., Grant, A., Fang, S. Y., & Li, P. (2019). A longitudinal investigation of structural brain changes during second language learning. *Brain and Language, 197*, 104661.

Lehtonen, M., Laine, M., Niemi, J., Thomsen, T., Vorobyev, V., & Hugdahl, K. (2005). Brain correlates of sentence translation in Finnish-Norwegian bilinguals. *Neuroreport, 16*(6), 607–610.

Lei, M., Akama, H., & Murphy, B. (2014). Neural basis of language switching in the brain: fMRI evidence from Korean–Chinese early bilinguals. *Brain & Language, 138*, 12–18.

Leivada, E., Westergaard, M., Duñabeitia, J. A., & Rothman, J. (2021). On the phantom-like appearance of bilingualism effects on neurocognition: (How) should we proceed? *Bilingualism: Language and Cognition, 24*(1), 197–210.

Leminen, A., Kimppa, L., Leminen, M. M., Lehtonen, M., Mäkelä, J. P., & Shtyrov, Y. (2016). Acquisition and consolidation of novel morphology in human neocortex: A neuromagnetic study. *Cortex, 83*, 1–16.

Lenneberg, E. H. (1967). *Biological foundations of language.* Wiley.

Levelt, W. J. (1993). *Speaking: From intention to articulation.* MIT.

Levelt, W. J., Praamsma, P., Meyer, A., Helenius, P., & Salmelin, R. (1998). An MEG study of picture naming. *Journal of Cognitive Neuroscience, 10*, 553–557.

Li, P., & Grant, A. (2016). Second language learning success revealed by brain networks. *Bilingualism: Language and Cognition, 19*(4), 657–664.

Li, P., Legault, J., & Litcofsky, K. (2014). Neuroplasticity as a function of second language learning: Anatomical changes in the human brain. *Cortex, 58*, 301–324.

Li, P., Zhang, F., Yu, A., & Zhao, X. (2020). Language History Questionnaire (LHQ3): An enhanced tool for assessing multilingual experience. *Bilingualism: Language and Cognition, 23*(5), 938–944.

Liao, C., & Chan, S. (2016). Direction matters: Event-related brain potentials reflect extra processing costs in switching from the dominant to the less dominant language. *Journal of Neurolinguistics, 40*, 79–97.

Libben, G., & Schwieter, J. W. (2019). Lexical organization and reorganization in the multilingual mind. In J. W. Schwieter (Ed.), *The handbook of the neuroscience of multilingualism* (pp. 297–312). Wiley-Blackwell.

Libben, G., Goral, M., & Baayen, H. (2017b). Dynamicity and compound processing in bilinguals. In M. Libben, M. Goral, & G. Libben (Eds.), *Bilingualism: A framework for understanding the mental lexicon* (pp. 199–218). Benjamins.

Libben, M., & Titone, D. (2009). Bilingual lexical access in context: Evidence from eye movements during reading. *Journal of Experimental Psychology: Learning, Memory, and Cognition, 35*, 381–390.

Libben, M., Goral, M., & Libben, G. (2017a). The dynamic lexicon: Complex words in bilingual minds. In M. Libben, M. Goral, & G. Libben

(Eds.), *Bilingualism: A framework for understanding the mental lexicon* (pp. 1–7). Benjamins.

Lichtheim, L. (1885). On aphasia. *Brain*, *7*, 433–484.

Liégeois, F., Baldeweg, T., Connelly, A., Gadian, D., Mishkin, M., & Vargha-Khadem, F. (2003). Language fMRI abnormalities associated with FOXP2 gene mutation. *Nature Neuroscience*, *6*, 1230–1237.

Linck, J. A., Kroll, J. F., & Sunderman, G. (2009). Losing access to the native language while immersed in a second language: Evidence for the role of inhibition in second-language learning. *Psychological Science*, *20*(12), 1507–1515.

Lindell, A. K. (2006). In your right mind: Right hemisphere contributions to language processing and production. *Neuropsychology Review*, *16*(3), 131–148.

Liu, C., de Bruin, A., Jiao, L., Li, Z., & Wang, R. (2021a). Second language learning tunes the language control network: A longitudinal fMRI study. *Language, Cognition and Neuroscience*, *36*(4), 462–473.

Liu, C., Jiao, L., Li, Z., Timmer, K., & Wang, R. (2021b). Language control network adapts to second language learning: A longitudinal rs-fMRI study. *Neuropsychologia*, *150*, 107688.

Liu, C., Jiao, L., Timmer, K., & Wang, R. (2021c). Structural brain changes with second language learning: A longitudinal voxel-based morphometry study. *Brain and Language*, *222*, 105015.

Liu, C., Yang, C. L., Jiao, L., Schwieter, J. W., Sun, X., & Wang, R. (2019). Training in language switching facilitates bilinguals' monitoring and inhibitory control. *Frontiers in Psychology*, *10*, 1839.

Liu, H., & Cao, F. (2016). L1 and L2 processing in the bilingual brain: A meta-analysis of neuroimaging studies. *Brain and Language*, *159*, 60–73.

Long, M. R., Vega-Mendoza, M., Rohde, H., Sorace, A., & Bak, T. H. (2020). Understudied factors contributing to variability in cognitive performance related to language learning. *Bilingualism: Language and Cognition*, *23*(4), 801–811.

Lorenzen, B., & Murray, L. (2008). Bilingual aphasia: A theoretical and clinical review. *The American Journal of Speech-Language Pathology*, *17*, 299–317.

Lowie, W., & Verspoor, M. (2004). Input versus transfer?: The role of frequency and similarity in the acquisition of L2 prepositions. In M. Achard & S. Niemeier (Eds.), *Cognitive linguistics, second language acquisition, and foreign language teaching* (pp. 77–94). de Gruyter.

Lucas, T., McKhann, G., & Ojemann, G. (2004). Functional separation of languages in the bilingual brain: A comparison of electrical stimulation language mapping in 25 bilingual patients and 117 monolingual control patients. *Journal of Neurosurgery*, *101*, 449–457.

Luck, S. J. (2014). *An introduction to the event-related potential technique.* MIT Press.

Luk, G., & Bialystok, E. (2013). Bilingualism is not a categorical variable: Interaction between language proficiency and usage. *Journal of Cognitive Psychology, 25*(5), 605–621.

Luk, G., & Grundy, J. G. (2023). The importance of recognizing social contexts in research on bilingualism. *Bilingualism: Language and Cognition, 26*(1), 25–27.

Luk, G., & Rothman, J. (2022). Experience-based individual differences modulate language, mind, and brain outcomes in multilinguals. *Brain and Language, 228*, 105107.

Luk, G., Anderson, J. A., Craik, F. I., Grady, C., & Bialystok, E. (2010). Distinct neural correlates for two types of inhibition in bilinguals: Response inhibition versus interference suppression. *Brain and Cognition, 74*(3), 347–357.

Luk, G., Bialystok, E., Craik, F. I., & Grady, C. L. (2011). Lifelong bilingualism maintains white matter integrity in older adults. *Journal of Neuroscience, 31*(46), 16808–16813.

Luk, G., Green, D., Abutalebi, J., & Grady, C. (2012). Cognitive control for language switching in bilinguals: A quantitative meta-analysis of functional neuroimaging studies. *Language and Cognitive Processes, 27*(10), 1479–1488.

Luo, X., Cheung, H., Bel, D., Li, L., Chen, L., & Mo, L. (2013). The roles of semantic sense and form-meaning connection in translation priming. *Psychological Record, 63*, 193–208.

MacDonald, M. (1999). Distributional information in language comprehension, production, and acquisition: Three puzzles and a moral. In B. MacWhinney (Ed.), *The emergence of language* (pp. 177–196). Erlbaum.

MacDonald, M. (2013). How language production shapes language form and comprehension. *Frontiers in Psychology, 4*(226), 1–16.

Macnamara, J., & Kushnir, S. (1971). Linguistic independence of bilinguals: The input switch. *Journal of Verbal Learning and Verbal Behavior, 10*(5), 480–487.

MacWhinney, B., Bates, E., & Kliegl, R. (1984). Cue validity and sentence interpretation in English, German, and Italian. *Journal of Verbal Learning and Verbal Behavior, 23*, 127–150.

Maguire, E. A., Gadian, D. G., Johnsrude, I. S., Good, C. D., Ashburner, J., Frackowiak, R. S., & Frith, C. D. (2000). Navigation-related structural change in the hippocampi of taxi drivers. *Proceedings of the National Academy of Sciences, 97*(8), 4398–4403.

Malcolm, T., Lerman, A., Korytkowska, M., Vonk, J., & Obler, L. (2019). Primary progressive aphasia in bilinguals and multilinguals. In J. W.

Schwieter (Ed.), *The handbook of the neuroscience of multilingualism* (pp. 572–591). Wiley-Blackwell.

Malins, J., & Joanisse, M. (2010). The roles of tonal and segmental information in Mandarin spoken word recognition: An eyetracking study. *Journal of Memory and Language, 62*(4), 407–420.

Mamiya, P. C., Richards, T. L., Coe, B. P., Eichler, E. E., & Kuhl, P. K. (2016). Brain white matter structure and COMT gene are linked to second-language learning in adults. *Proceedings of the National Academy of Sciences, 113*(26), 7249–7254.

Maragnolo, P., Rizzi, C., Peran, P., Piras, F., & Sabatini, U. (2009). Parallel recovery in a bilingual aphasic: A neurolinguistic and fMRI study. *Neuropsychology, 23*, 405–409.

Marian, V. (2008). Bilingual research methods. In J. Altarriba & R. R. Heredia (Eds.), *An introduction to bilingualism. Principles and processes* (pp. 13–37). Erlbaum.

Marian, V., & Hayakawa, S. (2021). Measuring bilingualism: The quest for a "bilingualism quotient". *Applied Psycholinguistics, 42*(2), 527–548.

Marian, V., & Spivey, M. (2003). Competing activation in bilingual language processing: Within-and between-language competition. *Bilingualism: Language and Cognition, 6*(2), 97–115.

Mariën, P., Abutalebi, J., Engelborghs, S., & De Deyn, P. P. (2005). Pathophysiology of language switching and mixing in an early bilingual child with subcortical aphasia. *Neurocase, 11*, 385–398.

Markiewicz, R., Mazaheri, A., & Krott, A. (2023). Bilingualism can cause enhanced monitoring and occasional delayed responses in a Flanker task. *European Journal of Neuroscience, 57(1)*, 129–147.

Martin-Rhee, M. M., & Bialystok, E. (2008). The development of two types of inhibitory control in monolingual and bilingual children. *Bilingualism: Language and Cognition, 11*(1), 81–93.

Masek, L. R., McMillan, B. T., Paterson, S. J., Tamis-LeMonda, C. S., Golinkoff, R. M., & Hirsh-Pasek, K. (2021). Where language meets attention: How contingent interactions promote learning. *Developmental Review, 60*, 1–12.

Matusevych, Y., Beekhuizen, B., & Stevenson, S. (2018). Crosslinguistic transfer as category adjustment: Modeling conceptual color shift in bilingualism. *Proceedings of the Annual Meeting of the Cognitive Science Society, 40*, 744–749.

McCabe, A., Tamis-LeMonda, C. S., Bornstein, M. H., Brockmeyer Cates, C., Golinkoff, R., Wishard Guerra, A., … & Song, L. (2013). Multilingual children beyond myths and toward best practices. *Society for Research in Child Development, 27*(4), 1–36.

McCrory, E., Frith, U., Brunswick, N., & Price, C. (2000). Abnormal functional activation during a simple word repetition task: A PET study of adult dyslexics. *Journal of Cognitive Neuroscience, 12*, 753–762.

McDermott, K. B., Buckner, R. L., Petersen, S. E., Kelley, W. M., & Sanders, A. L. (1999). Set-and code-specific activation in the frontal cortex: An fMRI study of encoding and retrieval of faces and words. *Journal of Cognitive Neuroscience, 11*(6), 631–640.

McLaughlin, B. (1984). *Second language acquisition in childhood* (Vol. 1). Erlbaum.

Mechelli, A., Crinion, J. T., Noppeney, U., O'Doherty, J., Ashburner, J., Frackowiak, R. S., & Price, C. J. (2004). Neurolinguistics: Structural plasticity in the bilingual brain. *Nature, 431*(7010), 757.

Meinzer, M., Obleser, J., Flaisch, T., Eulitz, C., & Rockstroh B. (2007). Recovery from aphasia as a function of language therapy in an early bilingual patient demonstrated by fMRI. *Neuropsychologia, 45*(6), 1247–1256.

Meisel, J. (1989). Early differentiation of languages in bilingual children. In K. Hyltenstam & L. Obler (Eds.), *Bilingualism across the lifespan: Aspects of acquisition, maturity and loss* (pp. 13–40). Cambridge University Press.

Meisel, J. (2011). *First and second language acquisition: Parallels and differences*. Cambridge University Press.

Melby-Lervag, M., & Lervag, A. (2011). Cross-linguistic transfer of oral language, decoding, phonological awareness and reading comprehension: A meta-analysis of the correlational evidence. *Journal of Research in Reading, 34*(1), 114–135.

Melo-Pfeifer, S. (2020). Intercomprehension in the mainstream language classroom at secondary school level: How online multilingual interaction fosters foreign language learning. In C. Kirsch & J. Duarte (Eds.), *Multilingual approaches for teaching and learning* (pp. 94–113). Routledge.

Meltzoff, A. N., Kuhl, P. K., Movellan, J., & Sejnowski, T. J. (2009). Foundations for a new science of learning. *Science, 325*(5938), 284–288.

Merkx, M., Rastle, K., & Davis, M. H. (2011). The acquisition of morphological knowledge investigated through artificial language learning. *The Quarterly Journal of Experimental Psychology, 64*(6), 1200–1220.

Mesulam, M., Rogalski, E., Wieneke, C., Hurley, R., Geula, C., ... & Weintraub, S. (2014). Primary progressive aphasia and the evolving neurology of the language network. *Nature Reviews: Neurology, 10*(10), 554–569.

Meuter, R., & Allport, A. (1999). Bilingual language switching in naming: Asymmetrical costs of language selection. *Journal of Memory and Language, 40*(1), 25–40.

Meznah, A. (2018). Investigating the negative impact of pragmatic transfer on the acquisition of English pragmatic as perceved by L2 Learners: A review. *International Journal of English and Literature, 9*(3), 18–24.

Michael, E. B., & Gollan, T. H. (2005). Being and becoming bilingual. In J. Kroll & A. de Groot (Eds.), *Handbook of bilingualism: Psycholinguistic approaches* (pp. 389–407). Oxford University Press.

Miertsch, B., Meisel, J., & Isel, F. (2009). Non-treated languages in aphasia therapy of polyglots benefit from improvement in the treated language. *Journal of Neurolinguistics, 22*, 135–150.

Miikkulainen, R., & Kiran, S. (2009). Modeling the bilingual lexicon of an individual subject. In J. Princípe & R. Miikkulainen (Eds.), *Proceedings of the 7th international workshop on advances in self-organizing maps* (pp. 191–199). Springer-Verlag.

Miller Amberber, A. (2012). Language intervention in French-English bilingual aphasia: Evidence of limited therapy transfer. *Journal of Neurolinguistics, 25*(6), 588–614.

Mion, M., Patterson, K., Acosta-Cabronero, J., Pengas, G., Izquierdo-Garcia, D., Hong, Y., ... & Nestor, P. (2010). What the left and right anterior fusiform gyri tell us about semantic memory. *Brain, 133*(11), 3256–3268.

Mishra, M., & Abutalebi, J. (Eds.). (2020). Cognitive consequences of bilingualism [Special issue]. *Journal of Cultural Cognitive Science, 4*(2), 123–291.

Mishra, R. K. (2015). Let's not forget about language proficiency and cultural variations while linking bilingualism to executive control. *Bilingualism: Language and Cognition, 18*(1), 39–40.

Mitchell, D., Cuetos, F., & Corley, M. (1992). Statistical versus linguistic determinants of parsing bias: Cross-linguistic evidence. Paper presented at the *Fifth Annual CUNY conference on Human Sentence Processing*, New York, NY.

Mitchell, D., Cuetos, F., Corley, M., & Brysbaert, M. (1995). Exposure-based models of human parsing: Evidence for the use of coarse-grained (non-lexical) statistical records. *Journal of Psycholinguistic Research, 24*, 469–488.

Miura, K., Nakamura, Y., Miura, F., Yamada, I., Takahashi, R., ... & Mizobata, T. (1999). Functional magnetic resonance imaging to word generation task in a patient with Broca's aphasia. *Journal of Neurolinguistics, 246*, 939–942.

Miyake, A., Friedman, N. P., Emerson, M. J., Witzki, A. H., Howerter, A., & Wager, T. D. (2000). The unity and diversity of executive functions and their contributions to complex "frontal lobe" tasks: A latent variable analysis. *Cognitive Psychology, 41*(1), 49–100.

Mohades, S. G., Van Schuerbeek, P., Rosseel, Y., Van De Craen, P., Luypaert, R., & Baeken, C. (2015). White-matter development is different in bilingual and monolingual children: A longitudinal DTI study. *PLoS One*, *10*(2), e0117968.

Monnier, C., Boiché, J., Armandon, P., Baudoin, S., & Bellocchi, S. (2022). Is bilingualism associated with better working memory capacity? A meta-analysis. *International Journal of Bilingual Education and Bilingualism*, *25*(6), 2229–2255.

Montanari, S. (2019). Facilitated language learning in multilinguals. In S. Montanari & S. Quay (Eds.), *Multidisciplinary perspectives on multilingualism: The fundamentals* (pp. 302–324). De Gruyter.

Morales, J., Padilla, F., Gómez-Ariza, C., & Bajo, M. T. (2015). Simultaneous interpretation selectively influences working memory and attentional networks. *Acta Psychologica*, *155,* 82–91.

Moreno, E. M., Federmeier, K. D., & Kutas, M. (2002). Switching languages, switching palabras (words): An electrophysiological study of code switching. *Brain and Language*, *80*, 188–207.

Mosca, M., & de Bot, K. (2017). Bilingual language switching: Production vs. recognition. *Frontiers in Psychology*, *8*(934), 1–18.

Mouthon, M., Annoni, J. M., & Khateb, A. (2013). The bilingual brain. *Swiss Archives of Neurology and Psychiatry*, *164*(8), 266–273.

Mukadam, N., Jichi, F., Green, D., & Livingston, G. (2018). The relationship of bilingualism to cognitive decline: The Australian longitudinal study of ageing. *International Journal of Geriatric Psychiatry*, *33*(2), e249–e256.

Muysken, P. (2000). *Bilingual speech: A typology of code-mixing.* Cambridge University Press.

Naatanen, R., Lehtokoski, A., Lennes, M., Cheour, M., Huotilainen, M., Livonen, A., … & Alho, K. (1997). Language-specific phoneme representations revealed by electric and magnetic brain responses. *Nature*, *385*, 432–434.

Nacar Garcia, L., Guerrero-Mosquera, C., Colomer, M., & Sebastian-Galles, N. (2018). Evoked and oscillatory EEG activity differentiates language discrimination in young monolingual and bilingual infants. *Scientific Reports*, *8*(1), 1–9.

Nadesan, M. H. (2002). Engineering the entrepreneurial infant: Brain science, infant development toys, and governmentality. *Cultural Studies*, *16*(3), 401–432.

Naeem, K., Filippi, R., Periche-Tomas, E., Papageorgiou, A., & Bright, P. (2018). The importance of socioeconomic status as a modulator of the bilingual advantage in cognitive ability. *Frontiers in Psychology*, *9*, 1818.

Nakayama, M., Ida, K., & Lupker, S. (2016). Cross-script L2-L1 noncognate translation priming in lexical decision depends on L2 proficiency: Evidence from Japanese-English bilinguals. *Bilingualism: Language and Cognition, 19*(5), 1001–1022.

Nakayama, M., Lupker, S., & Itaguchi, Y. (2018). An examination of L2-L1 noncognate translation priming in the lexical decision task: Insights from distributional and frequency-based analyses. *Bilingualism: Language and Cognition, 21*(2), 265–277.

National Aphasia Association. (2020). 2020 aphasia awareness survey. Retrieved on May 19, 2020 from www.aphasia.org/2020-aphasia-awareness-survey.

National Institute on Deafness and Other Communication Disorders. (2015). NIDCD fact sheet: Aphasia. Retrieved on May 19, 2020 from www.nidcd.nih.gov/sites/default/files/Documents/health/voice/Aphasia6-1-16.pdf.

Navarro-Torres, C. A., Beatty-Martínez, A. L., Kroll, J. F., & Green, D. W. (2021). Research on bilingualism as discovery science. *Brain and Language, 222*, 105014.

Nichols, E., & Joanisse, M. F. (2016). Functional activity and white matter microstructure reveal the independent effects of age of acquisition and proficiency on second-language learning. *NeuroImage, 143*, 15–25.

Nicoladis, E. (2008). Bilingual and language cognitive development. In J. Altarriba & R. R. Heredia (Eds.), *An introduction to bilingualism. Principles and processes* (pp. 167–181). Erlbaum.

Nicoladis, E., & Smithson, L. (2022). Gesture in bilingual language acquisition. In A. Morgenstern & S. Goldin-Meadow (Eds.), *Gesture in language: Development across the lifespan* (pp. 297–315). De Gruyter Mouton.

Nicoladis, E., Hui, D., & Wiebe, S. A. (2018). Language dominance and cognitive flexibility in French–English bilingual children. *Frontiers in Psychology, 9*, 1697.

Nielsen, M., & Haun, D. (2016). Why developmental psychology is incomplete without comparative and cross-cultural perspectives. *Philosophical Transactions of the Royal Society B: Biological Sciences, 371*(1686), 1–7.

Noble, K. G., Houston, S. M., Kan, E., & Sowell, E. R. (2012). Neural correlates of socioeconomic status in the developing human brain. *Developmental Science, 15*(4), 516–527.

Ochs, E., & Schieffelin, B. B. (2011). The theory of language socialization. In A. Duranti, E. Ochs, & B. B. Schieffelin (Eds.), *The handbook of language socialization* (pp. 1–21). Blackwell.

Odlin, T. (1989). *Language transfer: Cross-linguistic influence in language learning.* Cambridge University Press.

Odlin, T., & Jarvis, S. (2004). Same source, different outcomes: A study of Swedish influence on the acquisition of English in Finland. *International Journal of Multilingualism*, *1*, 123–140.

Ojemann, G., & Whitaker, H. (1978) The bilingual brain. *Archives of Neurology*, *35*, 409–412.

Olson, D. J. (2022). The Bilingual Code-Switching Profile (BCSP): Assessing the reliability and validity of the BCSP questionnaire. *Linguistic Approaches to Bilingualism*. https://doi.org/10.1075/lab.21039.ols.

Ortega, L. (2019). SLA and the study of equitable multilingualism. *The Modern Language Journal*, *103*, 23–38.

Ortega, L. (2020). The study of heritage language development from a bilingualism and social justice perspective. *Language Learning*, *70*, 15–53.

Osterhout, L., McLaughlin, J., Pitkänen, I., Frenck-Mestre, C., & Molinaro, N. (2006). Novice learners, longitudinal designs, and event-related potentials: A means for exploring the neurocognition of second language processing. *Language Learning*, *56*, 199–230.

Ouzia, J., & Filippi, R. (2016). The bilingual advantage in the auditory domain. In J. W. Schwieter (Ed.), *Cognitive control and consequences of multilingualism* (pp. 299–322). Benjamins.

Paap, K. (2023). *The bilingual advantage in executive functioning hypothesis: How the debate provides insight into psychology's replication crisis*. Routledge.

Paap, K. R., & Greenberg, Z. I. (2013). There is no coherent evidence for a bilingual advantage in executive processing. *Cognitive Psychology*, *66*(2), 232–258.

Paap, K. R., & Sawi, O. (2014). Bilingual advantages in executive functioning: Problems in convergent validity, discriminant validity, and the identification of the theoretical constructs. *Frontiers in Psychology*, *5*, 962.

Paap, K. R., & Sawi, O. (2016). The role of test-retest reliability in measuring individual and group differences in executive functioning. *Journal of Neuroscience Methods*, *274*, 81–93.

Paap, K. R., Anders-Jefferson, R., Mason, L., Alvarado, K., & Zimiga, B. (2018). Bilingual advantages in inhibition or selective attention: More challenges. *Frontiers in Psychology*, *9*, 1409.

Paap, K. R., Darrow, J., Dalibar, C., & Johnson, H. A. (2015a). Effects of script similarity on bilingual advantages in executive control are likely to be negligible or null. *Frontiers in Psychology*, *5*, 1539.

Paap, K. R., Johnson, H. A., & Sawi, O. (2015b). Bilingual advantages in executive functioning either do not exist or are restricted to very specific and undetermined circumstances. *Cortex*, *69*, 265–278.

Paap, K. R., Johnson, H. A., & Sawi, O. (2016). Should the search for bilingual advantages in executive functioning continue. *Cortex*, *74*(4), 305–314.

Paivio, A. (1986). *Mental representations: A dual coding approach.* Oxford University Press.

Paivio, A. (2010). Dual coding theory and the mental lexicon. *The Mental Lexicon, 5,* 205–230.

Pallier, C., Dehaene, S., Poline, J. B., LeBihan, D., Argenti, A. M., Dupoux, E., & Mehler, J. (2003). Brain imaging of language plasticity in adopted adults: Can a second language replace the first? *Cerebral Cortex, 13*(2), 155–161.

Palomar-García, M. Á., Bueichekú, E., Avila, C., Sanjuán, A., Strijkers, K., Ventura-Campos, N., & Costa, A. (2015). Do bilinguals show neural differences with monolinguals when processing their native language? *Brain and Language, 142,* 36–44.

Papageorgiou, A., Bright, P., Periche Tomas, E., & Filippi, R. (2019). Evidence against a cognitive advantage in the older bilingual population. *Quarterly Journal of Experimental Psychology, 72*(6), 1354–1363.

Paquot, M. (2017). L1 frequency in foreign language acquisition: Recurrent word combinations in French and Spanish EFL learner writing. *Second Language Research, 33*(1), 13–32.

Paradis, J. (2001). Do bilingual two-year-olds have separate phonological systems? *The International Journal of Bilingualism, 5*(1), 19–38.

Paradis, J. (2011). Individual differences in child English second language acquisition: Comparing child-internal and child-external factors. *Linguistic Approaches to Bilingualism, 1*(3), 213–237.

Paradis, J. (2016). The development of English as a second language with and without specific language impairment: Clinical implications. *Journal of Speech, Language, and Hearing Research, 59*(1), 171–182.

Paradis, J. (2019). English second language acquisition from early childhood to adulthood: The role of age, first language, cognitive, and input factors. *Proceedings of the BUCLD, 43,* 11–26.

Paradis, J., & Navarro, S. (2003). Subject realization and crosslinguistic interference in the bilingual acquisition of Spanish and English: What is the role of the input? *Journal of Child Language, 30,* 371–393.

Paradis, J., Rusk, B., Duncan, T. S., & Govindarajan, K. (2017). Children's second language acquisition of English complex syntax: The role of age, input, and cognitive factors. *Annual Review of Applied Linguistics, 37,* 148–167.

Paradis, M. (1977). Bilingualism and aphasia. In H. Whitaker & H. Whitaker (Eds.), *Studies in neurolinguistics, vol. 3* (pp. 65–121). Academic Press.

Paradis, M. (1987). *Bilingual aphasia test.* Erlbaum.

Paradis, M. (1990). Language lateralization in bilinguals: Enough already! *Brain and Language, 39,* 576–586.

Paradis, M. (2000). Prerequisites for a study of neurolinguistic processes involved in simultaneous interpreting. A synopsis. In B. Englund Dimitrova & K. Hyltenstam (Eds.), *Language processing and simultaneous interpreting: Interdisciplinary perspectives* (pp. 17–24). Benjamins.

Paradis, M. (2001). Bilingual and polyglot aphasia. In R. Berndt (Ed.), *Handbook of neuropsychology* (2nd ed.) (pp. 69–91). Elsevier.

Paradis, M. (2003). The bilingual Loch Ness Monster raises its non-asymmetric head again – Or, why bother with such cumbersome notions as validity and reliability? Comments on Evans et al. (2002). *Brain and Language, 87,* 441–448.

Paradis, M. (2004). *A neurolinguistic theory of bilingualism* (Vol. 18). Benjamins.

Paradis, M. (2011). Principles underlying the Bilingual Aphasia Test (BAT) and its uses. *Clinical Linguistics & Phonetics, 25*(6–7), 427–443.

Paradis, M., & Libben, G. (1987). *The assessment of bilingual aphasia.* Erlbaum.

Parker Jones, Ō., Green, D. W., Grogan, A., Pliatsikas, C., Filippopolitis, K., Ali, N., … & Price, C. J. (2012). Where, when, and why brain activation differs for bilinguals and monolinguals during picture naming and reading aloud. *Cerebral Cortex, 22*(4), 892–902.

Parkinson, B., Raymer, A., Chang, Y-L., Fitzgerald, D., & Crosson B. (2009). Lesion characteristics related to treatment improvement in object and action naming for patients with chronic aphasia. *Brain and Language, 110*(2), 61–70.

Pavlenko, A. (2009). Conceptual representation in the bilingual lexicon and second language vocabulary learning. In A. Pavlenko (Ed.), *The bilingual mental lexicon: Interdisciplinary approaches* (pp. 125–160). Multilingualism Matters.

Pavlenko, A., & Driagina, V. (2007). Russian emotion vocabulary in American learners' narratives. *Modern Language Journal, 91,* 213–234.

Pavlenko, A., & Jarvis, S. (2002). Bidirectional transfer. *Applied Linguistics, 23,* 190–214.

Pavlenko, A., & Malt, B. C. (2011). Kitchen Russian: Cross-linguistic differences and first-language object naming by Russian–English bilinguals. *Bilingualism: Language and Cognition, 14*(1), 19–45.

Pavlenko, A., Jarvis, S., Melnyk, S., & Sorokina, A. (2017). Communicative relevance: Color references in bilingual and trilingual speakers. *Bilingualism: Language and Cognition, 20,* 853–866.

Pedersen, P., Jørgensen, H., Nakayama, H., Raaschou, H., & Olsen, T. (1995). Aphasia in acute stroke: Incidence, determinants, and recovery. *Annals of Neurology, 38*(4), 659–666.

Peñaloza, C., & Kiran, S. (2019). Recovery and rehabilitation patterns in bilingual and multilingual aphasia. In J. W. Schwieter (Ed.), *The handbook of the neuroscience of multilingualism* (pp. 553–571). Wiley-Blackwell.

Peñaloza, C., Barrett, K., & Kiran, S. (2020). The influence of pre-stroke proficiency on post-stroke lexical-semantic performance in bilingual aphasia. *Aphasiology, 34*(10), 1223–1240.

Penfield, W., & Roberts, L. (1959). *Speech and brain mechanisms.* Princeton University Press.

Perani D., & Abutalebi J. (2015). Bilingualism, dementia, cognitive and neural reserve. *Current Opinion in Neurology, 28*, 618–625.

Perani, D., & Abutalebi, J. (2005). The neural basis of first and second language processing. *Current Opinion in Neurobiology, 15*, 202–206.

Perani, D., Abutalebi, J., Paulesu, E., Brambati, S., Scifo, P., Cappa, S. F., & Fazio, F. (2003). The role of age of acquisition and language usage in early, high-proficient bilinguals: An fMRI study during verbal fluency. *Human Brain Mapping, 19*(3), 170–182.

Perani, D., Dehaene, S., Grassi, F., Cohen, L., Cappa, S. F., Dupoux, E., ... & Mehler, J. (1996). Brain processing of native and foreign languages. *NeuroReport-International Journal for Rapid Communications of Research in Neuroscience, 7*(15), 2439–2444

Perani, D., Farsad, M., Ballarini, T., Lubian, F., Malpetti, M., Fracchetti, A., ... & Abutalebi, J. (2017). The impact of bilingualism on brain reserve and metabolic connectivity in Alzheimer's dementia. *Proceedings of the National Academy of Sciences, 114*(7), 1690–1695.

Perani, D., Paulesu, E., Sebastián-Gallés, N., Dupoux, E., Dehaene, S., Bertinatti, V., Cappa, S., Fazio, F., & Mehler, J. (1998). The bilingual brain: Proficiency and age of acquisition of the second language. *Brain, 121*, 1841–1852.

Peristeri, E., & Tsapkini, K. (2011). A comparison of the BAT and BDAE-SF batteries in determining the linguistic ability in Greek-speaking patients with Broca's aphasia. *Clinical Linguistics & Phonetics, 25*(6–7), 464–479.

Peyer, E., Kaiser, I., & Berthele, R. (2010). The multilingual reader: Advantages in understanding and decoding German sentence structure when reading German as an L3. *International Journal of Multilingualism, 7*(3), 225–239.

Pfenninger, S., Festman, J., & Singleton, D. (2023). *Second language acquisition and lifelong learning: An introduction and methodological guide.* Routledge.

Pham, G., Donovan, D., Dam, Q., & Contant, A. (2018). Learning words and definitions in two languages: What promotes cross-language transfer? *Language Learning, 68*(1), 206–223.

Pika, S., Nicoladis, E., & Marentette, P. F. (2006). A cross-cultural study on the use of gestures: Evidence for cross-linguistic transfer? *Bilingualism: Language and Cognition, 9*(3), 319–327.

Pinker, S. (1994). *The language instinct: The new science of language and mind.* Penguin.

Pisoni, D., Aslin, R., Perey, A., & Hennessy, B. (1982). Some effects of laboratory training on identification and discrimination of voicing contrasts in stop consonants. *Journal of Experimental Psychology: Human Perception and Performance, 8*, 297–314.

Pitres, A. (1895a). Aphasia in polyglots. In M. Paradis (Ed.) (1983), *Readings on aphasia in bilinguals and polyglots* (pp. 26–49). Marcel-Dieder.

Pitres, A. (1895b). Étude sur l'aphasie chez les polyglottes. *Revue de médicine, 15*, 873–899.

Pizzamiglio, L., Mammucari, A., & Razzano, C. (1985). Evidence for sex differences in brain organization in recovery in aphasia. *Brain and Language, 25*(2), 213–223.

Pliatsikas, C. (2020). Understanding structural plasticity in the bilingual brain: The dynamic restructuring model. *Bilingualism: Language and Cognition, 23*(2), 459–471.

Pliatsikas, C., DeLuca, V., & Voits, T. (2020). The many shades of bilingualism: Language experiences modulate adaptations in brain structure. *Language Learning, 70*(S2), 133–149.

Pliatsikas, C., DeLuca, V., Moschopoulou, E., & Saddy, J. D. (2017). Immersive bilingualism reshapes the core of the brain. *Brain Structure and Function, 222*(4), 1785–1795.

Pliatsikas, C., Meteyard, L., Veríssimo, J., DeLuca, V., & Shattuck, K. (2020). The effect of bilingualism on brain development from early childhood to young adulthood. *Brain Structure and Function, 225*, 2131–2152.

Pliatsikas, C., Moschopoulou, E., & Saddy, J. D. (2015). The effects of bilingualism on the white matter structure of the brain. *Proceedings of the National Academy of Sciences, 112*(5), 1334–1337.

Pliatsikas, C., Pereira Soares, S. M., Voits, T., DeLuca, V., & Rothman, J. (2021). Bilingualism is a long-term cognitively challenging experience that modulates metabolite concentrations in the healthy brain. *Scientific Reports, 11*(1), 1–12.

Poarch, G. J., & Krott, A. (2019). A bilingual advantage? An appeal for a change in perspective and recommendations for future research. *Behavioral Sciences, 9*(9), 95.

Poarch, G. J., & van Hell, J. G. (2012a). Executive functions and inhibitory control in multilingual children: Evidence from second-language learners, bilinguals, and trilinguals. *Journal of Experimental Child Psychology, 113*(4), 535–551.

Poarch, G., & van Hell, J. (2012b). Cross-language activation in children's speech production: Evidence from second language learners, bilinguals, and trilinguals. *Journal of Experimental Child Psychology*, *111*, 419–438.

Polyn, S. M., Natu, V. S., Cohen, J. D., & Norman, K. A. (2005). Category-specific cortical activity precedes retrieval during memory search. *Science*, *310*(5756), 1963–1966.

Postman-Caucheteux, W., Birn, R., Pursley, R., Butman, J., Solomon, J., ... & Braun, A. (2010). Single-trial fMRI shows contralesional activity linked to overt naming errors in chronic aphasic patients. *Journal of Cognitive Neuroscience*, *22*, 1299–1318.

Potter, C., So, Q-F, von Eckart, B., & Feldman, L. (1984). Lexical and conceptual representation in beginning and proficient bilinguals. *Journal of Verbal Learning and Verbal Behaviour*, *23*, 23–38.

Poulin-Dubois, D., Neumann, C., Masoud, S., & Gazith, A. (2022). Effect of bilingualism on infants' cognitive flexibility. *Bilingualism: Language and Cognition*, *25*(3), 484–497.

Poulisse, N. (1999). *Slips of the tongue: Speech errors in first and second language production.* Benjamins.

Poulisse, N., & Bongaerts, T. (1994). First language use in second language production. *Applied Linguistics*, *15*(1), 36–57.

Poulisse, N., Bongaerts, T., & Kellerman, E. (1984). On the use of compensatory strategies in second language performance. *Interlanguage Studies Bulletin*, 70–105.

Price, C. (2000). The anatomy of language: Contributions from functional neuroimaging. *Journal of Anatomy*, *197*, 335–359.

Price, C., Green, D., & von Studnitz, R. (1999). Functional imaging study of translation and language switching. *Brain*, *122*, 2221–2235.

Pruijn, L., Peacock, J., & Dijkstra, T. (in press). Mechanisms of word translation production: Empirical and simulation data.

Pulvermüller, F. (1999). Words in the brain's language. *Behavioral and Brain Sciences*, *22*, 253–279.

Pulvermüller, F. (2003). *The neuroscience of language: On brain circuits of word and serial order.* Cambridge University Press.

Quaresima, V., Ferrari, M., van der Sluijs, M., Menssen, J., & Colier, W. (2002). Lateral frontal cortex oxygenation changes during translation and language switching revealed by non-invasive near-infrared multi-point measurements. *Brain Research Bulletin*, *59*(3), 235–243.

Radman, N., Spierer, L., Laganaro, M., Annoni, J., & Colombo, F. (2016). Language specificity of lexical-phonological therapy in bilingual aphasia: A clinical and electrophysiological study. *Neuropsychological Rehabilitation*, *26*(4), 532–557.

Raichle, M. E. (2001). Functional neuroimaging: A historical and physiological perspective. In R. Cabeza & A. Kingstone (Eds.),

Handbook of functional neuroimaging of cognition (pp. 3–26). MIT Press.

Raviv, T., Kessenich, M., & Morrison, F. J. (2004). A mediational model of the association between socioeconomic status and three-year-old language abilities: The role of parenting factors. *Early Childhood Research Quarterly, 19*(4), 528–547.

Rekké, S. (2010). *Multilink: A model for multilingual processing*. Bachelor's thesis, Radboud University Nijmegen, The Netherlands. Retrieved on March 19, 2021 from https://kuifvlinder.uci.ru.nl/bitstream/handle/123456789/64/Rekk%c3%a9%2c_S.T._1.pdf?sequence=1.

Renninger, K. A., & Hidi, S. E. (Eds.). (2019). *The Cambridge handbook of motivation and learning*. Cambridge University Press.

Ribot, T. (1882). *Diseases of memory: An essay in the positive psychology*. Appleton.

Rilling, J. K., Glasser, M. F., Preuss, T. M., Ma, X., Zhao, T., Hu, X., & Behrens, T. E. (2008). The evolution of the arcuate fasciculus revealed with comparative DTI. *Nature Neuroscience, 11*(4), 426–428.

Riney, T., Takada, M., & Ota, M. (2000). Segmentals and global foreign accent: The Japanese flap in EFL. *TESOL Quarterly, 34*, 711–738.

Ringbom, H. (1987). *The role of the first language in foreign language learning*. Multilingual Matters.

Ringbom, H. (2001). Lexical transfer in L3 production. In J. Cenoz, B. Hufeisen, & U. Jessner (Eds.), *Cross-linguistic influence in third language acquisition: Psycholinguistic perspectives* (pp. 59–68). Multilingual Matters.

Ringbom, H. (2007). *The importance of cross-linguistic similarity in foreign language learning: Comprehension, learning, and production*. Multilingual Matters.

Rivera-Gaxiola, M., Silva-Pereyra, J., & Kuhl, P. K. (2005). Brain potentials to native and non-native speech contrasts in 7-and 11-month-old American infants. *Developmental Science, 8*(2), 162–172.

Rodriguez-Fornells, A., Krämer, U. M., Lorenzo-Seva, U., Festman, J., & Münte, T. F. (2012). Self-assessment of individual differences in language switching. *Frontiers in Psychology, 2*, 388.

Rodriguez-Fornells, A., Lugt, A. V. D., Rotte, M., Britti, B., Heinze, H. J., & Münte, T. F. (2005). Second language interferes with word production in fluent bilinguals: Brain potential and functional imaging evidence. *Journal of Cognitive Neuroscience, 17*(3), 422–433.

Rodriguez-Fornells, A., Rotte, M., Heinze, H., Nösselt, T., & Münte, T. (2002). Brain potential and functional MRI evidence for how to handle two languages with one brain. *Nature, 415*(6875), 1026–1029.

Rodríguez-Fornells, A., Van der Lugt, A., Rotte, M., Britti, B., Heinze, H.-J., & Münte, T. (2005). Second language interferes with word production in fluent bilinguals: Brain potential and functional imaging evidence. *Journal of Cognitive Neuroscience, 17*, 422–433.

Rogalski, E., Cobia, D., Harrison, T., Wieneke, C., Weintraub, S., & Mesulam, M. (2011). Progression of language decline and cortical atrophy in subtypes of primary progressive aphasia. *Neurology, 76*(21), 1804.

Rohde, A., Worrall, L., Godecke, E., O'Halloran, R., Farrell, A., & Massey, M. (2018). Diagnosis of aphasia in stroke populations: A systematic review of language tests. *PloS One, 13*(3), e0194143.

Rösler, F. (2011). *Psychophysiologie der Kognition: eine Einführung in die kognitive Neurowissenschaft*. Springer-Verlag.

Rossi, E., Cheng, H., Kroll, J. F., Diaz, M. T., & Newman, S. D. (2017). Changes in white-matter connectivity in late second language learners: Evidence from diffusion tensor imaging. *Frontiers in Psychology, 8*, 2040.

Rowe, M. L. (2012). A longitudinal investigation of the role of quantity and quality of child-directed speech in vocabulary development. *Child Development, 83*(5), 1762–1774.

Rumlich, D. (2020). Bilingual education in monolingual contexts: A comparative perspective. *The Language Learning Journal, 48*(1), 115–119.

Sala, A., Malpetti, M., Farsad, M., Lubian, F., Magnani, G., Frasca Polara, G., ... & Perani, D. (2022). Lifelong bilingualism and mechanisms of neuroprotection in Alzheimer dementia. *Human Brain Mapping, 43*(2), 581–592.

Sá-Leite, A. R., Fraga, I., & Comesaña, M. (2019). Grammatical gender processing in bilinguals: An analytic review. *Psychonomic Bulletin & Review, 26*(4), 1148–1173.

Salomé, F., Casalis, S., & Commissaire, E. (2022). Bilingual advantage in L3 vocabulary acquisition: Evidence of a generalized learning benefit among classroom-immersion children. *Bilingualism: Language and Cognition, 25*(2), 242–255.

Sánchez-Casas, R., & García-Albea, J. (2005). The representation of cognate and noncognate words in bilingual memory: Can cognate status be characterized as a special kind of morphological relation? In J. Kroll & A. de Groot (Eds.), *Handbook of bilingualism: Psycholinguistic approaches* (pp. 226–250). Oxford University Press.

Santilli, M., Gonzalez, M., Mikulan, E., Martorell, M., Muñoz, E., Sedeño, L., & García, A. (2019). Bilingual memory, to the extreme: Lexical processing in simultaneous interpreters. *Bilingualism: Language and Cognition, 22*(2), 331–348.

Scarborough, D., Gerard, L., & Cortese C. (1984). Independence of lexical access in bilingual word recognition. *Journal of Verbal Learning and Verbal Behavior, 23*, 84–99.

Schacter, D. L. (1987). Implicit memory: History and current status. *Journal of Experimental Psychology: Learning, Memory, and Cognition, 13*(3), 501–518.

Schirmer, A., Tang, S., Penney, T., Gunter, T., & Chen, H. (2005). Brain responses to segmentally and tonally induced semantic violations in Cantonese. *Journal of Cognitive Neuroscience, 17*(1), 1–12.

Schlaug, G., Norton, A., Overy, K., & Winner, E. (2005). Effects of music training on the child's brain and cognitive development. *Annals of the New York Academy of Sciences, 1060*(1), 219–230.

Schlegel, A. A., Rudelson, J. J., & Tse, P. U. (2012). White matter structure changes as adults learn a second language. *Journal of Cognitive Neuroscience, 24*(8), 1664–1670.

Schmid, M. (2010). Languages at play: The relevance of L1 attrition to the study of bilingualism. *Bilingualism: Language and Cognition, 13*, 1–7.

Schmidtke, J. (2018). Pupillometry in linguistic research: An introduction and review for second language researchers. *Studies in Second Language Acquisition, 40*(3), 529–549.

Schoenberg, M., &, Scott, J. (2011). Aphasia syndromes. In M. Schoenberg & J. Scott (Eds.), *The little black book of neuropsychology* (pp. 267–292). Springer.

Schoonbaert, S., Duyck, W., Brysbaert, M., & Hartsuiker, R. (2009). Semantic and translation priming from a first language to a second and back: Making sense of the findings. *Memory & Cognition, 37*, 569–586.

Schrauf, R. (2009). English use among older bilingual immigrants in linguistically concentrated neighborhoods: Social proficiency and internal speech as intracultural variation. *Journal of Cross-Cultural Gerontology, 24*(2), 157–179.

Schulz, P., & Grimm, A. (2019). The age factor revisited: Timing in acquisition interacts with age of onset in bilingual acquisition. *Frontiers in Psychology, 9*, 1–18.

Schulz, P., & Tracy, R. (2011). *LiSe-DaZ: Linguistische Sprachstandserhebung-Deutsch als Zweitsprache.* Hogrefe Vorschultests.

Schwanenflugel, P., & LaCount, K. (1988). Semantic relatedness and the scope of facilitation for upcoming words in sentences. *Journal of Experimental Psychology: Learning, Memory, and Cognition, 14*, 344–354.

Schwartz, A., & Kroll, J. (2006). Bilingual lexical activation in sentence context. *Journal of Memory and Language, 55*, 197–212.

Schwieter, J. W. (Ed.). (2016). *Cognitive control and consequences of multilingualism.* Benjamins.

Schwieter, J. W. (Ed.). (2019). *The handbook of the neuroscience of multilingualism.* Wiley-Blackwell.

Schwieter, J. W., & Ferreira, A. (2013). Language selection, control, and conceptual-lexical development in bilinguals and multilinguals. In J. W. Schwieter (Ed.), *Innovative research and practices in second language acquisition and bilingualism* (pp. 241–266). Benjamins.

Schwieter, J. W., & Sunderman, G. (2008). Language switching in bilingual speech production: In search of the language-specific selection mechanism. *The Mental Lexicon, 3*(2), 214–238.

Schwieter, J. W., & Sunderman, G. (2009). Concept selection and developmental effects in bilingual speech production. *Language Learning, 59,* 897–927.

Scoresby-Jackson, R. (1867). Case of aphasia with right hemiplegia. *Edinburgh Medical Journal, 12,* 696–706.

Sebastian, R. (2010). *Neural activation patterns in chronic stroke patients with aphasia: The role of lesion site, lesion size, and task difficulty.* Unpublished doctoral dissertation. University of Texas at Austin.

Sebastian, R., Laird, A., & Kiran, S. (2011). Meta-analysis of the neural representation of first language and second language. *Applied Linguistics, 32*(4), 799–819.

Sebastián-Gallés, N., Albareda-Castellot, B., Weikum, W. M., & Werker, J. F. (2012). A bilingual advantage in visual language discrimination in infancy. *Psychological Science, 23*(9), 994–999.

Selinker, L. (1969). Language transfer. *General Linguistics, 9,* 67–92.

Seniów, J., Litwin, M., & Leśniak, M. (2009). The relationship between non-linguistic cognitive deficits and language recovery in patients with aphasia. *Journal of the Neurological Sciences, 283*(1–2), 91–94.

Serafini, S., Grant, G., Haglund, M., et al. (2013). Reorganization and stability for motor and language areas using cortical stimulation. *Brain Sciences, 3*(4), 1597–1614.

Sheridan, M. A., & McLaughlin, K. A. (2014). Dimensions of early experience and neural development: Deprivation and threat. *Trends in Cognitive Sciences, 18*(11), 580–585.

Sheridan, M. A., Fox, N. A., Zeanah, C. H., McLaughlin, K. A., & Nelson III, C. A. (2012). Variation in neural development as a result of exposure to institutionalization early in childhood. *Proceedings of the National Academy of Sciences, 109*(32), 12927–12932.

Shi, L. (2002). How Western-trained Chinese TESOL professionals publish in their home environment. *TESOL Quarterly, 36,* 625–634.

Shook, A., & Marian, V. (2016). The influence of native-language tones on lexical access in the second language. *Journal of Acoustic Society of America, 139*(6), 3102–3109.

Shulman, E. P., Harden, K. P., Chein, J. M., & Steinberg, L. (2016). The development of impulse control and sensation-seeking in adolescence:

Independent or interdependent processes?. *Journal of Research on Adolescence, 26*(1), 37–44.

Sicard, J., & de Bot, K. (2013). Multilingual dreaming. *International Journal of Multilingualism, 10*(3), 331–354.

Signorelli, T., Haarmann, H., & Obler, L. (2012). Working memory in simultaneous interpreters: Effects of task and age. *International Journal of Bilingualism, 16*(2), 198–212.

Silver, A. H., & Zimmerman, J. E. (1965). Quantum transitions and loss in multiply connected superconductors. *Physical Review Letters, 15*, 369–385.

Silveri, M., Di Betta, A., Filippini, V., Leggio, M., & Molinari, M. (1998). Verbal short-term store-rehearsal system and the cerebellum. Evidence from a patient with a right cerebellar lesion. *Brain, 121*, 2175–2187.

Singh, N., & Mishra, R. K. (2013). Second language proficiency modulates conflict-monitoring in an oculomotor Stroop task: Evidence from Hindi-English bilinguals. *Frontiers in Psychology, 4*, 322.

Singleton, D., & Leśniewska, J. (2021). The critical period hypothesis for L2 acquisition: An unfalsifiable embarrassment? *Languages, 6*(3), 1–15.

Sinnatamby, R., Antoun, N., Freer, C., Miles, K., & Hodges, J. (1996). Neuroradiological findings in primary progressive aphasia: CT, fMRI, and cerebral perfusion SPECT. *Neuroradiology, 38*(3), 232–238.

Sjöholm, K. (1995). *The influence of crosslinguistic, semantic, and input factors on the acquisition of English phrasal verbs: A comparison between Finnish and Swedish learners at an intermediate and advanced level.* Åbo Akademi University Press.

Skeide, M. A. (2019). A neural blueprint of language acquisition. In C. Rowland & E. Kidd (Eds.), *Human language: From genes and brains to behavior* (pp. 147–161). MIT Press.

Smit, D. J., Boersma, M., Schnack, H. G., Micheloyannis, S., Boomsma, D. I., Hulshoff Pol, H. E., Stam, C. J., & de Geus, E. J. (2012). The brain matures with stronger functional connectivity and decreased randomness of its network. *PLoS One, 7*(5), 1–11.

Smolensky, P., Goldrick, M., & Mathis, D. (2014). Optimization and quantization in gradient symbol systems: A framework for integrating the continuous and the discrete in cognition. *Cognitive Science, 38*, 1102–1138.

Soares, S. M. P., Kubota, M., Rossi, E., & Rothman, J. (2021). Determinants of bilingualism predict dynamic changes in resting state EEG oscillations. *Brain and Language, 223*, 105030.

Somerville, L. H. (2013). The teenage brain: Sensitivity to social evaluation. *Current Directions in Psychological Science, 22*(2), 121–127.

Soveri, A., Laine, M., Hämäläinen, H., & Hugdahl, K. (2011). Bilingual advantage in attentional control: Evidence from the forced-attention dichotic listening paradigm. *Bilingualism: Language and Cognition, 14*(3), 371–378.

Soveri, A., Lehtonen, M., Karlsson, L. C., Lukasik, K., Antfolk, J., & Laine, M. (2018). Test–retest reliability of five frequently used executive tasks in healthy adults. *Applied Neuropsychology: Adult, 25*(2), 155–165.

Sperry, D. E., Sperry, L. L., & Miller, P. J. (2019). Reexamining the verbal environments of children from different socioeconomic backgrounds. *Child Development, 90*(4), 1303–1318.

Spivey, M., & Cardon, S. (2015). Methods for studying adult bilingualism. In J. W. Schwieter (Ed.), *The Cambridge handbook of bilingual processing* (pp. 108–132). Cambridge University Press.

Spreen, O., & Risser, A. (Eds.). (2003). *Assessment of aphasia.* Oxford University Press.

Squire, L. R., Stark, C. E., & Clark, R. E. (2004). The medial temporal lobe. *Annual Review of Neuroscience, 27*, 279–306.

Starreveld, P., de Groot, A., Rossmark, B., & van Hell, J. (2014). Parallel language activation during word processing in bilinguals: Evidence from word production in sentence context. *Bilingualism: Language and Cognition, 17*(2), 258–276.

Stein, M., Federspiel, A., Koenig, T., Wirth, M., Strik, W., Wiest, R., ... & Dierks, T. (2012). Structural plasticity in the language system related to increased second language proficiency. *Cortex, 48*(4), 458–465.

Steinberg, L. (2005). Cognitive and affective development in adolescence. *Trends in Cognitive Sciences, 9*(2), 69–74.

Stocco, A., & Prat, C. S. (2014). Bilingualism trains specific brain circuits involved in flexible rule selection and application. *Brain and Language, 137*, 50–61.

Stocco, A., Lebiere, C., O'Reilly, R. C., & Anderson, J. R. (2012). Distinct contributions of the caudate nucleus, rostral prefrontal cortex, and parietal cortex to the execution of instructed tasks. *Cognitive, Affective, & Behavioral Neuroscience, 12*(4), 611–628.

Su, I. (2001). Transfer of sentence processing strategies: A comparison of L2 learners of Chinese and English. *Applied Psycholinguistics, 22*, 83–112.

Sugiura, L., Ojima, S., Matsuba-Kurita, H., Dan, I., Tsuzuki, D., ... & Hiroko Hagiwara. (2011). Sound to language: Different cortical processing for first and second languages in elementary school children as revealed by a large-scale study using fNIRS. *Cerebral Cortex, 21*(10), 2374–2393.

Sulpizio, S., Del Maschio, N., Del Mauro, G., Fedeli, D., & Abutalebi, J. (2020). Bilingualism as a gradient measure modulates functional connectivity of language and control networks. *NeuroImage, 205*, 116306.

Surrain, S., & Luk, G. (2019). Describing bilinguals: A systematic review of labels and descriptions used in the literature between 2005–2015. *Bilingualism: Language and Cognition, 22*(2), 401–415.

Swain, M. (1976). Bilingual first-language acquisition. In W. von Raffler-Engel & Y. Lebrun (Eds.), *Baby talk and infant speech* (pp. 277–280). Swets & Zeitlinger.

Takahashi, S. (1996). Pragmatic transferability. *Studies in Second Language Acquisition, 18,* 189–223.

Takashima, A., Bakker-Marshall, I., Van Hell, J. G., McQueen, J. M., & Janzen, G. (2019). Neural correlates of word learning in children. *Developmental Cognitive Neuroscience, 37,* 100649.

Tao, L., Wang, G., Zhu, M., & Cai, Q. (2021). Bilingualism and domain-general cognitive functions from a neural perspective: A systematic review. *Neuroscience & Biobehavioral Reviews, 125,* 264–295.

Teicher, M. H., & Samson, J. A. (2016). Annual research review: Enduring neurobiological effects of childhood abuse and neglect. *Journal of Child Psychology and Psychiatry, 57*(3), 241–266.

Teicher, M. H., Samson, J. A., Anderson, C. M., & Ohashi, K. (2016). The effects of childhood maltreatment on brain structure, function, and connectivity. *Nature Reviews Neuroscience, 17*(10), 652–666.

Teubner-Rhodes, S. E., Mishler, A., Corbett, R., Andreu, L., Sanz-Torrent, M., Trueswell, J. C., & Novick, J. M. (2016). The effects of bilingualism on conflict monitoring, cognitive control, and garden-path recovery. *Cognition, 150,* 213–231.

Thatcher, B. (2000). L2 professional writing in a US and South American context. *Journal of Second Language Writing, 9,* 41–69.

Thierry, G., & Wu, Y. J. (2007). Brain potentials reveal unconscious translation during foreign-language comprehension. *Proceedings of the National Academy of Sciences, 104*(30), 12530–12535.

Thierry, G., Athanasopoulos, P., Wiggett, A., Dering, B., & Kuipers, J. (2009). Unconscious effects of language-specific terminology on pre-attentive color perception. *Proceedings of the National Academy of Sciences, 106*(11), 4567–4570.

Thompson, P. M., Giedd, J. N., Woods, R. P., MacDonald, D., Evans, A. C., & Toga, A. W. (2000). Growth patterns in the developing brain detected by using continuum mechanical tensor maps. *Nature, 404*(6774), 190–193.

Thompson-Schill, S., Swick, D., Farah, M., D'Epositos, M., Kan, I., & Knight, R. (1998). Verb generation in patients with focal frontal lesions: A neuropsychological test of neuroimaging findings. *Proceedings of the National Academy of Science of the United States of America, 95,* 15855–15860.

Thulborn, K., Carpenter, P., & Just, M. (1999). Plasticity of language-related brain function during recovery from stroke. *Stroke, 30,* 749–754.

Timmer, K., Costa, A., & Wodniecka, Z. (2021). The source of attention modulations in bilingual language contexts. *Brain and Language, 223,* 105040.

Timmer, K., Wodniecka, Z., & Costa, A. (2021). Rapid attentional adaptations due to language (monolingual vs bilingual) context. *Neuropsychologia, 159,* 107946.

Titone, D., Libben, M., Mercier, J., Whitford, V., & Pivneva, I. (2011). Bilingual lexical access during L1 sentence reading: The effects of L2 knowledge, semantic constraint, and L1-L2 intermixing. *Journal of Experimental Psychology: Learning, Memory, and Cognition, 37,* 1412–1431.

Tomé Lourido, G., & Evans, B. (2019). The effects of language dominance switch in bilinguals: Galician new speakers' speech production and perception. *Bilingualism: Language and Cognition, 22*(3), 637–654.

Tran, C. D., Arredondo, M. M., & Yoshida, H. (2019). Early executive function: The influence of culture and bilingualism. *Bilingualism: Language and Cognition, 22*(4), 714–732.

Trebits, A., Koch, M. J., Ponto, K., Bruhn, A. C., Adler, M., & Kersten, K. (2022). Cognitive gains and socioeconomic status in early second language acquisition in immersion and EFL learning settings. *International Journal of Bilingual Education and Bilingualism, 24*(7), 1–14.

Treffers-Daller, J., & Sakel, J. (2012). Why transfer is a key aspect of language use and processing in bilinguals and L2-users. *International Journal of Bilingualism, 16*(1), 3–10.

Tsinivits, D., & Unsworth, S. (2021). The impact of older siblings on the language environment and language development of bilingual toddlers. *Applied Psycholinguistics, 42*(2), 325–344.

Tulving, E. (1972). Episodic and semantic memory. In E. Tulving & W. Donaldson (Eds.), *Organization of memory* (pp. 381–403). Academic Press.

Tytus, A. (2014). Can psycholinguistics inform second language learning? Educational implications arising from the Shared Asymmetrical Model. *Cambridge Open-Review Educational Research e-Journal, 1*(1), 74–87.

Unsworth, S. (2013). Assessing the role of current and cumulative exposure in simultaneous bilingual acquisition: The case of Dutch gender. *Bilingualism: Language and Cognition, 16*(1), 86–110.

Unsworth, S. (2016). Quantity and quality of language input in bilingual language development. In E. Nicoladis & S. Montanari (Eds.), *Bilingualism across the lifespan: Factors moderating language proficiency* (pp. 103–121). American Psychological Association.

Ursache, A., & Noble, K. G. (2016). Neurocognitive development in socioeconomic context: Multiple mechanisms and implications for measuring socioeconomic status. *Psychophysiology, 53*(1), 71–82.

Vaid, J., & Hall, D. (1991). Neuropsychological perspectives on bilingualism: Right, left, and center. In A. Reynolds (Ed.), *Bilingualism, multiculturalism, and second language learning: The McGill conference in honor of Wallace E. Lambert* (pp. 81–112). Erlbaum.

Vaid, J., & Menon, G. (2000). Correlates of bilinguals' preferred language for mental computations. *Spanish Applied Linguistics, 4*(2), 325–342.

Vaid, J., & Meuter, R. (2017). Languages without borders: Reframing the study of the bilingual mental lexicon. In M. Libben, M. Goral, & G. Libben (Eds.), *Bilingualism: A framework for understanding the mental lexicon* (pp. 8–39). Benjamins.

Valian, V. (2016). Putting together bilingualism and executive function. *Linguistic Approaches to Bilingualism, 6,* 565–574.

Van Assche, E., Drieghe, D., Duyck, W., Welvaert, M., & Hartsuiker, R. (2011). The influence of semantic constraints on bilingual word recognition during sentence reading. *Journal of Memory and Language, 64,* 88–107.

Van Assche, E., Duyck, W., & Hartsuiker, R. (2012). Bilingual word recognition in a sentence context. *Frontiers in Psychology, 3*(174), 1–8.

Van Assche, E., Duyck, W., Hartsuiker, R. J., & Diependaele, K. (2009). Does bilingualism change native-language reading? Cognate effects in a sentence context. *Psychological Science, 20,* 923–927.

van de Putte, E., De Baene, W., García-Pentón, L., Woumans, E., Dijkgraaf, A., & Duyck, W. (2018). Anatomical and functional changes in the brain after simultaneous interpreting training: A longitudinal study. *Cortex, 99,* 243–257.

Van den Noort, M., Bosch, P., & Struys, E. (Eds.). (2020). Individual variation and the bilingual advantage: Factors that modulate the effect of bilingualism on cognitive control and cognitive reserve [Special issue]. *Behavioral Sciences, 9*(12).

Van Hell, J., & de Groot, A. (1998). Conceptual representation in bilingual memory: Effects of concreteness and cognate status in word association. *Bilingualism: Language and Cognition, 1,* 193–211.

Van Hell, J., & de Groot, A. (2008). Sentence context modulates visual word recognition and translation in bilinguals. *Acta Psychologica, 128,* 431–451.

Van Hell, J., & Dijkstra, T. (2002). Foreign language knowledge can influence native language performance in exclusively native contexts. *Psychonomic Bulletin & Review, 9,* 780–789.

Van Hell, J., & Tanner, D. (2012). Second language proficiency and cross-language lexical activation. *Language Learning, 62,* 148–171.

van Hell, J., Litcofsky, K., & Ting, C. (2015). Intra-sentential code-switching: Cognitive and neural approaches. In J. W. Schwieter (Ed.), *The Cambridge handbook of bilingual processing* (pp. 459–482). Cambridge University Press.

Van Heuven, W., Dijkstra, T., & Grainger, J. (1998). Orthographic neighborhood effects in bilingual word recognition. *Journal of Memory and Language*, *39*, 458–483.

Vanlangendonck, F., Peeters, D., Rueschemeyer, S., & Dijkstra, T. (2020). Mixing the stimulus list in bilingual lexical decision turns cognate facilitation effects into mirrored inhibition effects. *Bilingualism: Language and Cognition*, *23*(4), 836–844.

Vaughn, K. A., & Hernandez, A. E. (2018). Becoming a balanced, proficient bilingual: Predictions from age of acquisition & genetic background. *Journal of Neurolinguistics*, *46*, 69–77.

Vaughn, K. A., Nguyen, M. V., Ronderos, J., & Hernandez, A. E. (2021). Cortical Thickness in bilingual and monolingual children: Relationships to language use and language skill. *NeuroImage*, *243*, 118560.

Vega-Mendoza, M., Alladi, S., & Bak, T. H. (2019). Dementia and multilingualism. In J. W. Schwieter (Ed.), *The handbook of the neuroscience of multilingualism* (pp. 608–624). Wiley-Blackwell.

Vildomec, V. (1963). *Multilingualism*. Sythoff.

Vīnerte, S., & Sabourin, L. (2019). Reviewing the bilingual cognitive control literature: Can a brain-based approach resolve the debate? *Canadian Journal of Experimental Psychology/Revue canadienne de psychologie expérimentale*, *73*(2), 118.

Vingerhoets, G., Van Borsel, J., Tesink, C., van den Noort, M., Deblaere, K., Seurinck, R., Vandemaele, P., & Achten, E. (2003). Multilingualism: An fMRI study. *Neuroimage*, *20*(4), 2181–2196.

Vogel, A., Maruff, P., & Morgan, A. (2010). Evaluation of communication assessment practices during the acute stages post stroke. *Journal of Evaluation in Clinical Practice*, *16*, 1183–1188.

Voits, T., Pliatsikas, C., Robson, H., & Rothman, J. (2020). Beyond Alzheimer's disease: Can bilingualism be a more generalized protective factor in neurodegeneration?. *Neuropsychologia*, *147*, 107593.

Vygotsky, L. S. (1962). *Thought and language*. MIT Press.

Wallisch, A., Little, L. M., Dean, E., & Dunn, W. (2018). Executive function measures for children: A scoping review of ecological validity. *OTJR: Occupation, Participation and Health*, *38*(1), 6–14.

Wang, X., & Forster, K. (2010). Masked translation priming with semantic categorization: Testing the Sense Model. *Bilingualism: Language and Cognition*, *13*(3), 327–340.

Wang, X., Hui, B., & Chen, S. (2020). Language selective or non-selective in bilingual lexical access? It depends on lexical tones! *PLoS ONE*, *15*(3), e0230412.

Wang, X., Wang, J., & Malins, J. (2017). Do you hear "feather" when listening to "rain"? Lexical tone activation during unconscious translation: Evidence from Mandarin-English bilinguals. *Cognition*, *169*, 15–24.

Wang, Y., Xue, G., Chen, C., Xue, F., & Dong, Q. (2007). Neural bases of asymmetric language switching in second-language learners: An ER-fMRI study. *Neuroimage, 35*(2), 862–870.

Wartenburger, I., Heekeren, H., Abutalebi, J., Cappa, S., Villringer, A., & Perani, D. (2003). Early setting of grammatical processing in the bilingual brain. *Neuron, 37*, 159–170.

Watanabe, E., Maki, A., Kawaguchi, F., Takashiro, K., Yamashita, Y., Koizumi, H., & Mayanagi, Y. (1998). Non-invasive assessment of language dominance with near-infrared spectroscopic mapping. *Neuroscience Letters, 256*(1), 49–52.

Watila, M., & Balarabe S. (2015). Factors predicting post-stroke aphasia recovery. *Journal of the Neurological Sciences, 352*, 12–18.

Wattendorf, E., Festman, J., Westermann, B., Keil, U., Zappatore, D., Franceschini, R., … & Neville, H. (1996). Maturational constraints on functional specialization for language processing: ERP and behavioral evidence in bilingual speakers. *Journal of Cognitive Neuroscience, 8*, 231–256.

Wattendorf, E., Festman, J., Westermann, B., Keil, U., Zappatore, D., Franceschini, R., … & Nitsch, C. (2014). Early bilingualism influences early and subsequently later acquired languages in cortical regions representing control functions. *International Journal of Bilingualism, 18*(1), 48–66.

Weiller, C., Isensee, C., Rijntjes, M., Huber, W., Muller, S., & Bier, D. (1995). Recovery from Wernicke's aphasia: A positron emission tomographic study. *Annals of Neurology, 37*, 723–732.

Weinreich, U. (1953). *Languages in contact: Findings and problems.* Linguistic Circle of New York.

Weissberg, R., Durlak, J., Domitrovich, C., & Gullotta, T. (2015). Social and emotional learning: Past, present, and future. In J. Durlak, C. Domitrovich, R. Weissberg, & T. Gullotta (Eds.), *Handbook of social and emotional learning* (pp. 3–19). Guilford Press.

Werker, J. (2012). Perceptual foundations of bilingual acquisition in infancy. *Annals of the New York Academy of Sciences, 1251*(1), 50–61.

Wermelinger, S., Gampe, A., Helbling, N., & Daum, M. M. (2020). Do you understand what I want to tell you? Early sensitivity in bilinguals' iconic gesture perception and production. *Developmental Science, 23*(5), e12943.

Wernicke, C. (1874). *Der aphasische Symptomen-complex. Eine psychologische Studie auf anatomischer Basis.* Cohn und Weigert.

Wheeler, M. E., Petersen, S. E., & Buckner, R. L. (2000). Memory's echo: Vivid remembering reactivates sensory-specific cortex. *Proceedings of the National Academy of Sciences, 97*(20), 11125–11129.

Wicha, N. Y. Y., Moreno E. M., & Carrasco-Ortíz, H. (2019). Real-time measures of the multilingual brain. In J. W. Schwieter (Ed.), *The handbook of the neuroscience of multilingualism* (pp. 100–120). Wiley.

Witney, J., & Dewaele, J. M. (2018). Learning two or more languages. In A. Burns & J. C. Richards (Eds.), *The Cambridge guide to learning English as a second language* (pp. 43–52). Cambridge.

Woumans, E., & Duyck, W. (2015). The bilingual advantage debate: Moving toward different methods for verifying its existence. *Cortex, 73,* 356–357.

Woumans, E. V. Y., Santens, P., Sieben, A., Versijpt, J. A. N., Stevens, M., & Duyck, W. (2015). Bilingualism delays clinical manifestation of Alzheimer's disease. *Bilingualism: Language and Cognition, 18*(3), 568–574.

Wright, W. E., Boun, S., & García, O. (2017). *The handbook of bilingual and multilingual education.* Wiley.

Wu, Y. J., & Thierry, G. (2010). Investigating bilingual processing: The neglected role of language processing contexts. *Frontiers in Psychology, 1,* 178.

Wu, Y. J., & Thierry, G. (2013). Fast modulation of executive function by language context in bilinguals. *Journal of Neuroscience, 33*(33), 13533–13537.

Xia, V., & Andrews, S. (2015). Masked translation priming asymmetry in Chinese-English bilinguals: Making sense of the Sense Model. *Quarterly Journal of Experimental Psychology, 68*(2), 294–325.

Xu, M., Baldauf, D., Chang, C. Q., Desimone, R., & Tan, L. H. (2017). Distinct distributed patterns of neural activity are associated with two languages in the bilingual brain. *Science Advances, 3*(7), e1603309.

Xue, G., Dong, Q., Jin, Z., Zhang, L., & Wang, Y. (2004). An fMRI study with semantic access in low proficiency second language learners. *NeuroReport, 15*(5), 791–796.

Yan, S., & Nicoladis, E. (2009). Finding *le mot juste*: Differences between bilingual and monolingual children's lexical access in comprehension and production. *Bilingualism: Language and Cognition, 12*(3), 323–335.

Yang, M., Cooc, N., & Sheng, L. (2017). An investigation of cross-linguistic transfer between Chinese and English: A meta-analysis. *Asian-Pacific Journal of Second and Foreign Language Education, 2*(15), 1–21.

Ye, Z., & Zhou, X. (2009). Executive control in language processing. *Neuroscience & Biobehavioral Reviews, 33*(8), 1168–1177.

Yelland, G. W., Pollard, J., & Mercuri, A. (1993). The metalinguistic benefits of limited contact with a second language. *Applied Psycholinguistics, 14*(4), 423–444.

Yeo, B. T., Krienen, F. M., Sepulcre, J., Sabuncu, M. R., Lashkari, D., Hollinshead, M., ... & Buckner, R. L. (2011). The organization of the human cerebral cortex estimated by intrinsic functional connectivity. *Journal of Neurophysiology, 106*(3), 1125–1165.

Yim, O., & Clément, R. (2021). Acculturation and attitudes toward code-switching: A bidimensional framework. *International Journal of Bilingualism, 25*(5), 1369–1388.

Yu, C. L., Kovelman, I., & Wellman, H. M. (2021). How bilingualism informs theory of mind development. *Child Development Perspectives, 15*(3), 154–159.

Yu, M.-C. (2004). Interlinguistic variation and similarity in second language speech act behavior. *The Modern Language Journal, 88*, 102–119.

Yudes, C., Macizo, P., & Bajo, M. T. (2011). The influence of expertise in simultaneous interpreting on non-verbal executive processes. *Frontiers in Psychology, 2*, 309.

Yudes, C., Macizo, P., Morales, L., & Bajo, M. T. (2013). Comprehension and error monitoring in simultaneous interpreters. *Applied Psycholinguistics, 34*, 1039–1057.

Yue, J., Bastiaanse, R., & Alter, K. (2014). Cortical plasticity induced by rapid Hebbian learning of novel tonal word-forms: Evidence from mismatch negativity. *Brain and Language, 139*, 10–22.

Yusuf, H. O., & Enesi, A. O. (2012). Using sound in teaching reading in early childhood education. *Journal of Language Teaching & Research, 3*(4), 660–666.

Zahn, R., Drews, E., Specht, K., Kemeny, S., Reith, W., Willmes, K., ... & Huber, W. (2004). Recovery of semantic word processing in global aphasia: A functional MRI study. *Cognitive Brain Research, 18*, 322–336.

Zatorre, R. (1989). On the representation of multiple languages in the brain: Old problems and new directions. *Brain and Language, 36*, 127–147.

Zeller, J. (2020). Code-switching does not equal code-switching: An event-related potentials study on switching from L2 German to L1 Russian at prepositions and nouns. *Frontiers in Psychology, 11*(1387), 1–13.

Zhang D. (2013). Linguistic distance effect on cross-linguistic transfer of morphological awareness. *Applied Psycholinguistics, 34*, 917–942.

Zhang, H., Diaz, M. T., Guo, T., & Kroll, J. F. (2021). Language immersion and language training: Two paths to enhanced language regulation and cognitive control. *Brain and Language, 223*, 105043.

Zhang, J., Anderson, R., Li, H., Dong, Q., Wu, X., & Zhang, Y. (2010). Cross-language transfer of insight into the structure of compound words. *Reading and Writing, 23*, 311–336.

Zhang, T., Van Heuven, W., & Conklin, K. (2011). Fast automatic translation and morphological decomposition in Chinese-English bilinguals. *Psychological Science, 22*(10), 1237–1242.

Zhao, X., & Li, P. (2010). Bilingual lexical interactions in an unsupervised neural network model. *International Journal of Bilingual Education and Bilingualism, 13*, 505–524.

Zhu, J., Seymour, R., Szakay, A., & Sowman, P. (2020). Neuro-dynamics of executive control in bilingual language switching: An MEG study. *Cognition, 199*, 104247.

Zobl, H. (1992). Prior linguistic knowledge and the conservatism of the learning procedure: Grammaticality judgments of unilingual and multilingual learners. In S. Gass & L. Selinker (Eds.), *Language transfer in language learning* (pp. 176–196). Benjamins.

Index